A Harmony
of the Four Gospels

The New International Version, Second Edition

Orville E. Daniel

 Baker Books

A Division of Baker Book House Co
Grand Rapids, Michigan 49516

To
Blanche
who has been my priceless
companion for more than fifty years

© 1996 by Orville E. Daniel

First edition reprinted 1987 by Baker Book House Company
with permission of Welsh Publishing Company, Inc.
Also published in Canada under the title *An Interwoven Harmony of the
Gospels* by Welsh Publishing Company, Inc., Burlington, Ontario

Second edition published by Baker Books
a division of Baker Book House Company
P.O. Box 6287, Grand Rapids, Michigan, 49516-6287

ISBN: 0-8010-5642-X

Fourth printing, July 2000

Printed in the United States of America

Library of Congress Cataloging-in-Publication Data is on file at the
Library of Congress, Washington, D.C.

For information about academic books, resources for Christian leaders,
and all new releases available from Baker Book House, visit our web site:
http://www.bakerbooks.com/

A Harmony
of the Four Gospels

Contents

Part 6 — Christ's Great Galilean Ministry

Part 7 — The Intensive Training of the Twelve in Districts beyond Galilee

A. Jesus' First Withdrawal from Galilee 87

B. Jesus' Second Withdrawal from Galilee 96

C. Jesus' Third Withdrawal from Galilee 99

Part 8 — Christ's Later Judean Ministry

Part 9 — Christ's Perean Ministry

Part 10 — Christ's Final Ministry in Jerusalem

Part 11 — Jesus with the Twelve in the Shadow of the Cross

Part 12 — Christ's Crowning Sacrifice

Part 13 — Jesus' Resurrection, Appearances, and Ascension

Part 14 — Conclusion

Foreword

This book is a Harmony of the Gospels as opposed to a Synopsis or a Gospel Parallel.

A Gospel Parallel arranges Matthew, Mark, and Luke, and sometimes John, in parallel columns, to show the student where the Gospels agree and disagree. Sometimes noncanonical parallels also are included. Gospel Parallels have become prerequisite research tools for scholars using modern methods of historical criticism.

A Synopsis is not designed to show where the Gospels agree or disagree. It is intended to enable the reader to follow the words and deeds of Jesus' life recorded in the four Gospels without the distraction of having to turn back and forth in the pages of the New Testament. A Synopsis is a connected record of the life of Christ that unites passages from the four Gospels into one in the probable chronological order. The life of Christ is thus presented in a connected and orderly sequence.

Harmonies of the Gospels that have been published look more like Gospel Parallels. The accounts are arranged in parallel columns, and the reader must scan each column to follow the story line.

The great advantage of Dr. Daniel's Harmony of the Gospels is that the story line is in bold print. In this way he has provided us with a real Harmony of the Gospels. The Gospel passages are still printed in a parallel arrangement so that the student who so desires may study them; but the boldface text presents a smooth, connected account through the four Gospels.

Devoted Bible students are indebted to Dr. Daniel for providing them with this helpful aid for studying and understanding the life of our Lord.

After graduating in Arts and Theology from Mc-Master University in Ontario, Canada, the author took further studies (Ph.D. in New Testament Interpretation) at the Southern Baptist Theological Seminary in Louisville, Kentucky. He then served for nineteen years as a missionary in India; subsequently he became General Secretary of the Canadian Baptist Overseas Mission Board, from which executive office he retired in 1970.

During his career, Dr. Daniel has written a number of books, some in English and several in the Telugu language of India.

In the Preface to this book he has provided more adequate explanatory information.

David E. Garland

Preface

Bible students must face the fact that the dates and the order of events pertaining to Christ's earthly ministry cannot be entirely determined with indisputable accuracy. For this reason some New Testament scholars decry any attempt to put together in historical sequence the occurrences recorded in the Gospels. Others would limit any such arrangement to happenings described in the Synoptic Gospels (Matthew, Mark, and Luke), because John's Gospel is so unlike the other three.

This Harmony bespeaks the author's conviction that there is real value in arranging the records of the New Testament writers so as to produce a combined account of the life of Christ, however historically tentative in detail it may be. Moreover, John's Gospel is included because the compiler of this Harmony agrees with the opinion expressed by a considerable number of biblical scholars that the narrative in the Fourth Gospel does not contradict but rather supplements the Synoptic accounts.

So-called Harmonies of the Gospels, however, which have appeared hitherto in various New Testament translations have presented the Gospels paralleled, but not really harmonized. This book is an attempt not merely to parallel but actually to harmonize the Gospels, by drawing out from the paralleled narratives a complete connected account of the life of Christ, free from repetition and yet comprising every detail given to us by the inspired writers. For this purpose two styles of type have been used, and the complete connected story is obtained by simply following the boldface type back and forth from column to column down the page.

At the same time, the use of two styles of type enables the reader to see at a glance which of the Gospels presents items of information not included in other Gospels. In the few instances where two or more Gospels present parallel material differing not merely in quantity but in substance, this fact has been pointed out; and explanations have been suggested in footnotes for some of the seeming contradictions. The footnotes of the NIV have been retained and are distinguished from these explanatory notes by the use of a serif font; a sans serif font is used for explanatory notes.

Care has also been taken in this Harmony so that the important benefits to be derived from the special arrangement of material may be obtained with a minimum of conscious effort on the part of the reader; thus one's mind is left free to concentrate upon the developing story itself. For example, when a section of the story is recorded by only one Gospel writer, the section is set in a single column with labelled boxes indicating the other three Gospels, so that one may be instantly aware of which Gospel is being read. Where two or three Gospels are in parallel, the remaining ones are again indicated by labelled boxes to keep the distinction of the text flow clear. Parallel passages have been placed in exact juxtaposition as far as possible, to facilitate comparison.

It would be impossible to mention the names of all persons to whom I am indebted. I have made full use of the invaluable work done by many New Testament scholars. Special mention, however, should be made of the late Dr. A. T. Robertson, one of my revered mentors, whose numerous books, including more than a dozen related to the life of Christ, are still widely read. My particular gratitude should be expressed to several contemporary seminary professors and pastors, in Canada and the U.S.A., who have encouraged me to proceed with the production of this Harmony. Among them I am especially thankful to Dr. David Garland, Dr. Roy Bell, Rev. Robert Muse, and Dr. Allison Trites, whose written comments appear, in whole or in part, inside this book or elsewhere.

Sincere thanks are due also to the Zondervan Publishing House, by whose kind permission I have used the text of their New International Version of the Gospels, a popular modern translation of the early Greek New Testament manuscripts.

Orville E. Daniel

PART 1

Introduction

1. The Dedication to Luke's Gospel

Matt.	Mark	**Luke 1:1–4**	John

¹Many have undertaken to draw up an account of the things that have been fulfilledᵃ among us, ²just as they were handed down to us by those who from the first were eyewitnesses and servants of the word. ³Therefore, since I myself have carefully investigated everything from the beginning, it seemed good also to me to write an orderly account for you, most excellent Theophilus, ⁴so that you may know the certainty of the things you have been taught.

a. *1* Or *been surely believed*

2. Christ's Preincarnate Existence

Matt.	Mark	Luke	**John 1:1–5, 9–13**

¹In the beginning was the Word, and the Word was with God, and the Word was God. ²He was with God in the beginning.

³Through him all things were made; without him nothing was made that has been made. ⁴In him was life, and that life was the light of men. ⁵The light shines in the darkness, but the darkness has not understoodᵃ it.ᵇ

⁹The true light that gives light to every man was coming into the world.ᶜ

¹⁰He was in the world, and though the world was made through him, the world did not recognize him. ¹¹He came to that which was his own, but his own did not receive him. ¹²Yet to all who received him, to those who believed in his name, he gave the right to become children of God—¹³children born not of natural descent,ᵈ nor of human decision or a husband's will, but born of God.

a. *5* Or *darkness, and the darkness has not overcome*
b. The NIV reads: "but the darkness has not *understood* it," and a footnote suggests "overcome" as an alternative translation. The Greek verb has more than one meaning. Many translators concur with the opinion of Thayer and other authorities that "overcome" or a synonym is preferable in John 1:5.
c. *9* Or *This was the true light that gives light to every man who comes into the world*
d. *13* Greek *of bloods*

3. Jesus' Human Ancestry

<table>
<tr><td>Matt. 1:1–17</td><td>Mark</td><td>Luke</td><td>John</td></tr>
</table>

[1]A record of the genealogy of Jesus Christ the son of David, the son of Abraham:

[2]Abraham was the father of Isaac,
Isaac the father of Jacob,
Jacob the father of Judah and his brothers,
[3]Judah the father of Perez and Zerah, whose mother was Tamar,
Perez the father of Hezron,
Hezron the father of Ram,
[4]Ram the father of Amminadab,
Amminadab the father of Nahshon,
[5]Nahshon the father of Salmon,
Salmon the father of Boaz, whose mother was Rahab,
Boaz the father of Obed, whose mother was Ruth,
Obed the father of Jesse,
[6]and Jesse the father of King David.

David was the father of Solomon, whose mother had been Uriah's wife,
[7]Solomon the father of Rehoboam,
Rehoboam the father of Abijah,
Abijah the father of Asa,
[8]Asa the father of Jehoshaphat,
Jehoshaphat the father of Jehoram,
Jehoram the father of Uzziah,
[9]Uzziah the father of Jotham,
Jotham the father of Ahaz,
Ahaz the father of Hezekiah,
[10]Hezekiah the father of Manasseh,
Manasseh the father of Amon,
Amon the father of Josiah,
[11]and Josiah the father of Jeconiah[a] and his brothers at the time of the exile to Babylon.

[12]After the exile to Babylon:
Jeconiah was the father of Shealtiel,
Shealtiel the father of Zerubbabel,
[13]Zerubbabel the father of Abiud,
Abiud the father of Eliakim,
Eliakim the father of Azor,
[14]Azor the father of Zadok,
Zadok the father of Akim,
Akim the father of Eliud,
[15]Eliud the father of Eleazar,
Eleazar the father of Matthan,
Matthan the father of Jacob,

---

a. *11* That is, Jehoiachin; also in verse 12

Matt. 1

	Mark	Luke	John

16and Jacob the father of Joseph, the husband of Mary, of whom was born Jesus, who is called Christ.

17Thus there were fourteen generations in all from Abraham to David, fourteen from David to the exile to Babylon, and fourteen from the exile to the Christ.a

a. *17* Or *Messiah.* "The Christ" (Greek) and "the Messiah" (Hebrew) both mean "the Anointed One."

Luke 3:23b–38

Matt.	Mark		

He was the son, so it was thought, of Joseph,

the son of Heli,a 24the son of Matthat,
the son of Levi, the son of Melki,
the son of Jannai, the son of Joseph,
25the son of Mattathias, the son of Amos,
the son of Nahum, the son of Esli,
the son of Naggai, 26the son of Maath,
the son of Mattathias, the son of Semein,
the son of Josech, the son of Joda,
27the son of Joanan, the son of Rhesa,
the son of Zerubbabel, the son of Shealtiel,
the son of Neri, 28the son of Melki,
the son of Addi, the son of Cosam,
the son of Elmadam, the son of Er,
29the son of Joshua, the son of Eliezer,
the son of Jorim, the son of Matthat,
the son of Levi, 30the son of Simeon,
the son of Judah, the son of Joseph,
the son of Jonam, the son of Eliakim,
31the son of Melea, the son of Menna,
the son of Mattatha, the son of Nathan,
the son of David, 32the son of Jesse,
the son of Obed, the son of Boaz,
the son of Salmon,b the son of Nahshon,
33the son of Amminadab, the son of Ram,c
the son of Hezron, the son of Perez,
the son of Judah, 34the son of Jacob,
the son of Isaac, the son of Abraham,
the son of Terah, the son of Nahor,
35the son of Serug, the son of Reu,
the son of Peleg, the son of Eber,
the son of Shelah, 36the son of Cainan,

a. We are told in Matt. 1:16 that Joseph was the son of Jacob. Various suggestions have been offered to explain the differences between the two genealogies. Many scholars are of the opinion that Matthew records the legal ancestry of Jesus through Joseph, while Luke records the actual ancestry through Mary. If so, Joseph was the *son-in-law* of Heli.

b. *32* Some early manuscripts *Sala*

c. *33* Some manuscripts *Amminadab, the son of Admin, the son of Arni;* other manuscripts vary widely.

Matt.	Mark	Luke 3	John

the son of Arphaxad, the son of Shem,
the son of Noah, the son of Lamech,
[37]the son of Methuselah, the son of Enoch,
the son of Jared, the son of Mahalalel,
the son of Kenan, [38]the son of Enosh,
the son of Seth, the son of Adam,
the son of God.

PART 2

John the Baptist and Jesus from Birth to Manhood

B.C. *6* to A.D. *8*[a]

4. The Angel's Announcement to Zechariah

The temple, Jerusalem; B.C. *6*

Matt.	Mark	Luke 1:5–25	John

⁵In the time of Herod king of Judea there was a priest named Zechariah, who belonged to the priestly division of Abijah; his wife Elizabeth was also a descendant of Aaron. ⁶Both of them were upright in the sight of God, observing all the Lord's commandments and regulations blamelessly. ⁷But they had no children, because Elizabeth was barren; and they were both well along in years.

⁸Once when Zechariah's division was on duty and he was serving as priest before God, ⁹he was chosen by lot, according to the custom of the priesthood, to go into the temple of the Lord and burn incense. ¹⁰And when the time for the burning of incense came, all the assembled worshipers were praying outside.

¹¹Then an angel of the Lord appeared to him, standing at the right side of the altar of incense. ¹²When Zechariah saw him, he was startled and was gripped with fear. ¹³But the angel said to him: "Do not be afraid, Zechariah; your prayer has been heard. Your wife Elizabeth will bear you a son, and you are to give him the name John. ¹⁴He will be a joy and delight to you, and many will rejoice because of his birth, ¹⁵for he will be great in the sight of the Lord. He is never to take wine or other fermented drink, and he will be filled with the Holy Spirit even from birth.[b] ¹⁶Many of the people of Israel will he bring back to the Lord their God. ¹⁷And he will go on before the Lord, in the spirit and power of Elijah, to turn the hearts of the fathers to their children and the disobedient to the wisdom of the righteous—to make ready a people prepared for the Lord."

¹⁸Zechariah asked the angel, "How can I be sure of this? I am an old man and my wife is well along in years."

¹⁹The angel answered, "I am Gabriel. I stand in the presence of God, and I have been sent to speak to you and to tell you this good news. ²⁰And now you will be silent and not

a. Dates in this book are only probable dates, derived from references such as Matt. 2:19 (Herod died in B.C. 4), Luke 3:23, etc.
b. *15* Or *from his mother's womb*

Matt.	Mark	Luke 1	John

able to speak until the day this happens, because you did not believe my words, which will come true at their proper time."

21Meanwhile, the people were waiting for Zechariah and wondering why he stayed so long in the temple. 22When he came out, he could not speak to them. They realized he had seen a vision in the temple, for he kept making signs to them but remained unable to speak.

23When his time of service was completed, he returned home. 24After this his wife Elizabeth became pregnant and for five months remained in seclusion. 25"The Lord has done this for me," she said. "In these days he has shown his favor and taken away my disgrace among the people."

5. The Angel's Message to Mary

Nazareth; the end of B.C. 6 or beginning of B.C. 5

Matt.	Mark	Luke 1:26–38	John

26In the sixth month, God sent the angel Gabriel to Nazareth, a town in Galilee, 27to a virgin pledged to be married to a man named Joseph, a descendant of David. The virgin's name was Mary. 28The angel went to her and said, "Greetings, you who are highly favored! The Lord is with you."

29Mary was greatly troubled at his words and wondered what kind of greeting this might be. 30But the angel said to her, "Do not be afraid, Mary, you have found favor with God. 31You will be with child and give birth to a son, and you are to give him the name Jesus. 32He will be great and will be called the Son of the Most High. The Lord God will give him the throne of his father David, 33and he will reign over the house of Jacob forever; his kingdom will never end."

34"How will this be," Mary asked the angel, "since I am a virgin?"

35The angel answered, "The Holy Spirit will come upon you, and the power of the Most High will overshadow you. So the holy one to be born will be calleda the Son of God. 36Even Elizabeth your relative is going to have a child in her old age, and she who was said to be barren is in her sixth month. 37For nothing is impossible with God."

38"I am the Lord's servant," Mary answered. "May it be to me as you have said." Then the angel left her.

a. *35 Or So the child to be born will be called holy*

6. Mary's Visit to Elizabeth

Judea; the beginning of B.C. 5

Matt.	Mark	Luke 1:39–56	John

39At that time Mary got ready and hurried to a town in the hill country of Judea, 40where she entered Zechariah's home and greeted Elizabeth. 41When Elizabeth heard Mary's greeting, the baby leaped in her womb, and Elizabeth was filled with the Holy Spirit. 42In a loud voice she exclaimed: "Blessed are you among women, and blessed is the child you will bear! 43But why am I so favored, that the mother of my Lord should come to me? 44As soon

Matt.	Mark	Luke 1	John

as the sound of your greeting reached my ears, the baby in my womb leaped for joy. [45]Blessed is she who has believed that what the Lord has said to her will be accomplished!"

[46]And Mary said:

"My soul glorifies the Lord
   [47]and my spirit rejoices in God my Savior,
[48]for he has been mindful
   of the humble state of his servant.
From now on all generations will call me blessed,
[49]for the Mighty One has done great things for me—
   holy is his name.
[50]His mercy extends to those who fear him,
      from generation to generation.
[51]He has performed mighty deeds with his arm;
      he has scattered those who are proud in their inmost thoughts.
[52]He has brought down rulers from their thrones
      but has lifted up the humble.
[53]He has filled the hungry with good things
      but has sent the rich away empty.
[54]He has helped his servant Israel,
      remembering to be merciful
[55]to Abraham and his descendants forever,
      even as he said to our fathers."

[56]Mary stayed with Elizabeth for about three months and then returned home.

7. John the Baptist's Birth

Judea; the spring of B.C. 5

Matt.	Mark	Luke 1:57–79	John

[57]When it was time for Elizabeth to have her baby, she gave birth to a son. [58]Her neighbors and relatives heard that the Lord had shown her great mercy, and they shared her joy.

[59]On the eighth day they came to circumcise the child, and they were going to name him after his father Zechariah, [60]but his mother spoke up and said, "No! He is to be called John."

[61]They said to her, "There is no one among your relatives who has that name."

[62]Then they made signs to his father, to find out what he would like to name the child. [63]He asked for a writing tablet, and to everyone's astonishment he wrote, "His name is John." [64]Immediately his mouth was opened and his tongue was loosed, and he began to speak, praising God. [65]The neighbors were all filled with awe, and throughout the hill country of Judea people were talking about all these things. [66]Everyone who heard this wondered about it, asking, "What then is this child going to be?" For the Lord's hand was with him.

[67]His father Zechariah was filled with the Holy Spirit and prophesied:

[68]"Praise be to the Lord, the God of Israel,
      because he has come and has redeemed his people.

Matt.	Mark	Luke 1	John

⁶⁹He has raised up a horn^a

of salvation for us

  in the house of his servant David

⁷⁰(as he said through his holy prophets of long ago),

⁷¹salvation from our enemies

    and from the hand of all who hate us—

⁷²to show mercy to our fathers

    and to remember his holy covenant,

      ⁷³the oath he swore to our father Abraham:

⁷⁴to rescue us from the hand of our enemies,

    and to enable us to serve him without fear

      ⁷⁵in holiness and righteousness before him all our days.

⁷⁶And you, my child, will be called a prophet of the Most High;

    for you will go on before the Lord to prepare the way for him,

⁷⁷to give his people the knowledge of salvation

  through the forgiveness of their sins,

⁷⁸because of the tender mercy of our God,

  by which the rising sun will come to us from heaven

⁷⁹to shine on those living in darkness

  and in the shadow of death,

to guide our feet into the path of peace."

a. *69 Horn* here symbolizes strength.

8. The Angel's Advice to Joseph

Nazareth; B.C. *5*

Matt. 1:18–25a	Mark	Luke	John

¹⁸This is how the birth of Jesus Christ came about: His mother Mary was pledged to be married to Joseph, but before they came together, she was found to be with child through the Holy Spirit. ¹⁹Because Joseph her husband was a righteous man and did not want to expose her to public disgrace, he had in mind to divorce her quietly.

²⁰But after he had considered this, an angel of the Lord appeared to him in a dream and said, "Joseph son of David, do not be afraid to take Mary home as your wife, because what is conceived in her is from the Holy Spirit. ²¹She will give birth to a son, and you are to give him the name Jesus,^a because he will save his people from their sins."

²²All this took place to fulfill what the Lord had said through the prophet: ²³"The virgin will be with child and will give birth to a son, and they will call him Immanuel"^b—which means, "God with us."

²⁴When Joseph woke up, he did what the angel of the Lord had commanded him and took Mary home as his wife. ²⁵But he had no union with her until she gave birth to a son.

a. *21 Jesus* is the Greek form of *Joshua,* which means *the* LORD *saves.*

b. *23* Isa. 7:14

9. Jesus' Birth

Bethlehem; the autumn of B.C. 5

Matt.	Mark	Luke 2:1–7	John

Luke 2:1–7

¹In those days Caesar Augustus issued a decree that a census should be taken of the entire Roman world. ²(This was the first census that took place while Quirinius was governor of Syria.)ᵃ ³And everyone went to his own town to register.

⁴So Joseph also went up from the town of Nazareth in Galilee to Judea, to Bethlehem the town of David, because he belonged to the house and line of David. ⁵He went there to register with Mary, who was pledged to be married to him and was expecting a child. ⁶While they were there, the time came for the baby to be born, ⁷and she gave birth to her firstborn, a son. She wrapped him in cloths and placed him in a manger, because there was no room for them in the inn.

a. Augustus inaugurated a periodical census, to be taken every fourteen years from B.C. 8 on. The second census occurred in A.D. 6 (Acts 5:37). Quirinius was twice governor of Syria; the first time was during B.C. 10–7. But such an early date for the birth of Jesus is impossible in the light of other chronological references in the Gospels. So we must assume that there was some delay in carrying out the first census in Palestine.

John 1:14a

Luke

¹⁴Soᵃ the Word became flesh and made his dwelling among us.

a. In the original Greek the conjunction is "And;" the NIV omits it. "So" is inserted here to make the connected narrative run more smoothly.

10. The Angels' Proclamation to the Shepherds

Near Bethlehem

Matt.	Mark	Luke 2:8–20	John

Luke 2:8–20

⁸And there were shepherds living out in the fields nearby, keeping watch over their flocks at night. ⁹An angel of the Lord appeared to them, and the glory of the Lord shone around them, and they were terrified. ¹⁰But the angel said to them, "Do not be afraid. I bring you good news of great joy that will be for all the people. ¹¹Today in the town of David a Savior has been born to you; he is Christᵇ the Lord. ¹²This will be a sign to you: You will find a baby wrapped in cloths and lying in a manger."

¹³Suddenly a great company of the heavenly host appeared with the angel, praising God and saying,

¹⁴"Glory to God in the highest,
and on earth peace to men on whom his favor rests."

¹⁵When the angels had left them and gone into heaven, the shepherds said to one another, "Let's go to Bethlehem and see this thing that has happened, which the Lord has told us about."

¹⁶So they hurried off and found Mary and Joseph, and the baby, who was lying in the

b. *11* Or *Messiah.* "The Christ" (Greek) and "the Messiah" (Hebrew) both mean "the Anointed One"; also in verse 26.

Matt.	Mark	Luke 2	John
		manger. [17]When they had seen him, they spread the word concerning what had been told them about this child, [18]and all who heard it were amazed at what the shepherds said to them. [19]But Mary treasured up all these things and pondered them in her heart. [20]The shepherds returned, glorifying and praising God for all the things they had heard and seen, which were just as they had been told.	

11. The Circumcision and Naming of Jesus

Eight days after birth

Matt. 1:25b	Mark	Luke 2:21	John
And he gave him the name Jesus.		[21]On the eighth day, when it was time to circumcise him, he was named Jesus, the name the angel had given him before he had been conceived.	

12. The Presentation of Jesus

Jerusalem; forty days after birth

Matt.	Mark	Luke 2:22–39a	John
		[22]When the time of their purification according to the Law of Moses had been completed, Joseph and Mary took him to Jerusalem to present him to the Lord [23](as it is written in the Law of the Lord, "Every firstborn male is to be consecrated to the Lord"[a]), [24]and to offer a sacrifice in keeping with what is said in the Law of the Lord: "a pair of doves or two young pigeons."[b]	

[25]Now there was a man in Jerusalem called Simeon, who was righteous and devout. He was waiting for the consolation of Israel, and the Holy Spirit was upon him. [26]It had been revealed to him by the Holy Spirit that he would not die before he had seen the Lord's Christ. [27]Moved by the Spirit, he went into the temple courts. When the parents brought in the child Jesus to do for him what the custom of the Law required, [28]Simeon took him in his arms and praised God, saying:

[29]"Sovereign Lord, as you have promised,
    you now dismiss[c] your servant in peace.
[30]For my eyes have seen your salvation,
       [31]which you have prepared in the sight of all people,
[32]a light for revelation to the Gentiles
    and for glory to your people Israel."

[33]The child's father and mother marveled at what was said about him. [34]Then Simeon blessed them and said to Mary, his mother: "This child is destined to cause the falling and

---

a. *23* Exod. 13:2,12
b. *24* Lev. 12:8
c. *29* Or *promised, now dismiss*

Matt.	Mark	Luke 2	John

rising of many in Israel, and to be a sign that will be spoken against, [35]so that the thoughts of many hearts will be revealed. And a sword will pierce your own soul too."

[36]There was also a prophetess, Anna, the daughter of Phanuel, of the tribe of Asher. She was very old; she had lived with her husband seven years after her marriage, [37]and then was a widow until she was eighty-four.[a] She never left the temple but worshiped night and day, fasting and praying. [38]Coming up to them at that very moment, she gave thanks to God and spoke about the child to all who were looking forward to the redemption of Jerusalem.

[39]When Joseph and Mary had done everything required by the Law of the Lord, . . .

a. *37* Or *widow for eighty-four years*

13. The Visit of the Magi

Matt. 2:1–12

Mark	Luke	John

[1]After Jesus was born in Bethlehem in Judea, during the time of King Herod, Magi[a] from the east came to Jerusalem [2]and asked, "Where is the one who has been born king of the Jews? We saw his star in the east[b] and have come to worship him."

[3]When King Herod heard this he was disturbed, and all Jerusalem with him. [4]When he had called together all the people's chief priests and teachers of the law, he asked them where the Christ[c] was to be born. [5]"In Bethlehem in Judea," they replied, "for this is what the prophet has written:

[6]"'But you, Bethlehem, in the land of Judah,
   are by no means least among the rulers of Judah;
for out of you will come a ruler
   who will be the shepherd of my people Israel.'[d]"

[7]Then Herod called the Magi secretly and found out from them the exact time the star had appeared. [8]He sent them to Bethlehem and said, "Go and make a careful search for the child. As soon as you find him, report to me, so that I too may go and worship him."

[9]After they had heard the king, they went on their way, and the star they had seen in the east[e] went ahead of them until it stopped over the place where the child was. [10]When they saw the star, they were overjoyed. [11]On coming to the house, they saw the child with his mother Mary, and they bowed down and worshiped him. Then they opened their treasures and presented him with gifts of gold and of incense and of myrrh. [12]And having been warned in a dream not to go back to Herod, they returned to their country by another route.

14. The Flight into Egypt

Matt. 2:13–18

Mark	Luke	John

[13]When they had gone, an angel of the Lord appeared to Joseph in a dream. "Get up," he said, "take the child and his mother and escape to Egypt. Stay there until I tell you, for Herod is going to search for the child to kill him."

a. *1* Traditionally *Wise Men*
b. *2* Or *star when it rose*
c. *4* Or *Messiah*
d. *6* Mic. 5:2
e. *9* Or *seen when it rose*

Matt. 2 | Mark | Luke | John

[14]So he got up, took the child and his mother during the night and left for Egypt, [15]where he stayed until the death of Herod. And so was fulfilled what the Lord had said through the prophet: "Out of Egypt I called my son."[a]

[16]When Herod realized that he had been outwitted by the Magi, he was furious, and he gave orders to kill all the boys in Bethlehem and its vicinity who were two years old and under, in accordance with the time he had learned from the Magi. [17]Then what was said through the prophet Jeremiah was fulfilled:

[18]"A voice is heard in Ramah,
    weeping and great mourning,
Rachel weeping for her children
    and refusing to be comforted,
because they are no more."[b]

15. The Return to Nazareth

B.C. 4

Matt. 2:19–23 | Mark | Luke | John

[19]After Herod died, an angel of the Lord appeared in a dream to Joseph in Egypt [20]and said, "Get up, take the child and his mother and go to the land of Israel, for those who were trying to take the child's life are dead."

[21]So he got up, took the child and his mother and went to the land of Israel. [22]But when he heard that Archelaus was reigning in Judea in place of his father Herod, he was afraid to go there. Having been warned in a dream,

a. *15* Hos. 11:1
b. *18* Jer. 31:15

Mark	Luke 2:39b

he withdrew to the district of Galilee, [23]and[c] went and lived in a town called Nazareth. So was fulfilled what was said through the prophets: "He will be called a Nazarene."

[39b]they returned to Galilee to their own town of Nazareth.

c. The NIV inserts "he" although Matthew's Gospel reads just as well without the repeated pronoun; It is omitted in this Harmony because the connected narrative reads "they" (Luke 2:39).

16. John the Baptist's Childhood

Matt. | Mark | **Luke 1:80a** | John

[80]And the child grew and became strong in spirit;

17. Jesus' Childhood

B.C. 4 to A.D. 8

Matt.	Mark	Luke 2:40	John

40And the child grew and became strong; he was filled with wisdom, and the grace of God was upon him.

18. Jesus' Visit to Jerusalem

A.D. 8

Matt.	Mark	Luke 2:41–51	John

41Every year his parents went to Jerusalem for the Feast of the Passover. 42When he was twelve years old, they went up to the Feast, according to the custom. 43After the Feast was over, while his parents were returning home, the boy Jesus stayed behind in Jerusalem, but they were unaware of it. 44Thinking he was in their company, they traveled on for a day. Then they began looking for him among their relatives and friends. 45When they did not find him, they went back to Jerusalem to look for him. 46After three days they found him in the temple courts, sitting among the teachers, listening to them and asking them questions. 47Everyone who heard him was amazed at his understanding and his answers. 48When his parents saw him, they were astonished. His mother said to him, "Son, why have you treated us like this? Your father and I have been anxiously searching for you."

49"Why were you searching for me?" he asked. "Didn't you know I had to be in my Father's house?" 50But they did not understand what he was saying to them.

51Then he went down to Nazareth with them and was obedient to them. But his mother treasured all these things in her heart.

19. Jesus from Youth to Manhood

A.D. 8 to 26

Matt.	Mark	Luke 2:52	John

52And Jesus grew in wisdom and stature, and in favor with God and men.

20. John the Baptist's Secluded Wilderness Life

Matt.	Mark	Luke 1:80b	John

80band he lived in the desert until he appeared publicly to Israel.

PART 3

John the Baptist's Preparatory Ministry

From the Spring to the Autumn of A.D. 26

21. John the Baptist's First Public Appearance

Judea; the spring of A.D. 26

Matt.	**Mark 1:1–6**	Luke	John

[1]The beginning of the gospel about Jesus Christ, the Son of God.[a]

a. *1* Some manuscripts do not have *the Son of God.*

Mark	**Luke 3:1–6**

[1]In the fifteenth year of the reign of Tiberius Caesar—when Pontius Pilate was governor of Judea, Herod tetrarch of Galilee, his brother Philip tetrarch of Iturea and Traconitis, and Lysanias tetrarch of Abilene—[2]during the high priesthood of Annas and Caiaphas, the word of God came to John son of Zechariah in the desert.

Matt. 3:1–6	Mark	Luke

[1]In those days John the Baptist came, preaching in the Desert of Judea [2]and saying, "Repent, for the kingdom of heaven is near." [3]This is he who was spoken of

through the prophet Isaiah:

"A voice of one calling in the
   desert,
'Prepare the way for the Lord,
   make straight paths for
      him.'"[a]

a. *3* Isa. 40:3

[2]It is written in Isaiah the prophet:

   "I will send my messenger
      ahead of you,
   who will prepare your
      way"[b]—
[3]"a voice of one calling in the
   desert,
'Prepare the way for the Lord,
   make straight paths for
      him.'"[c]

b. *2* Mal. 3:1
c. *3* Isa. 40:3

[4]As is written in the book of the words of Isaiah the prophet:

"A voice of one calling in the
   desert,
'Prepare the way for the Lord,
   make straight paths for
      him.

Matt.	Mark	Luke 3	John

⁵Every valley shall be filled in,
  every mountain and hill made low.
The crooked roads shall become straight,
  the rough ways smooth.
⁶And all mankind will see God's salvation.'"ᵃ

a. *6* Isa. 40:3–5

Matt. 3	Mark 1	Luke 3	John 1:6–8
	⁴And so John came,		⁶There came a man who was sent from God;
		³He went into all the country around the Jordan,	his name was John.
	baptizing in the desert region and preaching a baptism of repentance for the forgiveness of sins.	preaching a baptism of repentance for the forgiveness of sins.	
			⁷He came as a witness to testify concerning that light,ᵃ so that through him all men might believe. ⁸He himself was not the light; he came only as a witness to the light.
⁴John's clothes were made of camel's hair, and he had a leather belt around his waist. His food was locusts and wild honey. ⁵People went out to him from Jerusalem and all Judea and the whole region of the Jordan. ⁶Confessing their sins, they were baptized by him in the Jordan River.	⁶John wore clothing made of camel's hair, with a leather belt around his waist, and he ate locusts and wild honey. ⁵The whole Judean countryside and all the people of Jerusalem went out to him. Confessing their sins, they were baptized by him in the Jordan River.		

a. The NIV reads *"that* light," in the context of John 1:1–5.

22. John the Baptist's Forceful Preaching

Matt. 3:7–10	Mark	Luke 3:7–14	John

⁷But when he saw many of the Pharisees and Sadducees coming to where he was baptizing, he said to them: "You brood of vipers! Who

⁷John said to the crowds coming out to be baptized by him, "You brood of vipers! Who warned you to flee from the coming wrath? ⁸Produce fruit

Matt. 3	Mark	Luke 3	John

warned you to flee from the coming wrath? [8]Produce fruit in keeping with repentance. [9]And do not think you can say to yourselves, 'We have Abraham as our father.' I tell you that out of these stones God can raise up children for Abraham. [10]The ax is already at the root of the trees, and every tree that does not produce good fruit will be cut down and thrown into the fire.[a]

in keeping with repentance. And do not begin to say to yourselves, 'We have Abraham as our father.' For I tell you that out of these stones God can raise up children for Abraham. [9]The ax is already at the root of the trees, and every tree that does not produce good fruit will be cut down and thrown into the fire."

a. This is the first of several sections (called the Logia passages) in which Matthew and Luke present similar material apart from Mark. New Testament scholars assume that in these passages the two writers drew upon an unknown common source, presumably a manuscript that recorded some sayings (Greek, *logia*) of Jesus; it is labelled *Q* for purposes of academic reference.

Matt.	Mark		

[10]"What should we do then?" the crowd asked.

[11]John answered, "The man with two tunics should share with him who has none, and the one who has food should do the same."

[12]Tax collectors also came to be baptized. "Teacher," they asked, "what should we do?"

[13]"Don't collect any more than you are required to," he told them.

[14]Then some soldiers asked him, "And what should we do?"

He replied, "Don't extort money and don't accuse people falsely—be content with your pay."

23. John the Baptist's Messianic Proclamation

Matt.	Mark	Luke 3:15–18	John

[15]The people were waiting expectantly and were all wondering in their hearts if John might possibly be the Christ.[a] [16]John answered them all,

a. 15 Or *Messiah*

Mark 1:7–8

Matt. 3:11–12

[11]"I baptize you with[b] water for repentance. But after me will come one who is more powerful than I, whose sandals I am not fit to carry. He will baptize you with the Holy Spirit and with fire. [12]His winnowing fork is in his hand, and he will clear his threshing floor, gathering his wheat into the barn and

[7]And this was his message:

"After me will come one more powerful than I, the thongs of whose sandals I am not worthy to stoop down and untie.[a] [8]I baptize you with[b] water, but he

"I baptize you with[b] water. But one more powerful than I will come, the thongs of whose sandals I am not worthy to untie. He

will baptize you with the Holy Spirit and with fire. [17]His winnowing fork is in his hand to clear

a. Note that the wording in Mark 1:7 and Luke 3:16 differs from Matt. 3:11 ("whose sandals I am unfit to carry").

b. 11 Or *in*

b. 8 Or *in*

b. 16 Or *in*

Matt 3	Mark 1	Luke 3	John
burning up the chaff with unquenchable fire."	will baptize you with the Holy Spirit."	his threshing floor and to gather the wheat into his barn, but he will burn up the chaff with unquenchable fire." [18]And with many other words John exhorted the people and preached the good news to them.	

Part 4

The Messiah's
First Public Appearance

The Autumn of A.D. *26*

24. Jesus' Baptism

The Jordan River

Matt. 3:13–17	Mark 1:9–11	Luke 3:21–23a	John
	9At that time		
		21When all the people were being baptized,	
13Then Jesus came from Galilee	Jesus came from Nazareth in Galilee		

to the Jordan to be baptized by John. 14But John tried to deter him, saying, "I need to be baptized by you, and do you come to me?"

15Jesus replied, "Let it be so now; it is proper for us to do this to fulfill all righteousness." Then John consented.

Matt.	Mark	Luke

	and was baptized by John in the Jordan.	Jesus was baptized too.
	10As Jesus was	And as he was praying,
16As soon as Jesus was baptized, he went up out of the water. At that moment heaven was opened, and he saw the Spirit of God	coming up out of the water, he saw heaven being torn open and the Spirit descending on him	heaven was opened 22and the Holy Spirit descended on him in bodily form
descending like a dove and lighting on him.	like a dove.	like a dove.
17And a voice from heaven said, "This is my Son, whom I love; with him I am well pleased."	11And a voice came from heaven: "You are my Son, whom I love; with you I am well pleased."	And a voice came from heaven: "You are my Son, whom I love; with you I am well pleased."
		23Now Jesus himself was about thirty years old when he began his ministry.

25. The Temptation

The wilderness of Judea

Matt. 4:1–11	Mark 1:12–13	Luke 4:1–13	John
		¹Jesus, full of the Holy Spirit, returned from the Jordan and	
	¹²At once the Spirit sent him		
¹Then Jesus was led by the Spirit into the desert to be tempted by the devil. ²After fasting forty days and forty nights, he was hungry.	out into the desert, ¹³and he was in the desert forty days, being tempted by Satan. He was with the wild animals,	was led by the Spirit in the desert, ²where for forty days he was tempted by the devil.	

Mark He ate nothing during those days, and at the end of them he was hungry.

³The tempter came to him and said, "If you are the Son of God, tell these stones to become bread."

⁴Jesus answered, "It is written: 'Man does not live on bread alone, but on every word that comes from the mouth of God.'ᵃ"

⁵Then the devil took him to the holy city and had him stand on the highest point of the temple.

⁶"If you are the Son of God," he said, "throw yourself down. For it is written:

"'He will command his angels concerning you,
    and they will lift you up in their hands,
so that you will not strike your foot against a stone.'ᵇ"

³The devil said to him, "If you are the Son of God, tell this stone to become bread."

⁴Jesus answered, "It is written: 'Man does not live on bread alone.'ᵃ"

⁹The devil led him to Jerusalem and had him stand on the highest point of the temple.

"If you are the Son of God," he said, "throw yourself down from here. ¹⁰For it is written:

"'He will command his angels concerning you
    to guard you carefully;
¹¹they will lift you up in their hands,
    so that you will not strike your foot against a stone.'ᵇ"

⁷Jesus answered him, "It is also written: 'Do not put the Lord your God to the test.'ᶜ"

⁸Again, the devil took him to a very high mountain and showed him all the kingdoms of the world and their splendor. ⁹"All this I will give you," he said, "if you will bow down and worship me."

¹²Jesus answered, "It says: 'Do not put the Lord your God to the test.'ᶜ"

⁵The devil led him up to a high place and showed him in an instant all the kingdoms of the world. ⁶And he said to him,

"I will give you all their authority and splendor, for it has been given to me, and I can give it to

---

a. *4* Deut. 8:3
b. *6* Ps. 91:11, 12
c. *7* Deut. 6:16

---

a. *4* Deut. 8:3
b. *11* Ps. 91:11, 12
c. *12* Deut. 6:16

Matt. 4	Mark 1	Luke 4	John
		anyone I want to. [7]So if you worship me, it will all be yours."	
[10]Jesus said to him, "Away from me, Satan! For it is written: 'Worship the Lord your God, and serve him only.'[a]"		[8]Jesus answered, "It is written: 'Worship the Lord your God and serve him only.'[a]"	
[11]Then the devil left him,		[13]When the devil had finished all this tempting, he left him until an opportune time.	
and angels came and attended him.	[13b]and angels attended him.		
a. *10* Deut. 6:13		a. *8* Deut. 6:13	

26. John the Baptist's Testimony

Bethany, beyond the Jordan

Matt.	Mark	Luke	John 1:15, 19–28
			[19]Now this was John's testimony when the Jews of Jerusalem sent priests and Levites to ask him who he was. [20]He did not fail to confess, but confessed freely, "I am not the Christ.[a]"

[21]They asked him, "Then who are you? Are you Elijah?"

He said, "I am not."

"Are you the Prophet?"

He answered, "No."

[22]Finally they said, "Who are you? Give us an answer to take back to those who sent us. What do you say about yourself?"

[23]John replied in the words of Isaiah the prophet, "I am the voice of one calling in the desert, 'Make straight the way for the Lord.'"[b]

[24]Now some Pharisees who had been sent [25]questioned him, "Why then do you baptize if you are not the Christ, nor Elijah, nor the Prophet?"

[26]"I baptize with[c] water," John replied, "but among you stands one you do not know. [27]He is the one who comes after me, the thongs of whose sandals I am not worthy to untie."

[15]John testified concerning him. He cried out,[d] saying, "This was he of whom I said, 'He who comes after me has surpassed me because he was before me.'"

[28]This all happened at Bethany on the other side of the Jordan, where John was baptizing.

a. *20* Or *Messiah.* "The Christ" (Greek) and "the Messiah" (Hebrew) both mean "the Anointed One"; also in verse 25.
b. *23* Isa. 40:3
c. *26* Or *in;* also in verses 31 and 33
d. The NIV reads "John *testifies* concerning him. He *cries* out."

27. John the Baptist's Introduction of Jesus

Matt.	Mark	Luke	John 1:29–34
			[29]The next day John saw Jesus coming toward him and said, "Look, the Lamb of God, who takes away the sin of the world! [30]This is the one I meant when I said, 'A man who

Matt.	Mark	Luke	John 1

comes after me has surpassed me because he was before me.' [31]I myself did not know him, but the reason I came baptizing with water was that he might be revealed to Israel."

[32]Then John gave this testimony: "I saw the Spirit come down from heaven as a dove and remain on him. [33]I would not have known him, except that the one who sent me to baptize with water told me, 'The man on whom you see the Spirit come down and remain is he who will baptize with the Holy Spirit.' [34]I have seen and I testify that this is the Son of God."

28. Christ's First Contact with Some of the Twelve

Matt.	Mark	Luke	John 1:35–51

[35]The next day John was there again with two of his disciples. [36]When he saw Jesus passing by, he said, "Look, the Lamb of God!"

[37]When the two disciples heard him say this, they followed Jesus. [38]Turning around, Jesus saw them following and asked, "What do you want?"

They said, "Rabbi" (which means Teacher), "where are you staying?"

[39]"Come," he replied, "and you will see."

So they went and saw where he was staying, and spent that day with him. It was about the tenth hour.[a]

[40]Andrew, Simon Peter's brother, was one of the two who heard what John had said and who had followed Jesus. [41]The first thing Andrew did was to find his brother Simon and tell him, "We have found the Messiah" (that is, the Christ). [42]And he brought him to Jesus.

Jesus looked at him and said, "You are Simon son of John. You will be called Cephas" (which, when translated, is Peter[b]).

[43]The next day Jesus decided to leave for Galilee. Finding Philip, he said to him, "Follow me."

[44]Philip, like Andrew and Peter, was from the town of Bethsaida. [45]Philip found Nathanael and told him, "We have found the one Moses wrote about in the Law, and about whom the prophets also wrote—Jesus of Nazareth, the son of Joseph."

[46]"Nazareth! Can anything good come from there?" Nathanael asked.

"Come and see," said Philip.

[47]When Jesus saw Nathanael approaching, he said of him, "Here is a true Israelite, in whom there is nothing false."

[48]"How do you know me?" Nathanael asked.

Jesus answered, "I saw you while you were still under the fig tree before Philip called you."

[49]Then Nathanael declared, "Rabbi, you are the Son of God; you are the King of Israel."

[50]Jesus said, "You believe[c] because I told you I saw you under the fig tree. You shall see greater things than that." [51]He then added, "I tell you[d] the truth, you[e] shall see heaven open, and the angels of God ascending and descending on the Son of Man."

---

a. The time was about 10 A.M. according to the Roman system of counting hours from midnight and noon (which in due course became universal practice). John evidently used this chronological system throughout his Gospel.

b. *42* Both *Cephas* (Aramaic) and *Peter* (Greek) mean *rock.*

c. *50* Or *Do you believe . . . ?*

d. *51* The Greek is plural.

e. *51* The Greek is plural.

PART 5

The Beginning of Christ's Public Ministry in Galilee, Judea, and Samaria

From the End of A.D. 26 to the Autumn of A.D. 27

29. The First Miracle

Cana, in Galilee

Matt.	Mark	Luke	

John 2:1–11

¹On the third day a wedding took place at Cana in Galilee. Jesus' mother was there, ²and Jesus and his disciples had also been invited to the wedding. ³When the wine was gone, Jesus' mother said to him, "They have no more wine."

⁴"Dear woman, why do you involve me?" Jesus replied. "My time has not yet come."

⁵His mother said to the servants, "Do whatever he tells you."

⁶Nearby stood six stone water jars, the kind used by the Jews for ceremonial washing, each holding from twenty to thirty gallons.ᵃ

⁷Jesus said to the servants, "Fill the jars with water"; so they filled them to the brim.

⁸Then he told them, "Now draw some out and take it to the master of the banquet."

They did so, ⁹and the master of the banquet tasted the water that had been turned into wine. He did not realize where it had come from, though the servants who had drawn the water knew. Then he called the bridegroom aside ¹⁰and said, "Everyone brings out the choice wine first and then the cheaper wine after the guests have had too much to drink; but you have saved the best till now."

¹¹This, the first of his miraculous signs, Jesus performed at Cana in Galilee. He thus revealed his glory, and his disciples put their faith in him.

---

a. *6* Greek *two to three metretes* (probably about 75 to 115 liters)

30. Jesus and His Family's Visit to Capernaum

Matt.	Mark	Luke	

John 2:12

¹²After this he went down to Capernaum with his mother and brothers and his disciples. There they stayed for a few days.

31. Christ's First[a] Cleansing of the Temple

The Passover Festival at Jerusalem; the spring of A.D. 27

Matt.	Mark	Luke	John 2:13–22
			[13]When it was almost time for the Jewish Passover, Jesus went up to Jerusalem. [14]In the temple courts he found men selling cattle, sheep and doves, and others sitting at tables exchanging money. [15]So he made a whip out of cords, and drove all from the temple area, both sheep and cattle; he scattered the coins of the money changers and overturned their tables. [16]To those who sold doves he said, "Get these out of here! How dare you turn my Father's house into a market!"

[17]His disciples remembered that it is written: "Zeal for your house will consume me."[b]

[18]Then the Jews demanded of him, "What miraculous sign can you show us to prove your authority to do all this?"

[19]Jesus answered them, "Destroy this temple, and I will raise it again in three days."

[20]The Jews replied, "It has taken forty-six years to build this temple, and you are going to raise it in three days?" [21]But the temple he had spoken of was his body. [22]After he was raised from the dead, his disciples recalled what he had said. Then they believed the Scripture and the words that Jesus had spoken.

---

a. Some New Testament scholars consider this incident to be identical with that recorded in the Synoptic Gospels as taking place three years later (see sec. 136). Other scholars, however, support the assumption that Jesus felt impelled on two occasions to express his indignation at the habitual desecration of the temple, and that John recorded what happened the first time.

b. *17*Ps. 69:9

32. Shallow Belief at Jerusalem

Matt.	Mark	Luke	John 2:23–25
			[23]Now while he was in Jerusalem at the Passover Feast, many people saw the miraculous signs he was doing and believed in his name.[c] [24]But Jesus would not entrust himself to them, for he knew all men. [25]He did not need man's testimony about man, for he knew what was in a man.

---

c. *23*Or *and believed in him*

33. Jesus and Nicodemus

Jerusalem; during the Passover Festival; A.D. 27

Matt.	Mark	Luke	John 3:1–21
			[1]Now there was a man of the Pharisees named Nicodemus, a member of the Jewish ruling council. [2]He came to Jesus at night and said, "Rabbi, we know you are a teacher who has come from God. For no one could perform the miraculous signs you are doing if God were not with him."

Matt.	Mark	Luke

John 3

³In reply Jesus declared, "I tell you the truth, no one can see the kingdom of God unless he is born again.ᵃ"

⁴"How can a man be born when he is old?" Nicodemus asked. "Surely he cannot enter a second time into his mother's womb to be born!"

⁵Jesus answered, "I tell you the truth, no one can enter the kingdom of God unless he is born of water and the Spirit. ⁶Flesh gives birth to flesh, but the Spiritᵇ gives birth to spirit. ⁷You should not be surprised at my saying, 'Youᶜ must be born again.' ⁸The wind blows wherever it pleases. You hear its sound, but you cannot tell where it comes from or where it is going. So it is with everyone born of the Spirit."

⁹"How can this be?" Nicodemus asked.

¹⁰"You are Israel's teacher," said Jesus, "and do you not understand these things? ¹¹I tell you the truth, we speak of what we know, and we testify to what we have seen, but still you people do not accept our testimony. ¹²I have spoken to you of earthly things and you do not believe; how then will you believe if I speak of heavenly things? ¹³No one has ever gone into heaven except the one who came from heaven—the Son of Man.ᵈ ¹⁴Just as Moses lifted up the snake in the desert, so the Son of Man must be lifted up, ¹⁵that everyone who believes in him may have eternal life.ᵉ

¹⁶"For God so loved the world that he gave his one and only Son,ᶠ that whoever believes in him shall not perish but have eternal life. ¹⁷For God did not send his Son into the world to condemn the world, but to save the world through him. ¹⁸Whoever believes in him is not condemned, but whoever does not believe stands condemned already because he has not believed in the name of God's one and only Son.ᵍ ¹⁹This is the verdict: Light has come into the world, but men loved darkness instead of light because their deeds were evil. ²⁰Everyone who does evil hates the light, and will not come into the light for fear that his deeds will be exposed. ²¹But whoever lives by the truth comes into the light, so that it may be seen plainly that what he has done has been done through God."ʰ

---

a. *3 Or born from above; also in verse 7*
b. *6 Or but spirit*
c. *7 The Greek is plural.*
d. *13 Some manuscripts Man, who is in heaven*
e. *15 Or believes may have eternal life in him*
f. *16 Or his only begotten Son*
g. *18 Or God's only begotten Son*
h. *21 Some interpreters end the quotation after verse 15.*

34. A Test of Loyalty

The spring to the autumn of A.D. 27

Matt.	Mark	Luke

John 3:22–36

²²After this, Jesus and his disciples went out into the Judean countryside, where he spent some time with them, and baptized. ²³Now John also was baptizing at Aenon near Salim, because there was plenty of water, and people were constantly coming to be baptized. ²⁴(This was before John was put in prison.) ²⁵An argument developed between some of John's disciples and a certain Jewⁱ over the matter of ceremonial washing. ²⁶They came to John and said to him, "Rabbi, that man who was with you on the other side of the Jordan— the one you testified about—well, he is baptizing, and everyone is going to him."

---

i. *25 Some manuscripts and certain Jews*

Matt.	Mark	Luke	John 3

27To this John replied, "A man can receive only what is given him from heaven. 28You yourselves can testify that I said, 'I am not the Christ[a] but am sent ahead of him.' 29The bride belongs to the bridegroom. The friend who attends the bridegroom waits and listens for him, and is full of joy when he hears the bridegroom's voice. That joy is mine, and it is now complete. 30He must become greater; I must become less.

31"The one who comes from above is above all; the one who is from the earth belongs to the earth, and speaks as one from the earth. The one who comes from heaven is above all. 32He testifies to what he has seen and heard, but no one accepts his testimony. 33The man who has accepted it has certified that God is truthful. 34For the one whom God has sent speaks the words of God, for God[b] gives the Spirit without limit. 35The Father loves the Son and has placed everything in his hands. 36Whoever believes in the Son has eternal life, but whoever rejects the Son will not see life, for God's wrath remains on him."[c]

a. *28* Or *Messiah*
b. *34* Greek *he*
c. *36* Some interpreters end the quotation after verse 30.

35. John the Baptist's Imprisonment

At Machaerus; the autumn of A.D. *27*

Matt. 14:3–5	Mark 6:17–20	Luke 3:19–20	John
		19But when John rebuked Herod the tetrarch because of Herodias, his brother's wife, and all the other evil things he had done, 20Herod added this to them all: He	
	17For Herod himself		
	had given orders to have John arrested, and he had him bound and put in prison. He did this because of Herodias, his brother Philip's wife, whom he had married. 18For John had been saying to Herod, "It is not lawful for you to have your brother's wife."	locked John up in prison.	
3Now Herod had arrested John and bound him and put him in prison because of Herodias, his brother Philip's wife, 4for John had been saying to him: "It is not lawful for you to have her."			
5Herod wanted to kill John, but he was afraid of the people, because they considered him a prophet.	19So		
	Herodias nursed a grudge against John and wanted to kill him. But she was not able to, 20because Herod feared John and protected him, knowing him to be a righteous and holy man. When Herod		

Matt.	Mark 6	Luke	John
	heard John, he was greatly puzzled[a]; yet he liked to listen to him.		

a. 20 Some early manuscripts *he did many things*

36. Christ's Reasons for Leaving Judea

Matt. 4:12	Mark 1:14a	Luke	John 4:1–3, 44
[12]When Jesus heard that John had been put in prison,	[14]After John had been[b] put in prison,		[1]The Pharisees heard that Jesus was gaining and baptizing more disciples than John, [2]although in fact it was not Jesus who baptized, but his disciples. [3]When the Lord learned of this, he left Judea and went back once more to Galilee. [44](Now Jesus himself had pointed out that a prophet has no honor in his own country.)
he returned to Galilee.	Jesus went into Galilee,		

b. The NIV reads "was."

37. Jesus and the Samaritan Woman

Sychar, in Samaria; the autumn of A.D. 27

Matt.	Mark	Luke	John 4:4–43
			[4]Now he had to go through Samaria. [5]So he came to a town in Samaria called Sychar, near the plot of ground Jacob had given to his son Joseph. [6]Jacob's well was there, and Jesus, tired as he was from the journey, sat down by the well. It was about the sixth hour.[a]

[7]When a Samaritan woman came to draw water, Jesus said to her, "Will you give me a drink?" [8](His disciples had gone into the town to buy food.)

[9]The Samaritan woman said to him, "You are a Jew and I am a Samaritan woman. How can you ask me for a drink?" (For Jews do not associate with Samaritans.[b])

[10]Jesus answered her, "If you knew the gift of God and who it is that asks you for a drink, you would have asked him and he would have given you living water."

[11]"Sir," the woman said, "you have nothing to draw with and the well is deep. Where can you get this living water? [12]Are you greater than our father Jacob, who gave us the well and drank from it himself, as did also his sons and his flocks and herds?"

[13]Jesus answered, "Everyone who drinks this water will be thirsty again, [14]but whoever drinks the water I give him will never thirst. Indeed, the water I give him will become in him a spring of water welling up to eternal life."

[15]The woman said to him, "Sir, give me this water so that I won't get thirsty and have to keep coming here to draw water."

a. The time was about 6 P.M. (See the footnote on page 34).
b. 9 Or *do not use dishes Samaritans have used*

Matt.	Mark	Luke

[16]He told her, "Go, call your husband and come back."

[17]"I have no husband," she replied.

Jesus said to her, "You are right when you say you have no husband. [18]The fact is, you have had five husbands, and the man you now have is not your husband. What you have just said is quite true."

[19]"Sir," the woman said, "I can see that you are a prophet. [20]Our fathers worshiped on this mountain, but you Jews claim that the place where we must worship is in Jerusalem."

[21]Jesus declared, "Believe me, woman, a time is coming when you will worship the Father neither on this mountain nor in Jerusalem. [22]You Samaritans worship what you do not know; we worship what we do know, for salvation is from the Jews. [23]Yet a time is coming and has now come when the true worshipers will worship the Father in spirit and truth, for they are the kind of worshipers the Father seeks. [24]God is spirit, and his worshipers must worship in spirit and in truth."

[25]The woman said, "I know that Messiah" (called Christ) "is coming. When he comes, he will explain everything to us."

[26]Then Jesus declared, "I who speak to you am he."

[27]Just then his disciples returned and were surprised to find him talking with a woman. But no one asked, "What do you want?" or "Why are you talking with her?"

[28]Then, leaving her water jar, the woman went back to the town and said to the people, [29]"Come, see a man who told me everything I ever did. Could this be the Christ[a]?" [30]They came out of the town and made their way toward him.

[31]Meanwhile his disciples urged him, "Rabbi, eat something."

[32]But he said to them, "I have food to eat that you know nothing about."

[33]Then his disciples said to each other, "Could someone have brought him food?"

[34]"My food," said Jesus, "is to do the will of him who sent me and to finish his work. [35]Do you not say, 'Four months more and then the harvest'? I tell you, open your eyes and look at the fields! They are ripe for harvest. [36]Even now the reaper draws his wages, even now he harvests the crop for eternal life, so that the sower and the reaper may be glad together. [37]Thus the saying 'One sows and another reaps' is true. [38]I sent you to reap what you have not worked for. Others have done the hard work, and you have reaped the benefits of their labor."

[39]Many of the Samaritans from that town believed in him because of the woman's testimony, "He told me everything I ever did." [40]So when the Samaritans came to him, they urged him to stay with them, and he stayed two days. [41]And because of his words many more became believers.

[42]They said to the woman, "We no longer believe just because of what you said; now we have heard for ourselves, and we know that this man really is the Savior of the world."

[43]After the two days he left for Galilee.

---

a. *29*Or *Messiah*

PART 6

Christ's Great Galilean Ministry

From the Autumn of A.D. 27 to the Spring of A.D. 29

38. The Arrival and Reception of Jesus in Galilee

Matt. 4:17	Mark 1:14b–15	Luke 4:14–15	John 4:45
	¹⁴ᵇJesus went into Galilee,	¹⁴Jesus returned to Galilee in the power of the Spirit,	⁴⁵When he arrived in Galilee,
			the Galileans welcomed him. They had seen all that he had done in Jerusalem at the Passover Feast, for they also had been there.
¹⁷From that time on Jesus began	proclaiming the good news of God.		
		and news about him spread through the whole countryside.	
to preach, "Repent, for the kingdom of heaven is near."	¹⁵"The time has come," he said. "The kingdom of God is near. Repent and believe the good news!"		
		¹⁵He taught in their synagogues, and everyone praised him.	

39. The Healing of a Capernaum Official's Son

At Cana, in Galilee

Matt.	Mark	Luke	John 4:46–54
			⁴⁶Once more he visited Cana in Galilee, where he had turned the water into wine. And there was a certain royal official whose son lay sick at Capernaum. ⁴⁷When this man heard

Matt.	Mark	Luke	John 4

that Jesus had arrived in Galilee from Judea, he went to him and begged him to come and heal his son, who was close to death.

48"Unless you people see miraculous signs and wonders," Jesus told him, "you will never believe."

49The royal official said, "Sir, come down before my child dies."

50Jesus replied, "You may go. Your son will live."

The man took Jesus at his word and departed. 51While he was still on the way, his servants met him with the news that his boy was living. 52When he inquired as to the time when his son got better, they said to him, "The fever left him yesterday at the seventh hour."

53Then the father realized that this was the exact time at which Jesus had said to him, "Your son will live." So he and all his household believed.

54This was the second miraculous sign that Jesus performed, having come from Judea to Galilee.

40. The First Rejection of Jesus at Nazareth

Matt.	Mark	Luke 4:16–30	John

16He went to Nazareth, where he had been brought up, and on the Sabbath day he went into the synagogue, as was his custom. And he stood up to read. 17The scroll of the prophet Isaiah was handed to him. Unrolling it, he found the place where it is written:

18"The Spirit of the Lord is on me,
  because he has anointed me
  to preach good news to the poor.
He has sent me to proclaim freedom for the prisoners
  and recovery of sight for the blind,
to release the oppressed,
  19to proclaim the year of the Lord's favor."a

20Then he rolled up the scroll, gave it back to the attendant and sat down. The eyes of everyone in the synagogue were fastened on him, 21and he began by saying to them, "Today this scripture is fulfilled in your hearing."

22All spoke well of him and were amazed at the gracious words that came from his lips. "Isn't this Joseph's son?" they asked.

23Jesus said to them, "Surely you will quote this proverb to me: 'Physician, heal yourself! Do here in your hometown what we have heard that you did in Capernaum.'"

24"I tell you the truth," he continued, "no prophet is accepted in his hometown. 25I assure you that there were many widows in Israel in Elijah's time, when the sky was shut for three and a half years and there was a severe famine throughout the land. 26Yet Elijah was not sent to any of them, but to a widow in Zarephath in the region of Sidon. 27And there were many in Israel with leprosyb in the time of Elisha the prophet, yet not one of them was cleansed—only Naaman the Syrian."

28All the people in the synagogue were furious when they heard this. 29They got up, drove him out of the town, and took him to the brow of the hill on which the town was

---

a. 19 Isa. 61:1, 2
b. 27 The Greek word was used for various diseases affecting the skin—not necessarily leprosy.

Matt.	Mark	Luke 4	John

built, in order to throw him down the cliff. [30]But he walked right through the crowd and went on his way.

41. Christ's New Home in Capernaum

Matt. 4:13–16	Mark	Luke 4:31a	John

[13]Leaving Nazareth, he went and lived in Capernaum,

[31]Then he went down to Capernaum,

a town in Galilee,

Mark	Luke

which was by the lake in the area of Zebulun and Naphtali—[14]to fulfill what was said through the prophet Isaiah:

[15]"Land of Zebulun and land of Naphtali,
the way to the sea, along the Jordan,
Galilee of the Gentiles—
[16]the people living in darkness
have seen a great light;
on those living in the land of the shadow of death
a light has dawned."[a]

a. *16* Isa. 9:1, 2

42. A Remarkable Catch of Fish

The Lake of Galilee

Matt.	Mark	Luke 5:1–11	John

[1]One day as Jesus was standing by the Lake of Gennesaret,[a] with the people crowding around him and listening to the word of God, [2]he saw at the water's edge two boats, left there by the fishermen, who were washing their nets. [3]He got into one of the boats, the one belonging to Simon, and asked him to put out a little from shore. Then he sat down and taught the people from the boat.

[4]When he had finished speaking, he said to Simon, "Put out into deep water, and let down[b] the nets for a catch."

[5]Simon answered, "Master, we've worked hard all night and haven't caught anything. But because you say so, I will let down the nets."

[6]When they had done so, they caught such a large number of fish that their nets began to break. [7]So they signaled their partners in the other boat to come and help them, and they came and filled both boats so full that they began to sink.

[8]When Simon Peter saw this, he fell at Jesus' knees and said, "Go away from me, Lord; I am a sinful man!" [9]For he and all his companions were astonished at the catch of fish they had taken, [10]and so were James and John, the sons of Zebedee, Simon's partners.
Then

a. *1* That is, Sea of Galilee
b. *4* The Greek verb is plural.

Matt. 4:18–22	Mark 1:16–20	Luke 5	John
[18]As Jesus was walking beside the Sea of Galilee, he saw two brothers, Simon called Peter and his brother Andrew. They were casting a net into the lake, for they were fishermen. [19]"Come, follow me," Jesus said, "and I will make you fishers of men." [20]At once they left their nets and followed him.	[16]As Jesus walked beside the Sea of Galilee, he saw Simon and his brother Andrew casting a net into the lake, for they were fishermen. [17]"Come, follow me," Jesus said, "and I will make you fishers of men." [18]At once they left their nets and followed him.	Jesus said to Simon, "Don't be afraid; from now on you will catch men."	
[21]Going on from there, he saw two other brothers, James son of Zebedee and his brother John. They were in a boat with their father Zebedee, preparing their nets. Jesus called them, [22]and immediately they left the boat and their father and followed him.	[19]When he had gone a little farther, he saw James son of Zebedee and his brother John in a boat, preparing their nets. [20]Without delay he called them, and they left their father Zebedee in the boat with the hired men and followed him.	[11]So they pulled their boats up on shore, left everything and followed him.	

43. A Busy Sabbath in Capernaum

Matt.	Mark 1:21–34	Luke 4:31b–41	John
	[21]They went to Capernaum, and when the Sabbath came, Jesus went into the synagogue and began to teach. [22]The people were amazed at his teaching, because he taught them as one who had authority, not as the teachers of the law.	[31b]and on the Sabbath began to teach the people. [32]They were amazed at his teaching, because his message had authority.	
	[23]Just then a man in their synagogue who was possessed by an evil[a] spirit cried out, [24]"What do you want with us, Jesus of Nazareth? Have you come to destroy us? I know who you are—the Holy One of God!"	[33]In the synagogue there was a man possessed by a demon, an evil[a] spirit. He cried out at the top of his voice, [34]"Ha! What do you want with us, Jesus of Nazareth? Have you come to destroy us? I know who you are—the Holy One of God!"	
	[25]"Be quiet!" said Jesus sternly. "Come out of him!" [26]The evil spirit shook the man violently and came out of him with a shriek.	[35]"Be quiet!" Jesus said sternly. "Come out of him!" Then the demon threw the man down before them all and came out without injuring him.	
	[27]The people were all so amazed that they asked each other, "What is this? A new teaching— and with authority! He even gives orders to evil spirits and they obey him." [28]News	[36]All the people were amazed and said to each other, "What is this teaching? With authority and power he gives orders to evil spirits and they come out!" [37]And the news	

---

a. *23* Greek *unclean;* also in verses 26 and 27

a. *33* Greek *unclean;* also in verse 36

Matt. 8:14–17	Mark 1	Luke 4	John
	about him spread quickly over the whole region of Galilee.	about him spread throughout the surrounding area.	
	[29]As soon as they left the synagogue, they went with James and John to the home of Simon and Andrew. [30]Simon's mother-in-law was in bed with a fever, and they told Jesus about her.	[38]Jesus left the synagogue and went to the home of Simon. Now Simon's mother-in-law was suffering from a high fever, and they asked him[a] to help her.	
[14]When Jesus came into Peter's house, he saw Peter's mother-in-law lying in bed with a fever. [15]He touched her hand and the fever left her, and she got up and began to wait on him.	[31]So he went to her, took her hand and helped her up. The fever left her and she began to wait on them.	[39]So he bent over her and rebuked the fever, and it left her. She got up at once and began to wait on them.	
[16]When evening came, many who were demon-possessed were brought to him,	[32]That evening after sunset the people brought to Jesus all the sick and demon-possessed. [33]The whole town gathered at the door, [34]and Jesus healed many who had various diseases.	[40]When the sun was setting, the people brought to Jesus all who had various kinds of sickness, and laying his hands on each one, he healed them. [41]Moreover, demons came out of many people,	
and he drove out the spirits with a word and healed all the sick.	He also drove out many demons, but he would not let the demons speak because they knew who he was.	shouting, "You are the Son of God!" But he rebuked them and would not allow them to speak, because they knew he was the Christ.[b]	

[17]This was to fulfill what was spoken through the prophet Isaiah: | **Mark**

"He took up our infirmities
and carried our diseases."[a]

a. For the sake of clarity, the NIV reads "Jesus"; but adherence to the pronoun "him" (which is an exact translation of the Greek) improves the wording of the connected narrative.
b. 41 Or Messiah

a. 17 Isa. 53:4

44. Christ's First Tour of Galilee

Matt.	Mark 1:35–39	Luke 4:42–44	John
	[35]Very early in the morning, while it was still dark, Jesus got up, left the house and went off to	[42]At daybreak Jesus went out to a solitary place.	

Matt. 4:23–25	Mark 1	Luke 4	John
	a solitary place, where he prayed. [36]Simon and his companions went to look for him, [37]and when they found him, they exclaimed: "Everyone is looking for you!" [38]Jesus replied, "Let us go somewhere else—to the nearby villages—so I can preach there also. That is why I have come."		
		The people were looking for him and when they came to where he was, they tried to keep him from leaving them. [43]But he said, "I must preach the good news of the kingdom of God to the other towns also, because that is why I was sent."	
[23]Jesus went throughout Galilee, teaching in their synagogues, preaching the good news of the kingdom, and healing every disease and sickness among the people.	[39]So he traveled throughout Galilee, preaching in their synagogues	[44]And he kept on preaching in the synagogues of Judea.[a]	
		a. *44*Or *the land of the Jews;* some manuscripts *Galilee*	
	and driving out demons.		

[24]News about him spread all over Syria, and people brought to him all who were ill with various diseases, those suffering severe pain, the demon-possessed, those having seizures, and the paralyzed, and he healed them. [25]Large crowds from Galilee, the Decapolis,[a] Jerusalem, Judea and the region across the Jordan followed him.

a. *25*That is, the Ten Cities

45. The Healing of a Leper

A town in Galilee

Matt. 8:2–4	Mark 1:40–45	Luke 5:12–16	John
		[12]While Jesus was in one of the towns, a man came along who was covered with leprosy.[b] When he saw Jesus, he fell	
[2]A man with leprosy[b] came and knelt before him and said,	[40]A man with leprosy[a] came to him and begged him		
	on his knees,		
		with his face to the ground and begged him, "Lord, if you are willing, you can make me clean."	
"Lord, if you are willing, you can make me clean."	"If you are willing, you can make me clean."		

b. *2*The Greek word was used for various diseases affecting the skin—not necessarily leprosy.

a. *40*The Greek word was used for various diseases affecting the skin—not necessarily leprosy.

b. *12*The Greek word was used for various diseases affecting the skin—not necessarily leprosy.

Matt. 8	Mark 1	Luke 5	John
³Jesus reached out his hand and touched the man. "I am willing," he said. "Be clean!" Immediately he was cured[a] of his leprosy.	⁴¹Filled with compassion, Jesus reached out his hand and touched the man. "I am willing," he said. "Be clean!" ⁴²Immediately the leprosy left him and he was cured.	¹³Jesus reached out his hand and touched the man. "I am willing," he said. "Be clean!" And immediately the leprosy left him.	
⁴Then Jesus said to him, "See that you don't tell anyone. But go, show yourself to the priest and offer the gift Moses commanded, as a testimony to them."	⁴³Jesus sent him away at once with a strong warning: ⁴⁴"See that you don't tell this to anyone. But go, show yourself to the priest and offer the sacrifices that Moses commanded for your cleansing, as a testimony to them." ⁴⁵Instead he went out and began to talk freely, spreading the news. As a result, Jesus could no longer enter a town openly but stayed outside in lonely places.	¹⁴Then Jesus ordered him, "Don't tell anyone, but go, show yourself to the priest and offer the sacrifices that Moses commanded for your cleansing, as a testimony to them."	
	Yet the people still came to him	¹⁵Yet the news about him spread all the more, so that crowds of people came	
	from everywhere.	to hear him and to be healed of their sicknesses. ¹⁶But Jesus often withdrew to lonely places and prayed.	

a. *3* Greek *made clean*

46. The Healing of a Paralytic

Capernaum

Matt. 9:2–8	Mark 2:1–12	Luke 5:17–26	John
	¹A few days later, when Jesus again entered Capernaum,	¹⁷One day	
		as he was teaching,	
	the people heard that he had come home. ²So many gathered that there was no room left, not even outside the door, and he preached the word to them.		
		Pharisees and teachers of the law, who had come from every village of Galilee and from Judea and Jerusalem, were sitting there. And the power of the Lord was present for him to heal the sick.	

Matt. 9	Mark 2	Luke 5	John
²Some men brought to him a paralytic, lying on a mat.	³Some men came, bringing to him a paralytic,	¹⁸Some men came carrying a paralytic on a mat	
	carried by four of them.		
	⁴Since they could not get him to Jesus because of the crowd, they	and tried to take him into the house to lay him before Jesus. ¹⁹When they could not find a way to do this because of the crowd, they went up on the roof and	
	made an opening in the roof above Jesus and, after digging through it, they[a]		
	lowered the mat the paralyzed man was lying on.	lowered him on his mat through the tiles into the middle of the crowd, right in front of Jesus.	
When Jesus saw their faith, he said to the paralytic, "Take heart, son; your sins	⁵When Jesus saw their faith, he said to the paralytic, "Son, your sins	²⁰When Jesus saw their faith, he said, "Friend, your sins are forgiven."	
are forgiven."	are forgiven." ⁶Now some	²¹The	
³At this, some of the teachers of the law said to themselves, "This fellow is blaspheming!"	teachers of the law were sitting there, thinking to themselves, ⁷"Why does this fellow talk like that? He's blaspheming! Who can forgive sins but God alone?"	Pharisees and the teachers of the law began thinking to themselves, "Who is this fellow who speaks blasphemy? Who can forgive sins but God alone?"	
⁴Knowing their thoughts, Jesus said,	⁸Immediately Jesus knew in his spirit that this was what they were thinking in their hearts, and he said to them,	²²Jesus knew what they were thinking	
"Why do you entertain evil thoughts in your hearts? ⁵Which is easier: to say, 'Your sins are forgiven,' or to say, 'Get up and walk'? ⁶But so that you may know that the Son of Man has authority on earth to forgive sins. . . ." Then he said to the paralytic, "Get up, take your mat and go home." ⁷And the man got up and went home.	"Why are you thinking these things? ⁹Which is easier: to say to the paralytic, 'Your sins are forgiven,' or to say, 'Get up, take your mat and walk'? ¹⁰But that you may know that the Son of Man has authority on earth to forgive sins. . . ." He said to the paralytic, ¹¹"I tell you, get up, take your mat and go home." ¹²He got up, took his mat	and asked, "Why are you thinking these things in your hearts? ²³Which is easier: to say, 'Your sins are forgiven,' or to say, 'Get up and walk'? ²⁴But that you may know that the Son of Man has authority on earth to forgive sins. . . ." He said to the paralyzed man, "I tell you, get up, take your mat and go home." ²⁵Immediately he stood up in front of them, took what he had been lying on	

a. To make the connected narrative run smoothly, "they" (omitted in the NIV) has been inserted; the pronoun is embodied in the Greek verb.

Matt. 9	Mark 2	Luke 5	John
	and walked out in full view of them all.		
8When the crowd saw this, they were filled with awe; and they praised God, who had given such authority to men.	This amazed everyone and they praised God, saying,	and went home praising God. 26Everyone was amazed and gave praise to God. They were filled with awe and said, "We have seen remarkable things today."	
	"We have never seen anything like this!"		

47. Christ's Enlistment of Matthew Levi

Capernaum

Matt. 9:9	Mark 2:13–14	Luke 5:27–28	John
	13Once again Jesus went out beside the lake. A large crowd came to him, and he began to teach them.		
9As Jesus went on from there, he saw a man named Matthew sitting at the tax collector's booth. "Follow me," he told him, and	14As he walked along, he saw Levi son of Alphaeus sitting at the tax collector's booth. "Follow me," Jesus told him, and	27After this, Jesus went out and saw a tax collector by the name of Levi sitting at his tax booth. "Follow me," Jesus said to him, 28and Levi got	
Matthew got up and followed him.	Levi got up and followed him.	up, left everything and followed him.	

48. A Question about Fasting

Capernaum

Matt. 9:10–17	Mark 2:15–22	Luke 5:29–39	John
10While Jesus was having dinner at Matthew's house, many tax collectors and "sinners" came and ate with him and his disciples. 11When the Pharisees saw this, they asked his disciples,	15While Jesus was having dinner at Levi's house, many tax collectors and "sinners" were eating with him and his disciples, for there were many who followed him. 16When the teachers of the law who were Pharisees	29Then Levi held a great banquet for Jesus at his house, and a large crowd of tax collectors and others were eating with them. 30But the Pharisees and the teachers of the law who belonged to their sect	

Matt. 9	Mark 2	Luke 5	John
	saw him eating with the "sinners" and tax collectors, they asked		
	his disciples:	complained to his disciples, "Why do you eat and drink with tax collectors and 'sinners'?"	
"Why does your teacher eat with tax collectors and 'sinners'?"	"Why does he eat with tax collectors and 'sinners'?"		
[12]On hearing this, Jesus said, "It is not the healthy who need a doctor, but the sick.	[17]On hearing this, Jesus said to them, "It is not the healthy who need a doctor, but the sick.	[31]Jesus answered them, "It is not the healthy who need a doctor, but the sick. [32]I have not come	
[13]But go and learn what this means: 'I desire mercy, not sacrifice.'[a] For			
I have not come to call the righteous, but sinners."	I have not come to call the righteous, but sinners."	to call the righteous, but sinners to repentance."	
	[18]Now John's disciples and the Pharisees were fasting.		
[14]Then John's disciples came and	Some people came and	[33]They said to him, "John's disciples	
asked him, "How is it that we and the Pharisees fast,	asked Jesus, "How is it that John's disciples and the disciples of the Pharisees		
		often fast and pray,	
but your disciples do not fast?"	are fasting, but yours are not?"	and so do the disciples of the Pharisees, but yours go on eating and drinking."	
[15]Jesus answered, "How can the guests of the bridegroom mourn while he is with them?	[19]Jesus answered, "How can the guests of the bridegroom fast while he is with them?	[34]Jesus answered, "Can you make the guests of the bridegroom fast while he is with them? [35]But	
	They cannot, so long as they have him with them. [20]But the time		
The time will come when the bridegroom	will come when the bridegroom	the time will come when the bridegroom	
will be taken from them; then they will fast.	will be taken from them, and on that day they will fast.	will be taken from them; in those days they will fast."	
		[36]He told them this parable: "No one tears a patch	
[16]"No one sews a patch of unshrunk cloth on an old garment,	[21]"No one sews a patch of unshrunk cloth on an old garment. If he does,		
		from a new garment and sews it on an old one. If he does, he will have torn the new garment, and	
for the patch will pull away from the garment, making the tear worse.	the new piece will pull away from the old, making the tear worse. [22]And		
		the patch from the new will not match the old. [37]And no one	
[17]Neither do men pour new wine into old wineskins. If they do, the	no one pours new wine into old wineskins. If he does, the wine will burst the skins, and	pours new wine into old wineskins. If he does, the new wine	

a. *13* Hos. 6:6

Matt. 9	Mark 2	Luke 5	John
skins will burst, the wine will run out and the wineskins will be ruined. No, they pour new wine into new wineskins, and both are preserved."	both the wine and the wineskins will be ruined. No, he pours new wine into new wineskins."	will burst the skins, the wine will run out and the wineskins will be ruined. 38No, new wine must be poured into new wineskins. 39And no one after drinking old wine wants the new, for he says, 'The old is better.'"	

49. A Sabbath Controversy

Probably during the Passover Festival; the spring of A.D. 28

Matt.	Mark	Luke	John 5
			1Some time later, Jesus went up to Jerusalem for a feasta of the Jews. 2Now there is in Jerusalem near the Sheep Gate a pool, which in Aramaic is called Bethesdab and which is surrounded by five covered colonnades. 3Here a great number of disabled people used to lie— the blind, the lame, the paralyzed.c 5One who was there had been an invalid for thirty-eight years. 6When Jesus saw him lying there and learned that he had been in this condition for a long time, he asked him, "Do you want to get well?"

7"Sir," the invalid replied, "I have no one to help me into the pool when the water is stirred. While I am trying to get in, someone else goes down ahead of me."

8Then Jesus said to him, "Get up! Pick up your mat and walk." 9At once the man was cured; he picked up his mat and walked.

The day on which this took place was a Sabbath, 10and so the Jews said to the man who had been healed, "It is the Sabbath; the law forbids you to carry your mat."

11But he replied, "The man who made me well said to me, 'Pick up your mat and walk.'"

12So they asked him, "Who is this fellow who told you to pick it up and walk?"

13The man who was healed had no idea who it was, for Jesus had slipped away into the crowd that was there.

14Later Jesus found him at the temple and said to him, "See, you are well again. Stop sinning or something worse may happen to you." 15The man went away and told the Jews that it was Jesus who had made him well.

16So, because Jesus was doing these things on the Sabbath, the Jews persecuted him. 17Jesus said to them, "My Father is always at his work to this very day, and I, too, am working." 18For this reason the Jews tried all the harder to kill him; not only was he breaking the Sabbath, but he was even calling God his own Father, making himself equal with God.

19Jesus gave them this answer: "I tell you the truth, the Son can do nothing by himself; he can do only what he sees his Father doing, because whatever the Father does the Son also does. 20For the Father loves the Son and shows him all he does. Yes, to your amazement he will show him even greater things than these. 21For just as the Father raises the dead

---

a. New Testament scholars differ in their opinions about the identity of this unnamed religious festival. The strongest arguments seem to be those which support the probability that it was the Passover Festival.
b. 2 Some manuscripts *Bethzatha;* other manuscripts *Bethsaida*
c. 3 Some less important manuscripts *paralyzed—and they waited for the moving of the waters.* 4 From time to time an angel of the Lord would come down and stir up the waters. The first one into the pool after each such disturbance would be cured of whatever disease he had.

Matt.	Mark	Luke

John 5

and gives them life, even so the Son gives life to whom he is pleased to give it. [22]Moreover, the Father judges no one, but has entrusted all judgment to the Son, [23]that all may honor the Son just as they honor the Father. He who does not honor the Son does not honor the Father, who sent him.

[24]"I tell you the truth, whoever hears my word and believes him who sent me has eternal life and will not be condemned; he has crossed over from death to life. [25]I tell you the truth, a time is coming and has now come when the dead will hear the voice of the Son of God and those who hear will live. [26]For as the Father has life in himself, so he has granted the Son to have life in himself. [27]And he has given him authority to judge because he is the Son of Man.

[28]"Do not be amazed at this, for a time is coming when all who are in their graves will hear his voice [29]and come out—those who have done good will rise to live, and those who have done evil will rise to be condemned. [30]By myself I can do nothing; I judge only as I hear, and my judgment is just, for I seek not to please myself but him who sent me.

[31]"If I testify about myself, my testimony is not valid. [32]There is another who testifies in my favor, and I know that his testimony about me is valid.

[33]"You have sent to John and he has testified to the truth. [34]Not that I accept human testimony; but I mention it that you may be saved. [35]John was a lamp that burned and gave light, and you chose for a time to enjoy his light.

[36]"I have testimony weightier than that of John. For the very work that the Father has given me to finish, and which I am doing, testifies that the Father has sent me. [37]And the Father who sent me has himself testified concerning me. You have never heard his voice nor seen his form, [38]nor does his word dwell in you, for you do not believe the one he sent. [39]You diligently study[a] the Scriptures because you think that by them you possess eternal life. These are the Scriptures that testify about me, [40]yet you refuse to come to me to have life.

[41]"I do not accept praise from men, [42]but I know you. I know that you do not have the love of God in your hearts. [43]I have come in my Father's name, and you do not accept me; but if someone else comes in his own name, you will accept him. [44]How can you believe if you accept praise from one another, yet make no effort to obtain the praise that comes from the only God[b]?

[45]"But do not think I will accuse you before the Father. Your accuser is Moses, on whom your hopes are set. [46]If you believed Moses, you would believe me, for he wrote about me. [47]But since you do not believe what he wrote, how are you going to believe what I say?"

a. *39* Or *Study diligently* (the imperative)
b. *44* Some early manuscripts *the Only One*

50. Another Sabbath Controversy

Toward the end of April or in early May, A.D. 28

Matt. 12:1–8	Mark 2:23–28	Luke 6:1–5	John
[1]At that time Jesus went through the grainfields on the Sabbath. His disciples were hungry and began	[23]One Sabbath Jesus was going through the grainfields, and as his disciples walked along, they began	[1]One Sabbath Jesus was going through the grainfields, and his disciples began to pick some heads of	

Matt. 12	Mark 2	Luke 6	John
to pick some heads of grain and eat them.	to pick some heads of grain.	grain, rub them in their hands and eat the kernels.	
2When the Pharisees saw this, they said to him,a "Look! Your disciples are doing what is unlawful on the Sabbath."	24The Pharisees said to him, "Look, why are they doing what is unlawful on the Sabbath?"	2Some of the Pharisees asked, "Why are you doing what is unlawful on the Sabbath?"	
3He answered, "Haven't you read what David did when he and his companions were hungry?	25He answered, "Have you never read what David did when he and his companions were hungry and in need? 26In the days of Abiathar the high priest, he entered the house of God and ate the consecrated bread, which is lawful only for priests to eat. And he also gave some to his companions."	3Jesus answered them, "Have you never read what David did when he and his companions were hungry?	
4He entered the house of God, and he and his companions ate the consecrated bread—which was not lawful for them to do, but only for the priests.		4He entered the house of God, and taking the consecrated bread, he ate what is lawful only for priests to eat. And he also gave some to his companions."	
5Or haven't you read in the Law that on the Sabbath the priests in the temple desecrate the day and yet are innocent? 6I tell you that oneb greater than the temple is here. 7If you had known what these words mean, 'I desire mercy, not sacrifice,'c you would not have condemned the innocent.			
	27Then he said to them, "The Sabbath was made for man, not man for the Sabbath. 28So the Son of Man is Lord even of the Sabbath."		
8For the Son of Man is Lord of the Sabbath."		5Then Jesus said to them, "The Son of Man is Lord of the Sabbath."	

---

a. Note that according to Luke's account (6:2), some of the Pharisees also addressed the disciples directly.

b. *6* Or *something;* also in verses 41 and 42

c. *7* Hos. 6:6

51. Another Sabbath Controversy

A synagogue in Galilee

Matt. 12:9–15a	Mark 3:1–6	Luke 6:6–11	John
9Going on from that place, he went into their synagogue, 10and a man with a shriveled hand was	1Another time he went into the synagogue, and a man with a shriveled hand was there. 2Some of them	6On another Sabbath he went into the synagogue and was teaching, and a man was there whose right hand was shriveled.	

Matt. 12	Mark 3	Luke 6	John
there. Looking for a reason to accuse Jesus, they asked him, "Is it lawful to heal on the Sabbath?" ¹¹He said	were looking for a reason to accuse Jesus, so they watched him closely to see if he would heal him on the Sabbath.	⁷The Pharisees and the teachers of the law were looking for a reason to accuse Jesus, so they watched him closely to see if he would heal on the Sabbath. ⁸But Jesus knew what they were thinking and said	
to them, "If any of you has a sheep and it falls into a pit on the Sabbath, will you not take hold of it and lift it out? ¹²How much more valuable is a man than a sheep! Therefore it is lawful to do good on the Sabbath." ¹³Then he said to the man,	³Jesus said to the man with the shriveled hand, "Stand up in front of everyone."	to the man with the shriveled hand, "Get up and stand in front of everyone." So he got up and stood there.	
	⁴Then Jesus asked them, "Which is lawful on the Sabbath: to do good or to do evil, to save life or to kill?"	⁹Then Jesus said to them, "I ask you, which is lawful on the Sabbath: to do good or to do evil, to save life or to destroy it?"	
"Stretch out your hand." So he stretched it out and it was completely restored, just as sound as the other.	But they remained silent. ⁵He looked around at them in anger and, deeply distressed at their stubborn hearts, said to the man, "Stretch out your hand." He stretched it out, and his hand was completely restored.	¹⁰He looked around at them all, and then said to the man, "Stretch out your hand." He did so, and his hand was completely restored.	
		¹¹But they were furious and began to discuss with one another what they might do to Jesus.	
¹⁴But the Pharisees went out and plotted how they might kill Jesus.	⁶Then the Pharisees went out and began to plot with the Herodians how they might kill Jesus.		
¹⁵Aware of this, Jesus withdrew from that place.			

52. The Healing of Multitudes

Matt. 12:15b–21	Mark 3:7–12	Luke	John
^{15b}Many followed him,	⁷Jesus withdrew with his disciples to the lake, and a large crowd from Galilee followed. ⁸When they heard all he was doing, many people came to him from Judea, Jerusalem, Idumea, and the		

Matt. 12	Mark 3	Luke	John
	regions across the Jordan and around Tyre and Sidon. [9]Because of the crowd he told his disciples to have a small boat ready for him, to keep the people from crowding him. [10]For he had		
and he healed all their sick,	healed many, so that those with diseases were pushing forward to touch him. [11]Whenever the evil[a] spirits saw him, they fell down before him and cried out, "You are the Son of God." [12]But he gave them strict orders		
[16]warning them not to tell who he was. [17]This was to fulfill what was spoken through the prophet Isaiah:	not to tell who he was.		

a. *11* Greek *unclean;* also in verse 30

Mark

[18]"Here is my servant whom I have chosen,
    the one I love, in whom I delight;
I will put my Spirit on him,
    and he will proclaim justice to the nations.
[19]He will not quarrel or cry out;
    no one will hear his voice in the streets.
[20]A bruised reed he will not break,
    and a smoldering wick he will not snuff out,
till he leads justice to victory.
    [21]In his name the nations will put their hope."[a]

a. *21* Isa. 42:1–4

53. Christ's Selection of the Twelve

Matt. 10:2–4	Mark 3:13–19	Luke 6:12–16	John
	[13]Jesus went up on a mountainside and called to him those he wanted, and they came to him. [14]He appointed twelve—designating them apostles[b]—	[12]One of those days Jesus went out to a mountainside to pray, and spent the night praying to God. [13]When morning came, he called his disciples to him and chose twelve of them, whom he also designated apostles:	
	that they might be with him and that he might send them out to preach [15]and to have authority to drive out demons. [16]These are		
[2]These are the names of the twelve apostles: first,	the twelve		
Simon (who is called Peter)	he appointed: Simon (to whom he gave the name Peter);	[14]Simon (whom he named Peter), his brother Andrew, James, John,	
and his brother Andrew; James	[17]James son of Zebedee and his	Philip, Bartholomew, [15]Matthew, Thomas, James son of Alphaeus,	

b. *14* Some manuscripts do not have *designating them apostles.*

Matt. 10	Mark 3	Luke 6	John
son of Zebedee, and his brother John;	brother John (to them he gave the name Boanerges, which means Sons of Thunder);		
³Philip and Bartholomew; Thomas and Matthew the tax collector; James	¹⁸Andrew, Philip, Bartholomew, Matthew, Thomas, James		
son of Alphaeus, and Thaddaeus; ⁴Simon the Zealot and Judas Iscariot, who betrayed him.	son of Alphaeus, Thaddaeus, Simon the Zealot ¹⁹and Judas Iscariot, who betrayed him.	Simon who was called the Zealot, ¹⁶Judasª son of James, and Judas Iscariot, who became a traitor.	

a. In Matt. 10:3 and Mark 3:18 this Judas is called Thaddaeus, which was probably his surname.

54. Christ's Sermon on a Mountainside

Matt. 5:1–8:1	Mark	Luke 6:17–49	John
		¹⁷He went down with them and stood on a level place. A large crowd of his disciples was there and a great number of people from all over Judea, from Jerusalem, and from the coast of Tyre and Sidon, ¹⁸who had come to hear him and to be healed of their diseases. Those troubled by evilᵇ spirits were cured, ¹⁹and the people all tried to touch him, because power was coming from him and healing them all.	
¹Now when he saw the crowds, he went up on a mountainside and sat down. His disciples came to him, ²and			
he began to teach them, saying:		²⁰Looking at his disciples, he said:	
³"Blessed are the poor in spirit, for theirs is the kingdom of heaven. ⁴Blessed are those who mourn, for they will be comforted. ⁵Blessed are the meek, for they will inherit the earth. ⁶Blessed are those who hunger and thirst for righteousness, for they will be filled. ⁷Blessed are the merciful, for they will be shown mercy. ⁸Blessed are the pure in heart, for they will see God. ⁹Blessed are the peacemakers,		"Blessed are you who are poor, for yours is the kingdom of God. ²¹Blessed are you who hunger now, for you will be satisfied. Blessed are you who weep now, for you will laugh.	

b. 18 Greek unclean

Matt. 5	Mark	**Luke 6**	John

Matt. 5

for they will be called sons of God.
  [10]Blessed are those who are persecuted be-
     cause of righteousness,
  for theirs is the kingdom of heaven.

  [11]"Blessed are you when people insult you,

persecute you and falsely say all kinds of evil
against you

because of me. [12]Rejoice and be glad, because great
is your reward in heaven, for in the same way they

persecuted the prophets who were before you.

Luke 6

  [22]Blessed are you when men hate you,
     when they exclude you and insult you

  and reject your name as evil,
     because of the Son of Man.

  [23]"Rejoice in that day and leap for joy, because
great is your reward in heaven. For that is how
their fathers
treated the prophets.

	Mark	Luke

[13]"You are the salt of the earth. But if the salt loses its saltiness, how can it be made salty again? It is no longer good for anything, except to be thrown out and trampled by men.

[14]"You are the light of the world. A city on a hill cannot be hidden. [15]Neither do people light a lamp and put it under a bowl. Instead they put it on its stand, and it gives light to everyone in the house. [16]In the same way, let your light shine before men, that they may see your good deeds and praise your Father in heaven.

[17]"Do not think that I have come to abolish the Law or the Prophets; I have not come to abolish them but to fulfill them. [18]I tell you the truth, until heaven and earth disappear, not the smallest letter, not the least stroke of a pen, will by any means disappear from the Law until everything is accomplished. [19]Anyone who breaks one of the least of these commandments and teaches others to do the same will be called least in the kingdom of heaven, but whoever practices and teaches these commands will be called great in the kingdom of heaven. [20]For I tell you that unless your righteousness surpasses that of the Pharisees and the teachers of the law, you will certainly not enter the kingdom of heaven.

[21]"You have heard that it was said to the people long ago, 'Do not murder,[a] and anyone who murders will be subject to judgment.' [22]But I tell you that anyone who is angry with his brother[b] will be subject to judgment. Again, anyone who says to his brother, 'Raca,[c]' is answerable to the Sanhedrin. But anyone who says, 'You fool!' will be in danger of the fire of hell.

[23]"Therefore, if you are offering your gift at the altar and there remember that your brother has something against you, [24]leave your gift there in front of the altar. First go and be reconciled to your brother; then come and offer your gift.

[25]"Settle matters quickly with your adversary who is taking you to court. Do it while you are still with him on the way, or he may hand you over to the judge, and the judge may hand you over to the officer, and you may be thrown into prison. [26]I tell you the truth, you will not get out until you have paid the last penny.[d]

[27]"You have heard that it was said, 'Do not commit adultery.'[e] [28]But I tell you that anyone who looks at a woman lustfully has already committed adultery with her in his heart. [29]If

---

a. *21* Exod. 20:13
b. *22* Some manuscripts *brother without cause*
c. *22* An Aramaic term of contempt
d. *26* Greek *kodrantes*
e. *27* Exod. 20:14

Matt. 5

your right eye causes you to sin, gouge it out and throw it away. It is better for you to lose one part of your body than for your whole body to be thrown into hell. 30And if your right hand causes you to sin, cut it off and throw it away. It is better for you to lose one part of your body than for your whole body to go into hell.

31"It has been said, 'Anyone who divorces his wife must give her a certificate of divorce.'a 32But I tell you that anyone who divorces his wife, except for marital unfaithfulness, causes her to become an adulteress, and anyone who marries the divorced woman commits adultery.

33"Again, you have heard that it was said to the people long ago, 'Do not break your oath, but keep the oaths you have made to the Lord.' 34But I tell you, Do not swear at all: either by heaven, for it is God's throne; 35or by the earth, for it is his footstool; or by Jerusalem, for it is the city of the Great King. 36And do not swear by your head, for you cannot make even one hair white or black. 37Simply let your 'Yes' be 'Yes,' and your 'No,' 'No'; anything beyond this comes from the evil one.

38"You have heard that it was said, 'Eye for eye, and tooth for tooth.'b 39But I tell you,

---

a. *31* Deut. 24:1
b. *38* Exod. 21:24; Lev. 24:20; Deut. 19:21

Mark

Do not resist an evil person. If someone strikes you on the right cheek, turn to him the other also. 40And if someone wants to sue you and take your tunic, let him have your cloak as well. 41If someone forces you to go one mile, go with him two miles. 42Give to the one who asks you, and do not turn away from the one who wants to borrow from you.

29If someone strikes you on one cheek, turn to him the other also. If someone takes your cloak, do not stop him from taking your tunic.

30Give to everyone who asks you,

and if anyone takes what belongs to you, do not demand it back.

43"You have heard that it was said, 'Love your neighborc and hate your enemy.'

44But I tell you: Love your enemiesd and pray for those who persecute you, 45that you may be sons of your Father in heaven. He causes his sun to rise on the evil and the good, and sends rain on the righteous and the unrighteous. 46If you love those who love you, what reward will you get? Are not even the tax collectors doing that?

27"But I tell you who hear me: Love your enemies, do good to those who hate you, 28bless those who curse you, pray for those who mistreat you.

32"If you love those who love you, what credit is that to you?

Even 'sinners' love those who love them. 33And if you do good to those who are good to you, what credit is that to you? Even 'sinners' do that. 34And if you lend to those from whom you expect repayment, what credit is that to you? Even 'sinners' lend to 'sinners,' expecting to be repaid in full.

---

c. *43* Lev. 19:18
d. *44* Some late manuscripts *enemies, bless those who curse you, do good to those who hate you*

Matt. 5–6	Mark	Luke 6	John

Matt. 5–6

47And if you greet only your brothers, what are you doing more than others? Do not even pagans do that?

Luke 6

35But love your enemies, do good to them, and lend to them without expecting to get anything back. Then your reward will be great, and you will be sons of the Most High, because he is kind to the ungrateful and wicked.

48Be perfect, therefore, as your heavenly Father is perfect.

26Woe to you when all men speak well of
you,
for that is how their fathers treated the
false prophets.

	Mark	Luke

1"Be careful not to do your 'acts of righteousness' before men, to be seen by them. If you do, you will have no reward from your Father in heaven.

2"So when you give to the needy, do not announce it with trumpets, as the hypocrites do in the synagogues and on the streets, to be honored by men. I tell you the truth, they have received their reward in full. 3But when you give to the needy, do not let your left hand know what your right hand is doing, 4so that your giving may be in secret. Then your Father, who sees what is done in secret, will reward you.

5"And when you pray, do not be like the hypocrites, for they love to pray standing in the synagogues and on the street corners to be seen by men. I tell you the truth, they have received their reward in full. 6But when you pray, go into your room, close the door and pray to your Father, who is unseen. Then your Father, who sees what is done in secret, will reward you. 7And when you pray, do not keep on babbling like pagans, for they think they will be heard because of their many words. 8Do not be like them, for your Father knows what you need before you ask him.

9"This, then, is how you should pray:

"'Our Father in heaven,
hallowed be your name,
10your kingdom come,
your will be done
  on earth as it is in heaven.
11Give us today our daily bread.
12Forgive us our debts,
   as we also have forgiven our debtors.
13And lead us not into temptation,
but deliver us from the evil one.a'

14For if you forgive men when they sin against you, your heavenly Father will also forgive you. 15But if you do not forgive men their sins, your Father will not forgive your sins.

16"When you fast, do not look somber as the hypocrites do, for they disfigure their faces to show men they are fasting. I tell you the truth, they have received their reward in full. 17But when you fast, put oil on your head and wash your face, 18so that it will not be obvious

---

a. *13* Or *from evil;* some late manuscripts *one, for yours is the kingdom and the power and the glory forever. Amen.*

| Matt. 6–7 | Mark | Luke 6 | John |

to men that you are fasting, but only to your Father, who is unseen; and your Father, who sees what is done in secret, will reward you.

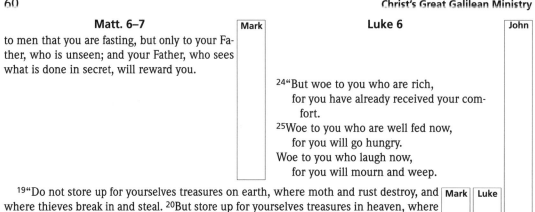

24"But woe to you who are rich,
  for you have already received your comfort.
25Woe to you who are well fed now,
  for you will go hungry.
Woe to you who laugh now,
  for you will mourn and weep.

Mark **Luke**

19"Do not store up for yourselves treasures on earth, where moth and rust destroy, and where thieves break in and steal. 20But store up for yourselves treasures in heaven, where moth and rust do not destroy, and where thieves do not break in and steal. 21For where your treasure is, there your heart will be also.

22"The eye is the lamp of the body. If your eyes are good, your whole body will be full of light. 23But if your eyes are bad, your whole body will be full of darkness. If then the light within you is darkness, how great is that darkness!

24"No one can serve two masters. Either he will hate the one and love the other, or he will be devoted to the one and despise the other. You cannot serve both God and Money.

25"Therefore I tell you, do not worry about your life, what you will eat or drink; or about your body, what you will wear. Is not life more important than food, and the body more important than clothes? 26Look at the birds of the air; they do not sow or reap or store away in barns, and yet your heavenly Father feeds them. Are you not much more valuable than they? 27Who of you by worrying can add a single hour to his life[a]?

28"And why do you worry about clothes? See how the lilies of the field grow. They do not labor or spin. 29Yet I tell you that not even Solomon in all his splendor was dressed like one of these. 30If that is how God clothes the grass of the field, which is here today and tomorrow is thrown into the fire, will he not much more clothe you, O you of little faith? 31So do not worry, saying, 'What shall we eat?' or 'What shall we drink?' or 'What shall we wear?' 32For the pagans run after all these things, and your heavenly Father knows that you need them. 33But seek first his kingdom and his righteousness, and all these things will be given to you as well. 34Therefore do not worry about tomorrow, for tomorrow will worry about itself. Each day has enough trouble of its own.

---

a. 27 Or *single cubit to his height*

1"Do not judge, or you too will be judged.

Mark

36Be merciful, just as your Father is merciful.
37"Do not judge, and you will not be judged. Do not condemn, and you will not be condemned. Forgive, and you will be forgiven. 38Give, and it will be given to you. A good measure, pressed down, shaken together and running over, will be poured into your lap.
For with the measure you use, it will be measured to you."

2For in the same way you judge others, you will be judged, and with the measure you use, it will be measured to you.

Matt. 7	Mark	Luke 6	John

Luke 6

[39]He also told them this parable: "Can a blind man lead a blind man? Will they not both fall into a pit? [40]A student is not above his teacher, but everyone who is fully trained will be like his teacher.

[3]"Why do you look at the speck of sawdust in your brother's eye and pay no attention to the plank in your own eye? [4]How can you say to your brother, 'Let me take the speck out of your eye,' when all the time there is a plank in your own eye? [5]You hypocrite, first take the plank out of your own eye, and then you will see clearly to remove the speck from your brother's eye.

[41]"Why do you look at the speck of sawdust in your brother's eye and pay no attention to the plank in your own eye? [42]How can you say to your brother, 'Brother, let me take the speck out of your eye,' when you yourself fail to see the plank in your own eye? You hypocrite, first take the plank out of your eye, and then you will see clearly to remove the speck from your brother's eye.

[6]"Do not give dogs what is sacred; do not throw your pearls to pigs. If you do, they may trample them under their feet, and then turn and tear you to pieces.

[7]"Ask and it will be given to you; seek and you will find; knock and the door will be opened to you. [8]For everyone who asks receives; he who seeks finds; and to him who knocks, the door will be opened.

[9]"Which of you, if his son asks for bread, will give him a stone? [10]Or if he asks for a fish, will give him a snake? [11]If you, then, though you are evil, know how to give good gifts to your children, how much more will your Father in heaven give good gifts to those who ask him! [12]So in everything, do to others what you would have them do to you, for this sums up the Law and the Prophets.

[31]Do to others as you would have them do to you.

[13]"Enter through the narrow gate. For wide is the gate and broad is the road that leads to destruction, and many enter through it. [14]But small is the gate and narrow the road that leads to life, and only a few find it.

[15]"Watch out for false prophets. They come to you in sheep's clothing, but inwardly they are ferocious wolves. [16]By their fruit you will recognize them.

[44]Each tree is recognized by its own fruit. People do not pick figs from thornbushes, or grapes from briers.

Do people pick grapes from thornbushes, or figs from thistles? [17]Likewise every good tree bears good fruit, but a bad tree bears bad fruit. [18]A good tree cannot bear bad fruit, and a bad tree cannot bear good fruit. [19]Every tree that does not bear good fruit is cut down and thrown into

[43]"No good tree bears bad fruit, nor does a bad tree bear good fruit.

Matt. 7–8	Mark	Luke 6	John

Matt. 7–8

the fire. [20]Thus, by their fruit you will recognize them.

[21]"Not everyone who says to me, 'Lord, Lord,' will enter the kingdom of heaven, but only he who does the will of my Father who is in heaven. [22]Many will say to me on that day, 'Lord, Lord, did we not prophesy in your name, and in your name drive out demons and perform many miracles?' [23]Then I will tell them plainly, 'I never knew you. Away from me, you evildoers!'

[24]"Therefore everyone who hears these words of mine and puts them into practice is like
a wise man
who built his house on the rock.
[25]The rain came down, the streams rose, and the winds blew and beat against that house; yet it did not fall, because it had its foundation on the rock. [26]But everyone who hears these words of mine and does not put them into practice is like a foolish man who built his house
on sand.
[27]The rain came down, the streams rose, and the winds blew and beat against that house, and it fell with a great crash."

Luke 6

[45]The good man brings good things out of the good stored up in his heart, and the evil man brings evil things out of the evil stored up in his heart. For out of the overflow of his heart his mouth speaks.
[46]"Why do you call me, 'Lord, Lord,' and do not do what I say?

[47]I will show you what he is like who comes to me and hears my words and puts them into practice. [48]He is like
a man
building a house, who dug down deep and laid the foundation on rock. When a flood came, the torrent struck that house but could not shake it, because it was well built.
[49]But the one who hears my words and does not put them into practice is like a man who built a house
on the ground without a foundation.

The moment the torrent struck that house, it collapsed

and its destruction was complete."

	Mark	Luke

[28]When Jesus had finished saying these things, the crowds were amazed at his teaching, [29]because he taught as one who had authority, and not as their teachers of the law. [1]When he came down from the mountainside, large crowds followed him.

55. The Healing of a Centurion's Servant

Capernaum

Matt. 8:5–13	Mark	Luke 7:1–10	John

Matt. 8:5–13

[5]When Jesus had entered Capernaum, a centurion came to him, asking for help. [6]"Lord," he said,

Luke 7:1–10

[1]When Jesus had finished saying all this in the hearing of the people, he entered Capernaum.

Matt. 8	Mark	Luke 7	John

Matt. 8

"my servant lies at home paralyzed and in terrible suffering."

[7]Jesus said,[a] "I will go and heal him."

[8]The centurion replied, "Lord, I do not deserve to have you come under my roof.

But just say the word, and my servant will be healed. [9]For I myself am a man under authority, with soldiers under me. I tell this one, 'Go,' and he goes; and that one, 'Come,' and he comes. I say to my servant, 'Do this,' and he does it."

[10]When Jesus heard this, he was astonished and said to those following him,

"I tell you the truth, I have not found anyone in Israel with such great faith. [11]I say to you that many will come from the east and the west, and will take their places at the feast with Abraham, Isaac and Jacob in the kingdom of heaven. [12]But the subjects of the kingdom will be thrown outside, into the darkness, where there will be weeping and gnashing of teeth."

[13]Then Jesus said to the centurion, "Go! It will be done just as you believed it would." And his servant was healed at that very hour.

---

a. Two words, "to him," have been omitted from Matthew's account in order to avoid ambiguity in the composite narrative.

Luke 7

[2]There a centurion's servant, whom his master valued highly, was sick and about to die. [3]The centurion heard of Jesus and sent some elders of the Jews to him, asking him to come and heal his servant.[a] [4]When they came to Jesus, they pleaded earnestly with him, "This man deserves to have you do this, [5]because he loves our nation and has built our synagogue."

[6]So Jesus went with them.

He was not far from the house when the centurion sent friends to say to him: "Lord, don't trouble yourself, for I do not deserve to have you come under my roof. [7]That is why I did not even consider myself worthy to come to you. But say the word, and my servant will be healed. [8]For I myself am a man under authority, with soldiers under me. I tell this one, 'Go,' and he goes; and that one, 'Come,' and he comes. I say to my servant, 'Do this,' and he does it."

[9]When Jesus heard this, he was amazed at him, and turning to the crowd following him, he said,

"I tell you, I have not found such great faith even in Israel."

[10]Then the men who had been sent returned to the house and found the servant well.

---

a. Matthew's Gospel reads as though the centurion came personally to Jesus, whereas Luke's account is more specific. Matthew, however, with reference to the servant's illness, provides information which Luke does not record, namely, that the servant was "paralyzed and in terrible suffering."

56. A Widow's Son Restored to Life

Nain

Matt.	Mark	Luke 7:11–17	John
		11Soon afterward, Jesus went to a town called Nain, and his disciples and a large crowd went along with him. 12As he approached the town gate, a dead person was being carried out—the only son of his mother, and she was a widow. And a large crowd from the town was with her. 13When the Lord saw her, his heart went out to her and he said, "Don't cry." 14Then he went up and touched the coffin, and those carrying it stood still. He said, "Young man, I say to you, get up!" 15The dead man sat up and began to talk, and Jesus gave him back to his mother. 16They were all filled with awe and praised God. "A great prophet has appeared among us," they said. "God has come to help his people." 17This news about Jesus spread throughout Judea[a] and the surrounding country.	

a. *17* Or *the land of the Jews*

57. An Inquiry from John the Baptist

Matt. 11:2–30	Mark	Luke 7:18–35	John
2When John heard in prison what Christ was doing, he sent his disciples 3to ask him, "Are you the one who was to come, or should we expect someone else?"		18John's disciples told him about all these things. Calling two of them, 19he sent them to the Lord to ask, "Are you the one who was to come, or should we expect someone else?" 20When the men came to Jesus, they said, "John the Baptist sent us to you to ask, 'Are you the one who was to come, or should we expect someone else?'" 21At that very time Jesus cured many who had diseases, sicknesses and evil spirits, and gave sight to many who were blind. 22So he replied to	
4Jesus replied, "Go back and report to John what you hear and see: 5The blind receive sight, the lame walk, those who have leprosy[a] are cured, the deaf hear, the dead are raised, and the good news is preached to the poor. 6Blessed is the man who does not fall away on account of me."		the messengers, "Go back and report to John what you have seen and heard: The blind receive sight, the lame walk, those who have leprosy[b] are cured, the deaf hear, the dead are raised, and the good news is preached to the poor. 23Blessed is the man who does not fall away on account of me."	
7As John's disciples were leaving, Jesus began to speak to the crowd about John: "What did you go out into the desert to see? A reed swayed by the wind? 8If not, what did you go out to see? A man dressed in fine clothes? No, those who wear fine		24After John's messengers left, Jesus began to speak to the crowd about John: "What did you go out into the desert to see? A reed swayed by the wind? 25If not, what did you go out to see? A man dressed in fine clothes? No, those who	

a. *5* The Greek word was used for various diseases affecting the skin—not necessarily leprosy.

b. *22* The Greek word was used for various diseases affecting the skin—not necessarily leprosy.

Matt. 11	Mark	**Luke 7**	John

Matt. 11

clothes are in kings' palaces. [9]Then what did you go out to see? A prophet? Yes, I tell you, and more than a prophet. [10]This is the one about whom it is written:

> "'I will send my messenger ahead of you,
>   who will prepare your way before you.'[a]

[11]I tell you the truth: Among those born of women there has not risen anyone greater than John the Baptist; yet he who is least in the kingdom of heaven is greater than he. [12]From the days of John the Baptist until now, the kingdom of heaven has been forcefully advancing, and forceful men lay hold of it. [13]For all the Prophets and the Law prophesied until John. [14]And if you are willing to accept it, he is the Elijah who was to come.

[15]He who has ears, let him hear.

[16]"To what can I compare this generation? They are like children sitting in the marketplaces and calling out to others:

> [17]"'We played the flute for you,
>   and you did not dance;
> we sang a dirge,
>   and you did not mourn.'

[18]For John came neither eating nor drinking, and they say, 'He has a demon.' [19]The Son of Man came eating and drinking, and they say, 'Here is a glutton and a drunkard, a friend of tax collectors and "sinners."' But wisdom is proved right by her actions."

[20]Then Jesus began to denounce the cities in which most of his miracles had been performed, because they did not repent. [21]"Woe to you, Korazin! Woe to you, Bethsaida! If the miracles that

Luke 7

wear expensive clothes and indulge in luxury are in palaces. [26]But what did you go out to see? A prophet? Yes, I tell you, and more than a prophet. [27]This is the one about whom it is written:

> "'I will send my messenger ahead of you,
>   who will prepare your way before you.'[a]

[28]I tell you, among those born of women there is no one greater than John; yet the one who is least in the kingdom of God is greater than he."

[29](All the people, even the tax collectors, when they heard Jesus' words, acknowledged that God's way was right, because they had been baptized by John. [30]But the Pharisees and experts in the law rejected God's purpose for themselves, because they had not been baptized by John.)

[31]"To what, then, can I compare the people of this generation? What are they like? [32]They are like children sitting in the marketplace and calling out to each other:

> "'We played the flute for you,
>   and you did not dance;
> we sang a dirge,
>   and you did not cry.'

[33]For John the Baptist came neither eating bread nor drinking wine, and you say, 'He has a demon.' [34]The Son of Man came eating and drinking, and you say, 'Here is a glutton and a drunkard, a friend of tax collectors and "sinners."' [35]But wisdom is proved right by all her children."[b]

---

a. *27* Mal. 3:1
b. Matthew's Gospel (v. 19) reads "by her actions." The meaning of both Gospels is the same, namely, that the worth of Christ's teaching is attested by the demonstrated results.

---

a. *10* Mal. 3:1

| | | | Mark | Luke | John |

Matt. 11

were performed in you had been performed in Tyre and Sidon, they would have repented long ago in sackcloth and ashes. 22But I tell you, it will be more bearable for Tyre and Sidon on the day of judgment than for you. 23And you, Capernaum, will you be lifted up to the skies? No, you will go down to the depths.a If the miracles that were performed in you had been performed in Sodom, it would have remained to this day. 24But I tell you that it will be more bearable for Sodom on the day of judgment than for you."

25At that time Jesus said, "I praise you, Father, Lord of heaven and earth, because you have hidden these things from the wise and learned, and revealed them to little children. 26Yes, Father, for this was your good pleasure.

27"All things have been committed to me by my Father. No one knows the Son except the Father, and no one knows the Father except the Son and those to whom the Son chooses to reveal him.

28"Come to me, all you who are weary and burdened, and I will give you rest. 29Take my yoke upon you and learn from me, for I am gentle and humble in heart, and you will find rest for your souls. 30For my yoke is easy and my burden is light."

a. *23* Greek *Hades*

58. A Penitent Woman

| Matt. | Mark | Luke 7:36–50 | John |

36Now one of the Pharisees invited Jesus to have dinner with him, so he went to the Pharisee's house and reclined at the table. 37When a woman who had lived a sinful life in that town learned that Jesus was eating at the Pharisee's house, she brought an alabaster jar of perfume, 38and as she stood behind him at his feet weeping, she began to wet his feet with her tears. Then she wiped them with her hair, kissed them and poured perfume on them.

39When the Pharisee who had invited him saw this, he said to himself, "If this man were a prophet, he would know who is touching him and what kind of woman she is—that she is a sinner."

40Jesus answered him, "Simon, I have something to tell you."

"Tell me, teacher," he said.

41"Two men owed money to a certain moneylender. One owed him five hundred denarii,a and the other fifty. 42Neither of them had the money to pay him back, so he canceled the debts of both. Now which of them will love him more?"

43Simon replied, "I suppose the one who had the bigger debt canceled."

"You have judged correctly," Jesus said.

44Then he turned toward the woman and said to Simon, "Do you see this woman? I came into your house. You did not give me any water for my feet, but she wet my feet with her tears and wiped them with her hair. 45You did not give me a kiss, but this woman, from the time I entered, has not stopped kissing my feet. 46You did not put oil on my head, but she has poured perfume on my feet. 47Therefore, I tell you, her many sins have been forgiven— for she loved much. But he who has been forgiven little loves little."

48Then Jesus said to her, "Your sins are forgiven."

a. *41* A denarius was a coin worth about a day's wages.

Matt.	Mark	Luke 7	John

⁴⁹The other guests began to say among themselves, "Who is this who even forgives sins?"

⁵⁰Jesus said to the woman, "Your faith has saved you; go in peace."

59. Christ's Second Tour of Galilee

Matt.	Mark	Luke 8:1–3	John

¹After this, Jesus traveled about from one town and village to another, proclaiming the good news of the kingdom of God. The Twelve were with him, ²and also some women who had been cured of evil spirits and diseases: Mary (called Magdalene) from whom seven demons had come out; ³Joanna the wife of Cuza, the manager of Herod's household; Susanna; and many others. These women were helping to support them out of their own means.

60. John the Baptist's Death

Matt. 14:6–13a

⁶On Herod's birthday the daughter of Herodias danced for them and pleased Herod so much ⁷that he promised with an oath to give her whatever she asked. ⁸Prompted by her mother, she said, "Give me here on a platter the head of John the Baptist." ⁹The king was distressed, but because of his oaths and his dinner guests, he ordered that her request be granted ¹⁰and had John beheaded in the prison. ¹¹His head was brought in on a platter and given to the girl, who carried it to her mother. ¹²John's disciples came and took his body and buried it.

Mark 6:21–29

²¹Finally the opportune time came. On his birthday Herod gave a banquet for his high officials and military commanders and the leading men of Galilee. ²²When the daughter of Herodias came in and danced, she pleased Herod and his dinner guests.

The king said to the girl, "Ask me for anything you want, and I'll give it to you." ²³And he promised her with an oath, "Whatever you ask I will give you, up to half my kingdom."

²⁴She went out and said to her mother, "What shall I ask for?"

"The head of John the Baptist," she answered.

²⁵At once the girl hurried in to the king with the request: "I want you to give me right now the head of John the Baptist on a platter."

²⁶The king was greatly distressed, but because of his oaths and his dinner guests, he did not want to refuse her. ²⁷So he immediately sent an executioner with orders to bring John's head. The man went, beheaded John in the prison, ²⁸and brought back his head on a platter. He presented it to the girl, and she gave it to her mother. ²⁹On hearing of this, John's disciples came and took his body and laid it in a tomb.

Luke	John

Then they went and told Jesus.

¹³When Jesus heard what had happened, he withdrew . . .

61. Christ's Intensive Ministry

Probably Capernaum

Matt. 12:22–50	Mark 3:20–35	Luke	John
	20Then Jesus entered a house, and again a crowd gathered, so that he and his disciples were not even able to eat. 21When his family heard about this, they went to take charge of him, for they said, "He is out of his mind."		
22Then they brought him a demon-possessed man who was blind and mute, and Jesus healed him, so that he could both talk and see. 23All the people were astonished and said, "Could this be the Son of David?"			
24But when the Pharisees	22And the teachers of the law who came down from Jerusalem		
heard this, they said,	said, "He is possessed by Beelzebub[a]!		
"It is only by Beelzebub,[a] the prince of demons, that this fellow drives out demons."	By the prince of demons he is driving out demons."		
25Jesus knew their thoughts and said to them, "Every kingdom divided against itself	23So Jesus called them and spoke to them in parables: "How can Satan drive out Satan? 24If a kingdom is divided against itself, that kingdom		
will be ruined, and every city or household divided against itself will not stand. 26If Satan drives out Satan, he is divided against himself. How then can his kingdom stand?	cannot stand. 25If a house is divided against itself, that house cannot stand. 26And if Satan opposes himself and is divided, he cannot stand;		
	his end has come.		
27And if I drive out demons by Beelzebub, by whom do your people drive them out? So then, they will be your judges. 28But if I drive out demons by the Spirit of God, then the kingdom of God has come upon you.			
29"Or again, how can anyone enter a strong man's house and carry off his possessions unless he first ties up the strong man? Then he can rob his house.	27In fact, no one can enter a strong man's house and carry off his possessions unless he first ties up the strong man. Then he can rob his house.		
30"He who is not with me is against me, and he who does not gather with me scatters.			
31And so I tell you, every sin and blasphemy will be forgiven men, but	28I tell you the truth, all the sins and blasphemies of men will be forgiven them. 29But		

a. *24* Greek *Beezeboul* or *Beelzeboul;* also in verse 27

a. *22* Greek *Beezeboul* or *Beelzeboul*

Matt. 12

the blasphemy against the Spirit will not be forgiven. ³²Anyone who speaks a word against the Son of Man will be forgiven, but anyone who speaks against the Holy Spirit will not be forgiven, either in this age or in the age to come.

³³"Make a tree good and its fruit will be good, or make a tree bad and its fruit will be bad, for a tree is recognized by its fruit. ³⁴You brood of vipers, how can you who are evil say anything good? For out of the overflow of the heart the mouth speaks. ³⁵The good man brings good things out of the good stored up in him, and the evil man brings evil things out of the evil stored up in him. ³⁶But I tell you that men will have to give account on the day of judgment for every careless word they have spoken. ³⁷For by your words you will be acquitted, and by your words you will be condemned."

³⁸Then some of the Pharisees and teachers of the law said to him, "Teacher, we want to see a miraculous sign from you."

³⁹He answered, "A wicked and adulterous generation asks for a miraculous sign! But none will be given it except the sign of the prophet Jonah. ⁴⁰For as Jonah was three days and three nights in the belly of a huge fish, so the Son of Man will be three days and three nights in the heart of the earth. ⁴¹The men of Nineveh will stand up at the judgment with this generation and condemn it; for they repented at the preaching of Jonah, and now one[a] greater than Jonah is here. ⁴²The Queen of the South will rise at the judgment with this generation and condemn it; for she came from the ends of the earth to listen to Solomon's wisdom, and now one greater than Solomon is here.

⁴³"When an evil[b] spirit comes out of a man, it goes through arid places seeking rest and does not find it. ⁴⁴Then it says, 'I will return to the house I left.' When it arrives, it finds the house unoccupied, swept clean and put in order. ⁴⁵Then it goes and takes with it seven other spirits more wicked than itself, and they go in and live there. And the final condition of that man is worse than the first. That is how it will be with this wicked generation."

a. *41* Or *something;* also in verse 42
b. *43* Greek *unclean*

Mark 3

whoever blasphemes against the Holy Spirit will never be forgiven;
he is guilty of an eternal sin."

³⁰He said this because they were saying, "He has an evil spirit."

Luke | John

Luke 8:19–21

Matt.	Mark	Luke
⁴⁶While Jesus was still talking to the crowd, his mother and brothers	³¹Then Jesus' mother and brothers	¹⁹Now Jesus' mother and brothers came to see him,
	arrived.	
		but they were not able to get near him because of the crowd.
stood outside, wanting to speak to him. ⁴⁷Someone told	Standing outside, they sent someone in to call him. ³²A crowd was	

Matt. 12	Mark 3	Luke 8	John
him, "Your mother and brothers are standing outside, wanting to speak to you."[a]	sitting around him, and they told him, "Your mother and brothers are outside looking for you."	20Someone told him, "Your mother and brothers are standing outside, wanting to see you."	
48He replied to him, "Who is my mother, and who are my brothers?"	33"Who are my mother and my brothers?" he asked.		
	34Then he looked at those seated in a circle around him and said, "Here are my mother and my brothers!		
49Pointing to his disciples, he said, "Here are my mother and my brothers.		21He replied,	
	35Whoever does God's will is my brother and sister and mother."	"My mother and brothers are those who hear God's word and put it into practice."	
50For whoever does the will of my Father in heaven is my brother and sister and mother."			

a. 47Some manuscripts do not have verse 47.

62. Parables about the Kingdom of God

Matt. 13:1–53	Mark 4:1–34	Luke 8:4–18	John
1That same day Jesus went out of the house and sat by the lake. 2Such large crowds gathered around him that he got into a boat and sat in it, while all the people stood on the shore. 3Then he told them many things in parables, saying: "A farmer went out to sow his seed. 4As he was scattering the seed, some fell along the path, and the birds came and ate it up. 5Some fell on rocky places, where it did not have much soil. It sprang up quickly, because the soil was shallow. 6But when the sun came up, the plants were scorched, and they withered because they had no root. 7Other seed fell among thorns, which grew up and choked the plants. 8Still other seed fell on good soil, where it produced a crop—a hundred, sixty or thirty times what	1Again Jesus began to teach by the lake. The crowd that gathered around him was so large that he got into a boat and sat in it out on the lake, while all the people were along the shore at the water's edge. 2He taught them many things by parables, and in his teaching said: 3"Listen! A farmer went out to sow his seed. 4As he was scattering the seed, some fell along the path, and the birds came and ate it up. 5Some fell on rocky places, where it did not have much soil. It sprang up quickly, because the soil was shal-	4While a large crowd was gathering and people were coming to Jesus from town after town, he told this parable: 5"A farmer went out to sow his seed. As he was scattering the seed, some fell along the path; it was trampled on, and the birds of the air ate it up. 6Some fell on rock, and when it came up, the plants withered	

Matt. 13	Mark 4	Luke 8	John
was sown.	low. [6]But when the sun came up, the plants were scorched,		
	and they withered because they had no root. [7]Other seed fell among thorns, which grew up	because they had no moisture. [7]Other seed fell among thorns, which grew up	
		with it	
	and choked the plants, so that they did not bear grain. [8]Still other seed fell on good soil. It came up, grew and produced a crop, multiplying thirty, sixty, or even	and choked the plants. [8]Still other seed fell on good soil. It came up and yielded a crop,	
	a hundred times."	a hundred times more than was sown."	
	[9]Then Jesus said,	When he said this, he called out,	
[9]He who has ears, let him hear." [10]The disciples	"He who has ears to hear, let him hear."	"He who has ears to hear, let him hear."	
came to him and asked, "Why do you speak to the people in parables?"	[10]When he was alone, the Twelve and the others around him asked him	[9]His disciples asked him what this parable meant. [10]He said, "The knowledge of the secrets of the kingdom of God has been given to you,	
[11]He replied, "The knowledge of the secrets of the kingdom of heaven has been given to you, but not to them. [12]Whoever has will be given more, and he will have an abundance. Whoever does not have, even what he has will be taken from him. [13]This is why	about the parables. [11]He told them, "The secret of the kingdom of God has been given to you.		
	But	but	
I speak to them in parables:	to those on the outside everything is said in parables [12]so that,	to others I speak in parables, so that,	
"Though seeing, they do not see; though hearing, they do not hear or understand.	"'they may be ever seeing but never perceiving, and ever hearing but never understanding; otherwise they might turn and be forgiven!'[a]"	"'though seeing, they may not see; though hearing, they may not understand.'[a]	

| | a. *12* Isa. 6:9, 10 | a. *10* Isa. 6:9 | |

[14]In them is fulfilled the prophecy of Isaiah:

"'You will be ever hearing but never understanding;
you will be ever seeing but never perceiving.
[15]For this people's heart has become calloused;
they hardly hear with their ears,

| | | Mark | Luke |

Matt. 13   Mark | Luke | John

and they have closed their eyes.
Otherwise they might see with their eyes,
   hear with their ears,
   understand with their hearts
and turn, and I would heal them.'[a]

[16]But blessed are your eyes because they see, and your ears because they hear. [17]For I tell you the truth, many prophets and righteous men longed to see what you see but did not see it, and to hear what you hear but did not hear it.

---

a. *15* Isa. 6:9, 10

Matthew	Mark	Luke
	[13]Then Jesus said to them, "Don't you understand this parable? How then will you understand any parable?	
[18]"Listen then to what the parable of the sower means:		[11]"This is the meaning of the parable: The seed is the word of God.
	[14]The farmer sows the word. [15]Some people are like seed along the path, where the word is sown. As soon as they hear	[12]Those along the path are the ones who hear,
[19]When anyone hears the message about the kingdom, not understanding[b] it, the evil one comes and snatches away what was sown in his heart. This is the seed sown along the path.	it, Satan comes and takes away the word that was sown in them.	and then the devil comes and takes away the word from their hearts, so that they may not believe and be saved.
[20]The one who received the seed that fell on rocky places is the man who hears the word and at once receives it with joy.	[16]Others, like seed sown on rocky places, hear the word and at once receive it with joy. [17]But since they have no root,	[13]Those on the rock are the ones who receive the word with joy when they hear it, but they have no root. They believe for a while, but
[21]But since he has no root, he lasts only a short time. When trouble or persecution comes because of the word, he quickly falls away.	they last only a short time. When trouble or persecution comes because of the word, they quickly fall away.	in the time of testing they fall away.
[22]The one who received the seed that fell among the thorns is the man who hears the word, but	[18]Still others, like seed sown among thorns, hear the word; [19]but	[14]The seed that fell among thorns stands for those who hear, but as they go on their way

---

b. The NIV reads "and does not understand." The wording has been slightly altered to avoid ambiguity in the composite narrative.

Matt. 13	Mark 4	Luke 8	John
the worries of this life and the deceitfulness of wealth choke it,	the worries of this life, the deceitfulness of wealth and the desires for other things come in and choke the word,	they are choked by life's worries, riches and pleasures,	
making it unfruitful. 23But the one who received the seed that fell on good soil is the man who hears the word and understands it. He produces a crop, yielding a hundred, sixty or thirty times what was sown."	making it unfruitful. 20Others, like seed sown on good soil, hear the word, accept it, and produce a crop—thirty, sixty or even a hundred times what was sown."	and they do not mature. 15But the seed on good soil stands for those with a noble and good heart, who hear the word, retain it, and by persevering produce a crop.	

Matt.

21He said to them, "Do you bring in a lamp to put it under a bowl or a bed?

16"No one lights a lamp and hides it in a jar or puts it under a bed. Instead, he puts it on a stand, so that those who come in can see the light. 17For there is nothing hidden that will not be disclosed, and nothing concealed that will not be known or brought out into the open.

Instead, don't you put it on its stand? 22For whatever is hidden is meant to be disclosed, and whatever is concealed is meant to be brought out into the open.

23If anyone has ears to hear, let him hear."

24"Consider carefully what you hear," he continued. "With the measure you use, it will be measured to you—and even more. 25Whoever has will be given more; whoever does not have, even what he has will be taken from him."

18Therefore consider carefully how you listen. Whoever has will be given more; whoever does not have, even what he thinks he has will be taken from him."

Luke

26He also said, "This is what the kingdom of God is like. A man scatters seed on the ground. 27Night and day, whether he sleeps or gets up, the seed sprouts and grows, though he does not know how. 28All by itself the soil produces grain—first the stalk, then the head, then the full kernel in the head. 29As soon as the grain is ripe, he puts the sickle to it, because the harvest has come."

Mark

24Jesus told them another parable: "The kingdom of heaven is like a man who sowed good seed in his field. 25But while everyone was sleeping, his enemy came and sowed weeds among the wheat, and went away. 26When the wheat sprouted and formed heads, then the weeds also appeared.

27"The owner's servants came to him and said, 'Sir, didn't you sow good seed in your field? Where then did the weeds come from?'

28"'An enemy did this,' he replied.

"The servants asked him, 'Do you want us to go and pull them up?'

29"'No,' he answered, 'because while you are pulling the weeds, you may root up the wheat with them. 30Let both grow together until the harvest. At that time I will tell the harvesters: First collect the weeds and tie them in bundles to be burned; then gather the wheat and bring it into my barn.'"

31He told them another parable:

30Again he said, "What shall we say the kingdom of God is like, or what parable shall we use to describe it?

Matt. 13	Mark 4	Luke	John

"The kingdom of heaven is like a mustard seed, which a man took and planted in his field. 32Though it is the smallest of all your seeds, yet when it grows, it is the largest of garden plants and becomes a tree,

so that the birds of the air come and perch in its branches."

33He told them still another parable: "The kingdom of heaven is like yeast that a woman took and mixed into a large amount[a] of flour until it worked all through the dough."

34Jesus spoke all these things

to the crowd

in parables; he did not say anything to them without using a parable.
35So was fulfilled what was spoken through the prophet:

"I will open my mouth in parables,
    I will utter things hidden since the cre-
        ation of the world."[b]

36Then he left the crowd and went into the house. His disciples came to him and said, "Explain to us the parable of the weeds in the field."

31It is like a mustard seed, which is the smallest seed you plant in the ground. 32Yet when planted, it grows and becomes the largest of all garden plants,

with such big branches that the birds of the air can perch in its shade."

33With many similar parables Jesus spoke the word

to them,

as much as they could understand. 34He did not say anything to them without using a parable.

But when he was alone with his own disciples, he explained everything.

---

a. *33* Greek *three satas* (probably about ½ bushel or 22 liters)
b. *35* Ps. 78:2

| | Mark |

37He answered, "The one who sowed the good seed is the Son of Man. 38The field is the world, and the good seed stands for the sons of the kingdom. The weeds are the sons of the evil one, 39and the enemy who sows them is the devil. The harvest is the end of the age, and the harvesters are angels.

40"As the weeds are pulled up and burned in the fire, so it will be at the end of the age. 41The Son of Man will send out his angels, and they will weed out of his kingdom everything that causes sin and all who do evil. 42They will throw them into the fiery furnace, where there will be weeping and gnashing of teeth. 43Then the righteous will shine like the sun in the kingdom of their Father. He who has ears, let him hear.

44"The kingdom of heaven is like treasure hidden in a field. When a man found it, he hid it again, and then in his joy went and sold all he had and bought that field.

45"Again, the kingdom of heaven is like a merchant looking for fine pearls. 46When he found one of great value, he went away and sold everything he had and bought it.

47"Once again, the kingdom of heaven is like a net that was let down into the lake and caught all kinds of fish. 48When it was full, the fishermen pulled it up on the shore. Then they sat down and collected the good fish in baskets, but threw the bad away. 49This is how it will be at the end of the age. The angels will come and separate the wicked from the righteous 50and throw them into the fiery furnace, where there will be weeping and gnashing of teeth.

Matt. 13

	Mark	Luke	John

51"Have you understood all these things?" Jesus asked.

"Yes," they replied.

52He said to them, "Therefore every teacher of the law who has been instructed about the kingdom of heaven is like the owner of a house who brings out of his storeroom new treasures as well as old."

53When Jesus had finished these parables, he moved on from there.

63. The Calming of a Storm

The Lake of Galilee

Matt. 8:18, 23–27	Mark 4:35–41	Luke 8:22–25	John
	35That day when evening came,	22One day Jesus said to his disciples, "Let's go over to the other side of the lake." So they got into a boat	
18When Jesus saw the crowd around him, he	he		
gave orders to cross	said to his disciples, "Let us go over		
to the other side of the lake.	to the other side."		
23Then he got into the boat and his disciples followed him.			
	36Leaving the crowd behind, they took him along, just as he was, in the boat. There were also other boats with him.	and set out.	
		23As they sailed, he fell asleep.	
24Without warning, a furious storm came up on the lake, so that the waves swept over	37A furious squall came up, and the waves broke over	A squall came down on the lake, so that the boat	
	the boat, so that it		
	was nearly swamped.	was being swamped, and they were in great danger.	
the boat. But Jesus was sleeping. 25The disciples went and woke him, saying,	38Jesus was in the stern, sleeping on a cushion.		
	The disciples woke him and said to him,	24The disciples went and woke him, saying, "Master, Master, we're going to drown!"	
"Lord, save us! We're going to drown!"	"Teacher, don't you care if we drown?"		
26He replied, "You of little faith, why are you so afraid?" Then he got up and rebuked the winds and the waves, and it was completely calm.	39He got up, rebuked the wind and said to the waves, "Quiet! Be still!" Then the wind died down and it was completely calm.	He got up and rebuked the wind and the raging waters; the storm subsided, and all was calm.	

Matt. 8	Mark 4	Luke 8	John
	40He said to his disciples, "Why are you so afraid? Do you still have no faith?" 41They were terrified and	25"Where is your faith?" he asked his disciples.	
27The men were amazed and asked, "What kind of man is this? Even the winds and the waves obey him!"	asked each other, "Who is this? Even the wind and the waves obey him!"	In fear and amazement they asked one another, "Who is this? He commands even the winds and the water, and they obey him."	

64. The Healing of a Demoniac

Southeast of the Lake of Galilee

Matt. 8:28–9:1a	Mark 5:1–20	Luke 8:26–39	John
28When he arrived at the other side in the region of the Gadarenes,a two demon-possessed men coming from the tombs met him. They were	1They went across the lake to the region of the Gerasenes.a 2When Jesus got out of the boat, a man with an evilb spirit came from the tombs to meet him. 3This man lived	26They sailed to the region of the Gerasenes,a which is across the lake from Galilee. 27When Jesus stepped ashore, he was met by a demon-possessed manb from the town. For a long time this man had not worn clothes or lived in a house, but had lived	
	in the tombs,	in the tombs.	
so violent that no one could pass that way.	and	29bMany times the demonc had seized him, and	
	no one could bind him any more, not even with a chain. 4For he had often been chained hand and foot,	though he was chained hand and foot	
	but he tore the chains apart and broke the irons on his feet.	and kept under guard, he had broken his chains and had been driven by the demon into solitary places.	
	No one was strong enough to subdue him. 5Night and day among the tombs and in the hills he would cry out and cut himself with stones.		

a. 1 Some manuscripts Gadarenes; other manuscripts Gergesenes
b. 2 Greek unclean; also in verses 8 and 13

a. 26 Some manuscripts Gadarenes; other manuscripts Gergesenes; also in verse 37
b. Matthew mentions two demoniacs. As Mark and Luke describe only one, it is probable that he was the more prominent one.
c. The NIV reads "it." The words "the demon" have been substituted for the sake of clarity.

a. 28 Some manuscripts Gergesenes; others Gerasenes

Matt. 8	Mark 5	Luke 8	John
	[6]When he saw Jesus from a distance, he ran and fell on his knees in front of him. [7]He shouted at the top of his voice, "What do you want with me, Jesus, Son of the Most High God? Swear to God that you won't torture me!" [8]For Jesus had said to him, "Come out of this man, you evil spirit!"	[28]When he saw Jesus, he cried out and fell at his feet, shouting at the top of his voice, "What do you want with me, Jesus, Son of the Most High God? I beg you, don't torture me!" [29]For Jesus had commanded the evil[a] spirit to come out of the man.	
[29]"What do you want with us, Son of God?" they shouted.			
	[9]Then Jesus asked him, "What is your name?" "My name is Legion," he replied, "for we are many."	[30]Jesus asked him, "What is your name?" "Legion," he replied, because many demons had gone into him.	
"Have you come here to torture us before the appointed time?" they cried.[a]	[10]And he begged Jesus again and again not to send them out of the area.	[31]And they begged him repeatedly not to order them to go into the Abyss.	
[30]Some distance from them a large herd of pigs was feeding.	[11]A large herd of pigs was feeding on the nearby hillside. [12]The demons begged Jesus,	[32]A large herd of pigs was feeding there on the hillside. The demons begged Jesus to let them go into them, and	
[31]The demons begged Jesus, "If you drive us out, send us into the herd of pigs." [32]He said to them, "Go!" So they came out and went into the pigs, and the	"Send us among the pigs; allow us to go into them." [13]He gave them permission, and the evil spirits came out	he gave them permission. [33]When the demons came out of the man,	
whole herd rushed down the steep bank into the lake and died in the water.	and went into the pigs. The herd, about two thousand in number, rushed down the steep bank into the lake and were drowned.	they went into the pigs, and the herd rushed down the steep bank into the lake and was drowned.	
[33]Those tending the pigs ran off, went into the town and reported all this, including what had happened to the demon-possessed men.	[14]Those tending the pigs ran off and reported this in the town and countryside, and the people went out to see what had happened. [15]When they came to Jesus, they saw the man	[34]When those tending the pigs saw what had happened, they ran off and reported this in the town and countryside, [35]and the people went out to see what had happened. When they came to Jesus, they found the man	

a. To make the composite narrative read smoothly, the words "they cried" have been inserted; they are not in the NIV.

a. *29 Greek* unclean

Matt. 8	Mark 5	Luke 8	John
34Then the whole town went out to meet Jesus.	who had been possessed by the legion of demons,		
	sitting there, dressed and in his right mind; and they were afraid. 16Those who had seen it told the people what had happened to the demon-possessed man—	from whom the demons had gone out, sitting at Jesus' feet, dressed and in his right mind; and they were afraid. 36Those who had seen it told the people how the demon-possessed man had been cured.	
	and told about the pigs as well. 17Then	37Then	
And when they saw him, they pleaded with him to leave their region.	the people	all the people of the region of the Gerasenes	
	began to plead with Jesus to leave their region.	asked Jesus to leave them,	
		because they were overcome with fear.	
1Jesus stepped into a boat,	18As Jesus was getting into the boat, the man who had been demon-possessed	So he got into the boat and left. 38The man	
		from whom the demons had gone out	
	begged to go with him. 19Jesus did not let him, but said, "Go home	begged to go with him, but Jesus sent him away, saying, 39"Return home	
	to your family and tell them how much the Lord has done for you, and how he has had mercy on you." 20So the man went away and began to tell in the Decapolisa how much Jesus had done for him. And all the people were amazed.	and tell how much God has done for you." So the man went away and told all over town how much Jesus had done for him.	

a. *20* That is, the Ten Cities

65. The Healing of a Woman and the Restoration of Jairus's Daughter

Capernaum

Matt. 9:1b, 18–26	Mark 5:21–43	Luke 8:40–56	John
[1aJesus . . .] 1bcrossed over and came to his own town.	21When Jesus had again crossed over by boat to the other side of the lake,	40Now when Jesus returned, a crowd	

Matt. 9	Mark 5	Luke 8	John
	a large crowd		
	gathered around him	welcomed him, for they were all expecting him.	
¹⁸While he was saying this, a ruler came	while he was by the lake. ²²Then one of the synagogue rulers, named Jairus, came there. Seeing Jesus, he fell at his feet		
and knelt before him		⁴¹Then a man named Jairus, a ruler of the synagogue, came and fell at Jesus' feet, pleading with	
	²³and pleaded earnestly with him, "My little	him to come to his house	
and said, "My daughter has just died. But come and put your hand on her, and she will live."	daughterᵃ is dying. Please come and put your hands on her so that she will be healed and live."	⁴²because his only daughter, a girl of about twelve, was dying.	
¹⁹Jesus got up and went with him, and so did his disciples.	²⁴So Jesus went with him.		
		As Jesus was on his way,	
	A large crowd followed and pressed around him. ²⁵And a	the crowds almost crushed him.	
²⁰Just then a woman who had been subject to bleeding for twelve years	woman was there who had been subject to bleeding for twelve years. ²⁶She had suffered a great deal under the care of many doctors and had spent all she had, yet instead of getting better she grew worse.	⁴³And a woman was there who had been subject to bleeding for twelve years,ᵃ	
		but no one could heal her.	
came up behind him and	²⁷When she heard about Jesus, she came up behind him in the crowd and		
touched the edge of his cloak. ²¹She said to herself, "If I only touch his cloak, I will be healed."	touched his cloak, ²⁸because she thought, "If I just touch his clothes, I will be healed."	⁴⁴She came up behind him and touched the edge of his cloak,	
	²⁹Immediately her bleeding stopped and she felt in her body that she was freed from her suffering.	and immediately her bleeding stopped.	
	³⁰At once Jesus realized that power had gone out from him. He turned around in the crowd and asked, "Who touched my clothes?"	⁴⁵"Who touched me?" Jesus asked.	
	³¹"You see the people crowding against you," his disciples answered, "and yet you can ask, 'Who touched me?'"		

---

a. Luke, in 8:42, compassionately adds that the girl was Jairus' only daughter.

a. *43* Many manuscripts *years, and she had spent all she had on doctors*

Matt. 9	Mark 5	Luke 8	John
	32But Jesus kept looking around to see who had done it.		
		When they all denied it, Peter said, "Master, the people are crowding and pressing against you." 46But Jesus said, "Someone touched me; I know that power has gone out from me."	
	33Then the woman, knowing what had happened to her, came and fell at his feet and, trembling with fear, told him the whole truth.	47Then the woman, seeing that she could not go unnoticed, came trembling and fell at his feet.	
22Jesus turned and saw her.	34He said to her, "Daughter,	In the presence of all the people, she told why she had touched him and how she had been instantly healed. 48Then he said to her,	
"Take heart, daughter," he said, "your faith has healed you."	your faith has healed you. Go in peace and be freed from your suffering."	"Daughter, your faith has healed you. Go in peace."	
And the woman was healed from that moment.			
	35While Jesus was still speaking, some men came from the house of Jairus, the synagogue ruler. "Your daughter is dead," they said. "Why bother the teacher any more?" 36Ignoring what they said, Jesus told the synagogue ruler,	49While Jesus was still speaking, someone came from the house of Jairus, the synagogue ruler. "Your daughter is dead," he said. "Don't bother the teacher any more." 50Hearing this, Jesus said to Jairus,	
23When Jesus entered the ruler's house and	"Don't be afraid; just believe."	"Don't be afraid; just believe, and she will be healed."	
	37He did not let anyone follow him except Peter, James and John the brother of James. 38When they came to the home of the synagogue ruler, Jesus	51When he arrived at the house of Jairus, he did not let anyone go in with him except Peter, John and James, and the child's father and mother. 52Meanwhile, all the people were wailing and mourning for her.	
saw the flute players and the noisy crowd,	saw a commotion, with people crying and wailing loudly. 39He went in and said to them, "Why all this commotion and wailing?		
24he said,		"Stop wailing," Jesus said. "She is not dead but asleep."	
"Go away. The girl is not dead but asleep." But	The child is not dead but asleep."		

Matt. 9	Mark 5	Luke 8	John
they laughed at him. 25After the crowd had been put outside,	40But they laughed at him.	53They laughed at him, knowing that she was dead.	
he went in and took the girl by the hand,	After he put them all out, he took the child's father and mother and the disciples who were with him, and went in where the child was. 41He took her by the hand and said to her, *"Talitha koum!"* (which means, "Little girl, I say to you, get up!"). 42Immediately the girl	54But he took her by the hand and said, "My child, get up!" 55Her spirit returned, and at once she	
and she got up.	stood up and walked around (she was twelve years old). At this they were completely astonished. 43He gave strict orders not to let anyone know about this, and told them to give her something to eat.	stood up. 56Her parents were astonished, but he ordered them not to tell anyone what had happened. 55bThen Jesus told them to give her something to eat.	
26News of this spread through all that region.			

66. The Healing of Two Blind Men and a Demoniac

Probably Capernaum

Matt. 9:27–34	Mark	Luke	John

27As Jesus went on from there, two blind men followed him, calling out, "Have mercy on us, Son of David!"

28When he had gone indoors, the blind men came to him, and he asked them, "Do you believe that I am able to do this?"

"Yes, Lord," they replied.

29Then he touched their eyes and said, "According to your faith will it be done to you"; 30and their sight was restored. Jesus warned them sternly, "See that no one knows about this." 31But they went out and spread the news about him all over that region.

32While they were going out, a man who was demon-possessed and could not talk was brought to Jesus. 33And when the demon was driven out, the man who had been mute spoke. The crowd was amazed and said, "Nothing like this has ever been seen in Israel."

34But the Pharisees said, "It is by the prince of demons that he drives out demons."

67. The Final[a] Rejection of Jesus at Nazareth

Matt. 13:54–58	Mark 6:1–6a	Luke	John

Matt. 13:54–58

54Coming to his hometown, he began teaching the people in their synagogue, and they were amazed. "Where did this man get this wisdom and these miraculous powers?" they asked. 55"Isn't this the carpenter's son? Isn't his mother's name Mary, and aren't his brothers James, Joseph, Simon and Judas?

56Aren't all his sisters with us? Where then did this man get all these things?" 57And they took offense at him.

But Jesus said to them, "Only in his hometown and in his own house is a prophet without honor." 58And he did not do many miracles there because of their lack of faith.

Mark 6:1–6a

1Jesus left there and went to his hometown, accompanied by his disciples. 2When the Sabbath came, he began to teach in the synagogue, and many who heard him were amazed.

"Where did this man get these things?" they asked. "What's this wisdom that has been given him, that he even does miracles! 3Isn't this the carpenter? Isn't this Mary's son and the brother of James, Joseph,[b] Judas and Simon? Aren't his sisters here with us?" And they took offense at him.

4Jesus said to them, "Only in his hometown, among his relatives and in his own house is a prophet without honor." 5He could not do any miracles there, except lay his hands on a few sick people and heal them. 6And he was amazed at their lack of faith.

a. It is not necessary to identify this visit to Nazareth with that recorded by Luke (in sec. 40) as taking place at the beginning of Christ's great Galilean ministry. It is only natural that after a long interval Jesus should give his own townspeople another opportunity to accept him and his message. Moreover, the recorded details of the two visits are different.
b. *3* Greek *Joses*, a variant of *Joseph*

68. Christ's Third Tour of Galilee

Matt. 9:35–38	Mark 6:6b	Luke	John

Matt. 9:35–38

35Jesus went through all the towns and villages, teaching in their synagogues, preaching the good news of the kingdom and healing every disease and sickness. 36When he saw the crowds, he had compassion on them, because they were harassed and helpless, like sheep without a shepherd. 37Then he said to his disciples, "The harvest is plentiful but the workers are few. 38Ask the Lord of the harvest, therefore, to send out workers into his harvest field."

Mark 6:6b

6bThen Jesus went around teaching from village to village.

(Mark)

69. Christ's Mission Instructions to the Twelve

Matt. 10:1, 5–11:1	Mark 6:7–13	Luke 9:1–6	John

Matt. 10:1, 5–11:1

1He called his twelve disciples to him

Mark 6:7–13

7Calling the Twelve to him,

Luke 9:1–6

1When Jesus had called the Twelve together,

Matt. 10	Mark 6	Luke 9	John
and gave them authority to drive out evil[a] spirits and to heal every disease and sickness.	he	he gave them power and authority to drive out all demons and to cure diseases, [2]and he	
	sent them out two by two	sent them out to preach the kingdom of God	
[5]These twelve Jesus sent out with the following instructions:	and gave them authority over evil[a] spirits. [8]These were his instructions:	and to heal the sick. [3]He told them:	
"Do not go among the Gentiles or enter any town of the Samaritans. [6]Go rather to the lost sheep of Israel. [7]As you go, preach this message: 'The kingdom of heaven is near.' [8]Heal the sick, raise the dead, cleanse those who have leprosy,[b] drive out demons. Freely you have received, freely give.			
	"Take nothing for the journey	"Take nothing for the journey—no staff, no bag, no bread, no money, no extra tunic.	
[9]Do not take along any gold or silver or copper in your belts; [10]take no bag for the journey, or extra tunic, or sandals or a staff;[c]	except a staff— no bread,		
for the worker is worth his keep.	no bag, no money in your belts.		
[11]"Whatever town or village you enter, search for some worthy person there and stay at his house until you leave. [12]As you enter the home, give it your greeting.	[9]Wear sandals but not an extra tunic. [10]Whenever you enter a house, stay there until you leave that town.	[4]Whatever house you enter, stay there until you leave that town.	
[13]If the home is deserving, let your peace rest on it; if it is not, let your peace return to you. [14]If anyone will not welcome you or listen to your words, shake the dust off your feet when you	[11]And if any place will not welcome you or listen to you, shake the dust off your feet when you	[5]If people do not welcome you, shake the dust off your feet when you	

a. *1* Greek *unclean*
b. *8* The Greek word was used for various diseases affecting the skin—not necessarily leprosy.
c. It should be noticed that according to Mark the instructions included permission to carry staves and to wear sandals. This would seem to indicate that in this respect the instructions to all the disciples were not the same, and that Peter (who is believed to be the main source for Mark's Gospel) and his companion, at least, were permitted this additional equipment probably because they were being sent to a more rugged part of the country.

a. *7* Greek *unclean*

Matt. 10	Mark 6	Luke 9	John
leave that home or town.	leave, as a testimony against them."	leave their town, as a testimony against them."	

15I tell you the truth, it will be more bearable for Sodom and Gomorrah on the day of judgment than for that town. 16I am sending you out like sheep among wolves. Therefore be as shrewd as snakes and as innocent as doves.

17"Be on your guard against men; they will hand you over to the local councils and flog you in their synagogues. 18On my account you will be brought before governors and kings as witnesses to them and to the Gentiles. 19But when they arrest you, do not worry about what to say or how to say it. At that time you will be given what to say, 20for it will not be you speaking, but the Spirit of your Father speaking through you.

21"Brother will betray brother to death, and a father his child; children will rebel against their parents and have them put to death. 22All men will hate you because of me, but he who stands firm to the end will be saved. 23When you are persecuted in one place, flee to another. I tell you the truth, you will not finish going through the cities of Israel before the Son of Man comes.

24"A student is not above his teacher, nor a servant above his master. 25It is enough for the student to be like his teacher, and the servant like his master. If the head of the house has been called Beelzebub,a how much more the members of his household!

26"So do not be afraid of them. There is nothing concealed that will not be disclosed, or hidden that will not be made known. 27What I tell you in the dark, speak in the daylight; what is whispered in your ear, proclaim from the roofs. 28Do not be afraid of those who kill the body but cannot kill the soul. Rather, be afraid of the One who can destroy both soul and body in hell. 29Are not two sparrows sold for a pennyb? Yet not one of them will fall to the ground apart from the will of your Father. 30And even the very hairs of your head are all numbered. 31So don't be afraid; you are worth more than many sparrows.

32"Whoever acknowledges me before men, I will also acknowledge him before my Father in heaven. 33But whoever disowns me before men, I will disown him before my Father in heaven.

34"Do not suppose that I have come to bring peace to the earth. I did not come to bring peace, but a sword. 35For I have come to turn

"'a man against his father,
  a daughter against her mother,
  a daughter-in-law against her mother-in-law—
  36a man's enemies will be the members of his own household.'c

37"Anyone who loves his father or mother more than me is not worthy of me; anyone who loves his son or daughter more than me is not worthy of me; 38and anyone who does not take his cross and follow me is not worthy of me. 39Whoever finds his life will lose it, and whoever loses his life for my sake will find it.

40"He who receives you receives me, and he who receives me receives the one who sent me. 41Anyone who receives a prophet because he is a prophet will receive a prophet's reward, and anyone who receives a righteous man because he is a righteous man will receive a righteous man's reward. 42And if anyone gives even a cup of cold water to one of these

a. 25 Greek *Beezeboul* or *Beelzeboul*
b. 29 Greek *an assarion*
c. 36 Mic. 7:6

Matt. 10	Mark 6	Luke 9	John
little ones because he is my disciple, I tell you the truth, he will certainly not lose his reward." [1]After Jesus had finished instructing his twelve disciples, he went on from there to teach and preach in the towns of Galilee.[a]			
	[12]They went out and preached	[6]So they set out and went from village to village, preaching the gospel	
	that people should repent. [13]They drove out many demons and anointed many sick people with oil and healed them.	and healing people everywhere.	

a. *1* Greek *in their towns*

70. Herod Antipas's Agitation

Probably Tiberias

Matt. 14:1–2	Mark 6:14–16	Luke 9:7–9	John
[1]At that time Herod the tetrarch heard the reports about Jesus, [2]and	[14]King Herod heard about this,	[7]Now Herod the tetrarch heard	
	for Jesus' name had become well known.	about all that was going on.	
he said	Some were saying,[a]	And he was perplexed, because some were saying	
to his attendants, "This is John the Baptist; he has risen from the dead! That is why miraculous powers are at work in him."	"John the Baptist has been raised from the dead, and that is why miraculous powers are at work in him." [15]Others said, "He is Elijah." And still others claimed, "He is a prophet, like one of the prophets of long ago." [16]But when Herod heard this, he said,	that John had been raised from the dead, [8]others that Elijah had appeared, and still others that one of the prophets of long ago had come back to life. [9]But Herod said, "I beheaded John. Who, then, is this I hear such things about?"	

a. *14* Some early manuscripts *He was saying*

Matt.	Mark 6	Luke 9	John
	"John, the man I beheaded, has been raised from the dead!"	And he tried to see him.	

71. The Return of the Twelve from Their Mission

Matt.	Mark 6:30	Luke 9:10a	John
	30The apostles gathered around Jesus and reported to him all they had done and taught.	10When the apostles returned, they reported to Jesus what they had done.	

PART 7

The Intensive Training of the Twelve in Districts beyond Galilee

From the Spring to the Autum of A.D. 29

A. Jesus' First Withdrawal from Galilee[a]

72. The Feeding of the Five Thousand

Northeast shore of the Lake of Galilee

Matt. 14:13b–21	Mark 6:31–44	Luke 9:10b–17	John 6:1–13
	[31]Then, because so many people were coming and going that they did not even have a chance to eat, he said to them, "Come with me by yourselves to a quiet place and get some rest." [32]So	[10b]Then	[1]Some time after this, Jesus
		he took them with him and	
[13b]he withdrew by boat privately	they went away by themselves in a boat	they withdrew by themselves	crossed to the far shore of the Sea of Galilee (that is, the Sea of Tiberias),
	a. During this six-month period Jesus retired three times from Galilee to outlying districts, seeking privacy with the Twelve. Leaving the hot shores of the lake, he planned to spend the summer on the cooler plateaus for more intensive training of those whom he had chosen to become apostles.	to a town called Bethsaida,[a]	
		a. This was evidently Bethsaida Julias (so named by the tetrarch Philip), near the northeast shore of the Lake of Galilee.	

Matt. 14	Mark 6	Luke 9	John 6
to a solitary place.	to a solitary place. ³³But	¹¹but the crowds learned about it and	
Hearing of this,			
the crowds followed him on foot from the towns.	many who saw them leaving recognized them and ran on foot from all the towns and got there ahead of them.	followed him.	²and a great crowd of people followed him
			because they saw the miraculous signs he had performed on the sick. ³Then Jesus
¹⁴When Jesus landed and	³⁴When Jesus landed and		
			went up on a mountainside and sat down with his disciples. ⁴The Jewish Passover Feast was near.
saw a large crowd,	saw a large crowd,		⁵When Jesus looked up and saw a great crowd coming toward him,

Matt. 14	Mark 6	Luke 9	John
he had compassion on them	he had compassion on them, because they were like sheep without a shepherd. So he began teaching them many things.	He welcomed them and spoke to them	
		about the kingdom of God, and healed those who needed healing.	
and healed their sick.			
	³⁵By this time it was late in the day,	¹²Late in the afternoon	
¹⁵As evening approached, the disciples came to him and said, "This is a remote place, and it's already getting late. Send the crowds away, so they can go to the villages and buy themselves some food."	so his disciples came to him. "This is a remote place," they said, "and it's already very late. ³⁶Send the people away so they can go to the surrounding countryside and villages and buy themselves something to eat."	the Twelve came to him and said, "Send the crowd away so they can go to the surrounding villages and countryside and find food and lodging, because we are in a remote place here."	
¹⁶Jesus replied, "They do not need to go away. You give them something to eat."	³⁷But he answered, "You give them something to eat."	¹³He replied, "You give them something to eat." And[a]	

a. The NIV omits "and," which is optional in the original Greek. The conjunction makes the interwoven narrative run smoothly.

Matt. 14	Mark 6	Luke 9	John 6
			he said to Philip, "Where shall we buy bread for these people to eat?" [6]He asked this only to test him, for he already had in mind what he was going to do.
	They said to him, "That would take eight months of a man's wages[a]!		[7]Philip answered him, "Eight months' wages[a] would not buy enough bread for each one to have a bite!"
	Are we to go and spend that much on bread and give it to them to eat?" [38]"How many loaves do you have?" he asked. "Go and see." When they found out,		[8]Another of his disciples, Andrew, Simon Peter's brother, spoke up, [9]"Here is a boy with five small barley loaves and two small fish, but how far will they go among so many?"
[17]"We have here only five loaves of bread and two fish," they answered.	they said, "Five—and two fish."	They answered, "We have only five loaves of bread and two fish—unless we go and buy food for all this crowd."	
		[14b]But he	[10]Jesus said,
[18]"Bring them here to me,"			
he said. [19]And he directed the people to sit down on the grass.	[39]Then Jesus directed them to have all the people sit down in groups on the green grass.	said to his disciples, "Have them sit down in groups of about fifty each." [15]The disciples did so,	"Have the people sit down."
			There was plenty of grass in that place, and the men sat down,
	[40]So they sat down in groups of hundreds and fifties.	and everybody sat down.	
Taking the five loaves and the two fish and looking up to heaven, he gave thanks and broke the loaves.	[41]Taking the five loaves and the two fish and looking up to heaven, he gave thanks and broke	[16]Taking the five loaves and the two fish and looking up to heaven, he gave thanks and broke	[11]Jesus then took the loaves, gave thanks, and distributed to those who were seated
Then he gave them to the disciples, and the disciples gave them to the people.	the loaves. Then he gave them to his disciples to set before the people.	them. Then he gave them to the disciples to set before the people.	
			as much as they wanted.

---

a. *37* Greek *take two hundred denarii*

a. *7* Greek *two hundred denarii*

Matt. 14	Mark 6	Luke 9	John 6
	He also divided the two fish among them all.		He did the same with the fish.
²⁰They all ate and were satisfied,	⁴²They all ate and were satisfied,	¹⁷They all ate and were satisfied,	¹²When they had all had enough to eat,
			he said to his disciples, "Gather the pieces that are left over. Let nothing be wasted." ¹³So they gathered them and filled twelve baskets with the pieces of the five barley loaves
and the disciples picked up twelve basketfuls of broken pieces	⁴³and the disciples picked up twelve basketfuls of broken pieces of bread	and the disciples picked up twelve basketfuls of broken pieces	
	and fish.		
that were left over.		that were left over.	left over by those who had eaten.
²¹The number of those who ate was about five thousand men, besides women and children.	⁴⁴The number of the men who had eaten was five thousand.	¹⁴(About five thousand men were there.)	¹⁰ᵇabout five thousand of them.

73. Christ's Rejection of Political Kingship

Northeast shore of the Lake of Galilee

Matt. 14:22–23	Mark 6:45–46	Luke	John 6:14–17a
			¹⁴After the people saw the miraculous sign that Jesus did, they began to say, "Surely this is the Prophet who is to come into the world." ¹⁵Jesus, knowing that they intended to come and make him king by force,
²²Immediately Jesus urgedᵃ the disciples get into the boat and go on ahead of him to the other side,	⁴⁵Immediately Jesus made his disciples get into the boat and go on ahead of him		withdrew again to a mountain by himself.
	to Bethsaida,ᵃ		¹⁶When evening came, his disciples went down to the lake, ¹⁷where they got into a boat and set off across the lake for Capernaum.

a. The NIV reads "made." But "urged" provides for a logical understanding of the sequence of events in the composite narrative; the reluctant disciples apparently delayed their departure until after Jesus repeatedly entreated them to leave.

a. This was evidently not Bethsaida Julias, but the other Bethsaida on the western shore of the Lake of Galilee, south of Capernaum, by the plain of Gennesaret (see sec. 75).

Matt. 14	Mark 6	Luke	John
while he dismissed the crowd.	while he dismissed the crowd.		
²³After he had dismissed them, he went up on a mountainside by himself to pray. When evening came, he was there alone,	⁴⁶After leaving them, he went up on a mountainside to pray.		

74. Jesus' Walking on the Water

The Lake of Galilee

Matt. 14:24–33	Mark 6:47–52	Luke	John 6:17b–21a
	⁴⁷When evening came, the boat was in the middle of the lake, and he was alone on land.		¹⁷ᵇBy now it was dark, and Jesus had not yet joined them. ¹⁸A strong wind was blowing and the waters grew rough. ¹⁹When
²⁴but the boat was already a considerable distanceª from land, buffeted by the waves			
because the wind was against it.	⁴⁸He saw the disciples straining at the oars, because the wind was against them.		
²⁵During the fourth watch of the night Jesus went out to them, walking on the lake. ²⁶When the disciples	About the fourth watch of the night he went out to them,		they had rowed three or three and a half miles,ª they saw Jesus approaching the boat,
saw him walking on the lake,	walking on the lake. He was about to pass by them, ⁴⁹but when they saw him walking on the lake,		walking on the water; and they were terrified. ²⁰But he said to them, "It is I; don't be afraid."
they were terrified. "It's a ghost," they said, and cried out in fear.	they thought he was a ghost. They cried out, ⁵⁰because they all saw him and were terrified.		
²⁷But Jesus immediately said to them: "Take courage! It is I. Don't be afraid."	Immediately he spoke to them and said, "Take courage! It is I. Don't be afraid."		
²⁸"Lord, if it's you," Peter replied, "tell me to come to you on the water."			
²⁹"Come," he said.			

---

a. *24 Greek many stadia*

a. *19 Greek rowed twenty-five or thirty stadia* (about 5 or 6 kilometers)

Matt. 14	Mark 6	Luke	John 6
Then Peter got down out of the boat, walked on the water and came toward Jesus. 30But when he saw the wind, he was afraid and, beginning to sink, cried out, "Lord, save me!" 31Immediately Jesus reached out his hand and caught him. "You of little faith," he said, "why did you doubt?"	51Then		21Then they were willing to take him into the boat,
32And when they climbed into the boat,	he climbed into the boat with them,		
the wind died down. 33Then those who were in the boat worshiped him, saying, "Truly you are the Son of God."	and the wind died down.		

Matt.	Mark	Luke	John
	They were completely amazed, 52for they had not understood about the loaves; their hearts were hardened.		

75. Jesus and the Twelve's Return to Galilee

Western shore of the Lake of Galilee

Matthew 14:34–36	Mark 6:53–56	Luke	John 6:21b
34When they had crossed over, they landed at Gennesaret.	53When they had crossed over, they landed at Gennesaret and anchored there. 54As soon as they got out of the boat, people		21band immediately the boat reached the shore where they were heading.
35And when the men of that place recognized Jesus, they	recognized Jesus. 55They ran throughout that whole region and		
sent word to all the surrounding country. People brought all their sick	carried the sick		
to him	on mats to wherever they heard he was. 56And wherever he went—into villages, towns or countryside—they placed the sick in the marketplaces. They		
36and begged him to let the sick just touch the edge of his cloak, and all who touched him were healed.	begged him to let them touch even the edge of his cloak, and all who touched him were healed.		

76. Christ's Discourse on the Bread of Life

The synagogue in Capernaum

Matt.	Mark	Luke	John 6:22–71

John 6:22–71

[22]At that time[a] the crowd that had stayed on the opposite shore of the lake realized that only one boat had been there, and that Jesus had not entered it with his disciples, but that they had gone away alone. [23]Then some boats from Tiberias landed near the place where the people had eaten the bread after the Lord had given thanks. [24]Once the crowd realized that neither Jesus nor his disciples were there, they got into the boats and went to Capernaum in search of Jesus.

[25]When they found him on the other side of the lake, they asked him, "Rabbi, when did you get here?"

[26]Jesus answered, "I tell you the truth, you are looking for me, not because you saw miraculous signs but because you ate the loaves and had your fill. [27]Do not work for food that spoils, but for food that endures to eternal life, which the Son of Man will give you. On him God the Father has placed his seal of approval."

[28]Then they asked him, "What must we do to do the works God requires?"

[29]Jesus answered, "The work of God is this: to believe in the one he has sent."

[30]So they asked him, "What miraculous sign then will you give that we may see it and believe you? What will you do? [31]Our forefathers ate the manna in the desert; as it is written: 'He gave them bread from heaven to eat.'[b]"

[32]Jesus said to them, "I tell you the truth, it is not Moses who has given you the bread from heaven, but it is my Father who gives you the true bread from heaven. [33]For the bread of God is he who comes down from heaven and gives life to the world."

[34]"Sir," they said, "from now on give us this bread."

[35]Then Jesus declared, "I am the bread of life. He who comes to me will never go hungry, and he who believes in me will never be thirsty. [36]But as I told you, you have seen me and still you do not believe. [37]All that the Father gives me will come to me, and whoever comes to me I will never drive away. [38]For I have come down from heaven not to do my will but to do the will of him who sent me. [39]And this is the will of him who sent me, that I shall lose none of all that he has given me, but raise them up at the last day. [40]For my Father's will is that everyone who looks to the Son and believes in him shall have eternal life, and I will raise him up at the last day."

[41]At this the Jews began to grumble about him because he said, "I am the bread that came down from heaven." [42]They said, "Is this not Jesus, the son of Joseph, whose father and mother we know? How can he now say, 'I came down from heaven'?"

[43]"Stop grumbling among yourselves," Jesus answered. [44]"No one can come to me unless the Father who sent me draws him, and I will raise him up at the last day. [45]It is written in the Prophets: 'They will all be taught by God.'[c] Everyone who listens to the Father and learns from him comes to me. [46]No one has seen the Father except the one who is from God; only he has seen the Father. [47]I tell you the truth, he who believes has everlasting life.

---

a. The NIV reads "the next day," in accord with the original Greek. Substitution of the phrase "at that time" helps to connnect the events recorded in John 6:22–71 with those described by Matthew and Mark in sec. 75. Christ's discourse in the Capernaum synagogue apparently occurred during the time of his healing ministry in the nearby Gennesaret region.

b. *31* Exod. 16:4; Neh. 9:15; Ps. 78:24, 25

c. *45* Isa. 54:13

Matt.	Mark	Luke

John 6

[48]I am the bread of life. [49]Your forefathers ate the manna in the desert, yet they died. [50]But here is the bread that comes down from heaven, which a man may eat and not die. [51]I am the living bread that came down from heaven. If anyone eats of this bread, he will live forever. This bread is my flesh, which I will give for the life of the world."

[52]Then the Jews began to argue sharply among themselves, "How can this man give us his flesh to eat?"

[53]Jesus said to them, "I tell you the truth, unless you eat the flesh of the Son of Man and drink his blood, you have no life in you. [54]Whoever eats my flesh and drinks my blood has eternal life, and I will raise him up at the last day. [55]For my flesh is real food and my blood is real drink. [56]Whoever eats my flesh and drinks my blood remains in me, and I in him. [57]Just as the living Father sent me and I live because of the Father, so the one who feeds on me will live because of me. [58]This is the bread that came down from heaven. Your forefathers ate manna and died, but he who feeds on this bread will live forever." [59]He said this while teaching in the synagogue in Capernaum.

[60]On hearing it, many of his disciples said, "This is a hard teaching. Who can accept it?"

[61]Aware that his disciples were grumbling about this, Jesus said to them, "Does this offend you? [62]What if you see the Son of Man ascend to where he was before! [63]The Spirit gives life; the flesh counts for nothing. The words I have spoken to you are spirit[a] and they are life. [64]Yet there are some of you who do not believe." For Jesus had known from the beginning which of them did not believe and who would betray him. [65]He went on to say, "This is why I told you that no one can come to me unless the Father has enabled him."

[66]From this time many of his disciples turned back and no longer followed him.

[67]"You do not want to leave too, do you?" Jesus asked the Twelve.

[68]Simon Peter answered him, "Lord, to whom shall we go? You have the words of eternal life. [69]We believe and know that you are the Holy One of God."

[70]Then Jesus replied, "Have I not chosen you, the Twelve? Yet one of you is a devil!" [71](He meant Judas, the son of Simon Iscariot, who, though one of the Twelve, was later to betray him.)

a. 63 Or *Spirit*

77. Conflict with the Pharisees

Matt. 15:1–20	Mark 7:1–23	Luke	John

Matt. 15:1–20	Mark 7:1–23
[1]Then some Pharisees and teachers of the law came to Jesus from Jerusalem and asked, [2]"Why do your disciples break the tradition of the elders?	[1]The Pharisees and some of the teachers of the law who had come from Jerusalem gathered around Jesus and [2]saw some of his disciples eating food with hands that were "unclean," that is, unwashed. [3](The Pharisees and all the Jews do not eat unless they give their hands a ceremonial washing, holding to the tradition of the elders. [4]When they come from the marketplace they do not eat unless they wash. And they observe many other traditions, such as the washing of cups, pitchers and kettles.[a])

a. 4 Some early manuscripts *pitchers, kettles and dining couches*

Matt. 15	Mark 7	Luke	John

Mark 7

5So the Pharisees and teachers of the law asked Jesus, "Why don't your disciples live according to the tradition of the elders instead of eating their food with 'unclean' hands?"

Matt. 15

They don't wash their hands before they eat!"

3Jesus replied, 7You hypocrites! Isaiah was right when he prophesied about you:

6He replied, "Isaiah was right when he prophesied about you hypocrites; as it is written:

8"'These people honor me with their lips,
  but their hearts are far from me.
9They worship me in vain;
    their teachings are but rules taught by
    men.'a"

"'These people honor me with their lips,
  but their hearts are far from me.
7They worship me in vain;
    their teachings are but rules taught by
    men.'a

3b"And why do you break the command of God for the sake of your tradition?

8You have let go of the commands of God and are holding on to the traditions of men."

9And he said to them: "You have a fine way of setting aside the commands of God in order to observeb your own traditions! 10For Moses said,

4For God said, 'Honor your father and mother'b and 'Anyone who curses his father or mother must be put to death.'c 5But you say that if a man says to his father or mother, 'Whatever help you might otherwise have received from me is a gift devoted to God,' 6he is not to 'honor his fatherd' with it. Thus you nullify the word of God for the sake of your tradition.

'Honor your father and your mother,'c and, 'Anyone who curses his father or mother must be put to death.'d 11But you say that if a man says to his father or mother: 'Whatever help you might otherwise have received from me is Corban' (that is, a gift devoted to God), 12then you no longer let him do anything for his father or mother. 13Thus you nullify the word of God by your tradition that you have handed down. And you do many things like that."

10Jesus called the crowd to him and said, "Listen and understand. 11What goes into a man's mouth does not make him 'unclean,' but what comes out of his mouth, that is what makes him 'unclean.'"

14Again Jesus called the crowd to him and said, "Listen to me, everyone, and understand this. 15Nothing outside a man can make him 'unclean' by going into him. Rather, it is what comes out of a man that makes him 'unclean.'e"

12Then

17After he had left the crowd and entered the house,

the disciples came to him and asked, "Do you know that the Pharisees were offended when they heard this?"

13He replied, "Every plant that my heavenly Father has not planted will be pulled up by the roots. 14Leave them; they are blind guides.e If a blind man leads a blind man, both will fall into a pit."

---

a. *9* Isa. 29:13
b. *4* Exod. 20:12; Deut. 5:16
c. *4* Exod. 21:17; Lev. 20:9
d. *6* Some manuscripts *father or his mother*
e. *14* Some manuscripts *guides of the blind*

a. *6, 7* Isa. 29:13
b. *9* Some manuscripts *set up*
c. *10* Exod. 20:12; Deut. 5:16
d. *10* Exod. 21:17; Lev. 20:9
e. *15* Some early manuscripts *'unclean.' 16 If anyone has ears to hear, let him hear.*

Matt. 15	Mark 7	Luke	John
[15]Peter said, "Explain the parable to us." [16]"Are you still so dull?" Jesus asked them. [17]"Don't you see that	his disciples asked him about this parable. [18]"Are you so dull?" he asked. "Don't you see that nothing that enters a man from the outside can make him 'unclean'? [19]For		
whatever enters the mouth goes into the stomach and then out of the body?	it doesn't go into his heart but into his stomach, and then out of his body." (In saying this, Jesus declared all foods "clean.") [20]He went on:		
[18]But the things that come out of the mouth come from the heart, and these make a man 'unclean.' [19]For	"What comes out of a man is what makes him 'unclean.' [21]For		
out of the heart come evil thoughts, murder, adultery, sexual immorality, theft,	from within, out of men's hearts, come evil thoughts, sexual immorality, theft, murder, adultery, [22]greed, malice, deceit, lewdness, envy,		
false testimony, slander. [20]These	slander, arrogance and folly. [23]All these evils come from inside		
are what make a man 'unclean'; but eating with unwashed hands does not make him 'unclean.'"	and make a man 'unclean.'"		

B. Jesus' Second Withdrawal from Galilee

78. A Syrophoenician Woman's Faith

The region of Tyre and Sidon

Matt. 15:21–28	Mark 7:24–30	Luke	John
[21]Leaving that place, Jesus withdrew to the region of Tyre and Sidon.	[24]Jesus left that place and went to the vicinity of Tyre.[a] He entered a house and did not want anyone to know it; yet he could not keep his presence secret. [25]In fact, as soon as she heard about him, a		
[22]A Canaanite woman from that vicinity	woman whose little daughter was possessed by an evil[b] spirit came and fell at his feet.		
came to him, crying out, "Lord, Son of David, have mercy on me! My daughter is suffering terribly from demon-possession."			
	[26]The woman was a Greek, born in Syrian Phoe-		

a. *24* Many early manuscripts *Tyre and Sidon*
b. *25* Greek *unclean*

Matt. 15	Mark 7	Luke	John
	nicia. She begged Jesus to drive the demon out of her daughter.		
23Jesus did not answer a word. So his disciples came to him and urged him, "Send her away, for she keeps crying out after us."			
24He answered, "I was sent only to the lost sheep of Israel."			
25The woman came and knelt before him. "Lord, help me!" she said.			
	27"First let the children eat all they want," he told her, "for it is not right to take the children's bread and toss it to their dogs."		
26He replied, "It is not right to take the children's bread and toss it to their dogs."			
27"Yes, Lord," she said, "but even the dogs eat the crumbs that fall from their masters' table."	28"Yes, Lord," she replied, "but even the dogs under the table eat the children's crumbs."		
28Then Jesus answered, "Woman, you have great faith! Your request is granted."	29Then he told her,		
	"For such a reply, you may go; the demon has left your daughter."		
And her daughter was healed from that very hour.			
	30She went home and found her child lying on the bed, and the demon gone.		

79. The Healing of a Deaf Man and Many Others

Matt. 15:29–31	Mark 7:31–37	Luke	John
29Jesus left there and went along the Sea of Galilee.	31Then Jesus left the vicinity of Tyre and went through Sidon, down to the Sea of Galilee and		

Matt. into the region of the Decapolis.a 32There some people brought to him a man who was deaf and could hardly talk, and they begged him to place his hand on the man.

33After he took him aside, away from the crowd, Jesus put his fingers into the man's ears. Then he spit and touched the man's tongue. 34He looked up to heaven and with a deep sigh said to him, *"Ephphatha!"* (which means, "Be opened!"). 35At this, the man's ears were opened, his tongue was loosened and he began to speak plainly.

36Jesus commanded them not to tell anyone. But the more he did so, the more they kept talking about it. 37People were overwhelmed with amazement. "He has done everything well," they said. "He even makes the deaf hear and the mute speak."

---

a. *31* That is, the Ten Cities

Then he went up on a mountainside and sat down. 30Great crowds came to him, bringing **Mark** the lame, the blind, the crippled, the mute and many others, and laid them at his feet; and he healed them. 31The people were amazed when they saw the mute speaking, the crippled made well, the lame walking and the blind seeing. And they praised the God of Israel.

80. The Feeding of the Four Thousand

The Decapolis

Matt. 15:32–39a	Mark 8:1–9	Luke	John

Matt. 15:32–39a

32Jesus called his disciples to him and said, "I have compassion for these people; they have already been with me three days and have nothing to eat. I do not want to send them away hungry, or they may collapse on the way."

33His disciples answered, "Where could we get enough bread in this remote place to feed

such a crowd?"
34"How many loaves do you have?" Jesus asked.
"Seven," they replied, "and a few small fish."
35He told the crowd to sit down on the ground.
36Then he took the seven loaves and the fish, and when he had given thanks, he broke them and gave them to the disciples, and they in turn

to the people. 37They all ate and were satisfied. Afterward the disciples picked up seven basketfuls of broken pieces that were left over. 38The number of those who ate was
four thousand,
besides women and children. 39After Jesus had sent the crowd away, [39bhe got into the boat . . .]

Mark 8:1–9

1During those days another large crowd gathered. Since they had nothing to eat, Jesus called his disciples to him and said, 2"I have compassion for these people; they have already been with me three days and have nothing to eat. 3If I send them home hungry, they will collapse on the way, because some of them have come a long distance."

4His disciples answered, "But where in this remote place can anyone get enough bread to feed
them?"
5"How many loaves do you have?" Jesus asked.
"Seven," they replied.
6He told the crowd to sit down on the ground. When he had taken the seven loaves and given thanks, he broke them and gave them to his disciples to set before the people, and they did so. 7They had a few small fish as well; he gave thanks for them also and told the disciples to distribute them.
8The people ate and were satisfied. Afterward the disciples picked up seven basketfuls of broken pieces that were left over. 9About

four thousand men
were present. And having sent them away, [10he got into the boat . . .]

81. Jesus' Second Brief Return to Gailiee

Dalmanutha or Magadan in Galilee

Matt. 15:39b–16:4a	Mark 8:10–12	Luke	John

Matt. 15:39b–16:4a

39bhe got into the boat and went

to the vicinity of Magadan. 1The Pharisees and Sadducees
came to Jesus and tested him

by asking him to show them a sign from heaven.

Mark 8:10–12

10he got into the boat with his disciples and went to the region of Dalmanutha.
11The Pharisees

came and began to question Jesus. To test him, they asked him
for a sign from heaven.

Matt. 16	Mark 8	Luke	John
[2]He replied,[a] "When evening comes, you say, 'It will be fair weather, for the sky is red,' [3]and in the morning, 'Today it will be stormy, for the sky is red and overcast.' You know how to interpret the appearance of the sky, but you cannot interpret the signs of the times. [4]A wicked and adulterous generation looks for a miraculous sign, but none will be given it except the sign of Jonah."	[12]He sighed deeply and said, "Why does this generation ask for a miraculous sign? I tell you the truth, no sign will be given to it."		

a. [2] Some early manuscripts do not have the rest of verse 2 and all of verse 3.

C. Jesus' Third Withdrawal from Galilee

82. Warning and Surprise

Northeast shore of the Lake of Galilee

Matt. 16:4b–12	Mark 8:13–21	Luke	John
[4b]Jesus then left them and went away.	[13]Then he left them, got back into the boat and crossed to the other side.		
[5]When they went across the lake, the disciples forgot to take bread.	[14]The disciples had forgotten to bring bread, except for one loaf they had with them in the boat.		
[6]"Be careful," Jesus said to them. "Be on your guard against the yeast of the Pharisees and Sadducees."	[15]"Be careful," Jesus warned them. "Watch out for the yeast of the Pharisees and that of Herod."		
[7]They discussed this among themselves and said, "It is because we didn't bring any bread."	[16]They discussed this with one another and said, "It is because we have no bread."		
[8]Aware of their discussion, Jesus asked, "You of little faith, why are you talking among yourselves about having no bread? [9]Do you still not understand? Don't you remember the five loaves for the five thousand, and how many basketfuls you gathered?	[17]Aware of their discussion, Jesus asked them: "Why are you talking about having no bread? Do you still not see or understand? Are your hearts hardened? [18]Do you have eyes but fail to see, and ears but fail to hear? And don't you remember? [19]When I broke the five loaves for the five thousand, how many basketfuls of pieces did you pick up?"		

Matt. 16	Mark 8	Luke	John
	"Twelve," they replied.		
10Or the seven loaves for the four thousand, and how many basketfuls you gathered?	20"And when I broke the seven loaves for the four thousand, how many basketfuls of pieces did you pick up?"		
	They answered, "Seven."		
11How is it you don't understand that I was not talking to you about bread? But be on your guard against the yeast of the Pharisees and Sadducees." 12Then they understood that he was not telling them to guard against the yeast used in bread, but against the teaching of the Pharisees and Sadducees.	21He said to them, "Do you still not understand?"		

83. The Healing of a Blind Man

Matt.	Mark 8:22–26	Luke	John
	22They came to Bethsaida,a and some people brought a blind man and begged Jesus to touch him. 23He took the blind man by the hand and led him outside the village. When he had spit on the man's eyes and put his hands on him, Jesus asked, "Do you see anything?" 24He looked up and said, "I see people; they look like trees walking around." 25Once more Jesus put his hands on the man's eyes. Then his eyes were opened, his sight was restored, and he saw everything clearly. 26Jesus sent him home, saying, "Don't go into the village."b		

a. This village, northeast of the Lake of Galilee, in the tetrarchy of Philip, was named by him Bethsaida Julias. It was near the place where Jesus miraculously fed more than five thousand people (see pages 87–90). Another village called Bethsaida was located on the western shore of the lake (see page 90).

b. *26* Some manuscripts *Don't go and tell anyone in the village*

84. A Test and a Declaration of Faith

Matt. 16:13–20	Mark 8:27–30	Luke 9:18–21	John
13When Jesus came to the region of Caesarea Philippi, he asked his disciples,	27Jesus and his disciples went on to the villages around Caesarea Philippi. On the way	18Once	
		when Jesus was praying in private and his disciples were with him,	
	he asked them,	he asked them, "Who do the	
"Who do people say the Son of Man is?"	"Who do people say I am?"	crowds say I am?"	
14They replied, "Some say John the Baptist; others say Elijah; and still others,	28They replied, "Some say John the Baptist; others say Elijah; and still	19They replied, "Some say John the Baptist; others say Elijah; and still	
		others, that	
Jeremiah or one of the prophets."	others, one of the prophets."	one of the prophets of long ago has	

Matt. 16	Mark 8	Luke 9	John
		come back to life."	
¹⁵"But what about you?" he asked. "Who do you say I am?"	²⁹"But what about you?" he asked. "Who do you say I am?"	²⁰"But what about you?" he asked. "Who do you say I am?"	
¹⁶Simon Peter answered, "You are the Christ,ᵃ the Son of the living God."	Peter answered, "You are the Christ.ᵃ"	Peter answered, "The Christᵃ of God."	
¹⁷Jesus replied, "Blessed are you, Simon son of Jonah, for this was not revealed to you by man, but by my Father in heaven. ¹⁸And I tell you that you are Peter,ᵇ and on this rock I will build my church, and the gates of Hadesᶜ will not overcome it.ᵈ ¹⁹I will give you the keys of the kingdom of heaven; whatever you bind on earth will beᵉ bound in heaven, and whatever you loose on earth will beᶠ loosed in heaven." ²⁰Then he warned			
	³⁰Jesus warned them not to tell anyone about him.	²¹Jesus strictly warned them not to tell this to anyone.	
his disciples not to tell anyone that he was the Christ.			

a. *16* Or *Messiah;* also in verse 20
b. *18 Peter* means *rock.*
c. *18* Or *hell*
d. *18* Or *not prove stronger than it*
e. *19* Or *have been*
f. *19* Or *have been*

a. *29* Or *Messiah.* "The Christ" (Greek) and "the Messiah" (Hebrew) both mean "the Anointed One."

a. *20* Or *Messiah*

85. Christ's Prediction of His Death, His Resurrection, and the Coming of His Kingdom

Matt. 16:21–28	Mark 8:31—9:1	Luke 9:22–27	John
²¹From that time on Jesus began to explain to his disciples that he	³¹He then began to teach them that		
	the Son of Man	²²And he said, "The Son of Man must suffer many things and be rejected by the elders, chief priests and teachers of the law, and he must be killed and on the third day be raised to life."	
must go to Jerusalem and suffer many things at the hands of the elders, chief priests and teachers of the law, and that he must be killed and on the third day be raised to life.	must suffer many things and be rejected by the elders, chief priests and teachers of the law, and that he must be killed and after three days rise again.		
²²Peter took him aside and	³²He spoke plainly about this, and Peter		

Matt. 16	Mark 8	Luke 9	John

Matt. 16 | **Mark 8** | **Luke 9**

began to rebuke him. "Never, Lord!" he said. "This shall never happen to you!"

²³Jesus turned and said to Peter, "Get behind me, Satan! You are a stumbling block to me; you do not have in mind the things of God, but the things of men."

²⁴Then Jesus said to his disciples, "If anyone would come after me, he must deny himself and take up his cross and follow me. ²⁵For whoever wants to save his life[a] will lose it, but whoever loses his life for me will find it. ²⁶What good will it be for a man if he gains the whole world, yet forfeits his soul? Or what can a man give in exchange for his soul?

²⁷For the Son of Man is going to come in his Father's glory with his angels, and then he will reward each person according to what he has done. ²⁸I tell you the truth, some who are standing here will not taste death before they see the Son of Man coming in his kingdom."

---

took him aside and began to rebuke him.

³³But when Jesus turned and looked at his disciples, he rebuked Peter. "Get behind me, Satan!" he said. "You do not have in mind the things of God, but the things of men."

³⁴Then he called the crowd to him along with his disciples and said: "If anyone would come after me, he must deny himself and take up his cross and follow me. ³⁵For whoever wants to save his life[a] will lose it, but whoever loses his life for me and for the gospel will save it. ³⁶What good is it for a man to gain the whole world, yet forfeit his soul?

³⁷Or what can a man give in exchange for his soul? ³⁸If anyone is ashamed of me and my words in this adulterous and sinful generation, the Son of Man will be ashamed of him when he comes in his Father's glory with the holy angels." ¹And he said to them, "I tell you the truth, some who are standing here will not taste death before they see the kingdom of God come with power."[b]

---

²³Then he said to them all: "If anyone would come after me, he must deny himself and take up his cross daily and follow me. ²⁴For whoever wants to save his life will lose it, but whoever loses his life for me will save it. ²⁵What good is it for a man to gain the whole world, and yet lose or forfeit his very self?

²⁶If anyone is ashamed of me and my words, the Son of Man will be ashamed of him when he comes in his glory and in the glory of the Father and of the holy angels.

²⁷I tell you the truth, some who are standing here will not taste death before they see the kingdom of God."

---

a. *25* The Greek word means either *life* or *soul;* also in verse 26.

a. *35* The Greek word means either *life* or *soul;* also in verse 36.

b. Note the different wording in Matt. 16:28.

86. The Transfiguration

Probably Mount Hermon

Matt. 17:1–8	Mark 9:2–8	Luke 9:28–36a	John
¹After six days Jesus took	²After six days Jesus took	²⁸About eight days after Jesus said this, he took	
with him Peter, James and John the brother of James, and led them up a high mountain by themselves.	Peter, James and John with him and led them up a high mountain,	Peter, John and James with him and went up onto a mountain	
	where they were all alone. There	to pray. ²⁹As he was praying, the appearance of his face changed, and	
²There he was transfigured before them.			
	he was transfigured before them.		
His face shone like the sun, and his clothes became	³His clothes became dazzling white,	his clothes became	
as white as the light.		as bright as a flash of lightning.	
	whiter than anyone in the world could bleach them. ⁴And there		
³Just then there appeared before them Moses and Elijah, talking with Jesus.	appeared before them Elijah and Moses,	³⁰Two men, Moses and Elijah, ³¹appeared	
	who were talking with Jesus.	in glorious splendor, talking with Jesus. They spoke about his departure, which he was about to bring to fulfillment at Jerusalem. ³²Peter and his companions were very sleepy, but when they became fully awake, they saw his glory and the two men standing with him. ³³As the men were	
⁴Peter said to Jesus, "Lord, it is good for us to be here.	⁵Peter said to Jesus, "Rabbi, it is good for us to be here.	leaving Jesus, Peter said to him, "Master, it is good for us to be here.	
If you wish, I will put up three shelters—one for you, one for Moses and one for Elijah."	Let us put up three shelters—one for you, one for Moses and one for Elijah." ⁶(He did not know what to say, they were so frightened.)	Let us put up three shelters—one for you, one for Moses and one for Elijah." (He did not know what he was saying.)	
⁵While he was still speaking, a bright cloud enveloped them,	⁷Then a cloud appeared and enveloped them,	³⁴While he was speaking, a cloud appeared and enveloped them,	
		and they were afraid as they entered the cloud. ³⁵A voice came from the cloud, saying, "This is my	
and a voice from the cloud said, "This is my Son, whom I love;	and a voice came from the cloud: "This is my		

Matt. 17	Mark 9	Luke 9	John
	beloved Son,[a]	Son, whom I have chosen;	
with him I am well pleased. Listen to him!” ⁶When the disciples heard this, they fell facedown to the ground, terrified. ⁷But Jesus came and touched them. “Get up,” he said. “Don’t be afraid.” ⁸When they looked up, they saw no one except Jesus.	Listen to him!” ⁸Suddenly, when they looked around, they no longer saw anyone with them except Jesus.	listen to him.” ³⁶When the voice had spoken, they found that Jesus was alone.	

a. The NIV reads “my Son, whom I love”—a good translation of the original Greek. The rendering “my beloved Son,” which has been used in several English versions, simplifies the reading of the interwoven narrative in this Harmony of the Gospels.

87. The Perplexity of the Disciples

On their way down the mountain

Matt. 17:9–13	Mark 9:9–13	Luke 9:36b	John
⁹As they were coming down the mountain, Jesus instructed them, “Don’t tell anyone what you have seen, until the Son of Man has been raised from the dead.”	⁹As they were coming down the mountain, Jesus gave them orders not to tell anyone what they had seen until the Son of Man had risen from the dead. ¹⁰They kept the matter to themselves, discussing what “rising from the dead” meant.	 ³⁶ᵇThe disciples kept this to themselves,	
¹⁰The disciples asked him, “Why then do the teachers of the law say that Elijah must come first?” ¹¹Jesus replied, “To be sure, Elijah comes and will restore all things.	¹¹And they asked him, “Why do the teachers of the law say that Elijah must come first?” ¹²Jesus replied, “To be sure, Elijah does come first, and restores all things. Why then is it written that the Son of Man must suffer much and be rejected?		
¹²But I tell you, Elijah has already come, and they did not recognize him, but have done to him everything they wished.	¹³But I tell you, Elijah has come, and they have done to him everything they wished, just as it is written about him.”		

Matt. 17	Mark	Luke 9	John
In the same way the Son of Man is going to suffer at their hands." ¹³Then the disciples understood that he was talking to them about John the Baptist.			
		and they[a] told no one at that time what they had seen.	
		a. The NIV omits the word "they"; it is inserted here to improve the reading of the composite narrative.	

88. The Healing of a Demoniac Boy

The region of Caesarea Philippi

Matt. 17:14–20	Mark 9:14–29	Luke 9:37–43a	John
		³⁷The next day, when they came down from the mountain,	
¹⁴When they came to the crowd,	¹⁴When they came to the other disciples, they saw a large crowd around them and the teachers of the law arguing with them. ¹⁵As soon as all the people saw Jesus, they were overwhelmed with wonder and ran to greet him.	a large crowd met him.	
	¹⁶"What are you arguing with them about?" he asked.		
a man	¹⁷A man in the crowd	³⁸A man in the crowd called out,	
approached Jesus and knelt before him. ¹⁵"Lord, have mercy on my	answered, "Teacher, I brought you my	"Teacher, I beg you to look at my son, for he is	
son," he said.	son,	my only child.	
	who is possessed by a spirit that has robbed him of speech.		
"He has seizures and is suffering greatly.	¹⁸Whenever it seizes him, it throws him		
		³⁹A spirit seizes him and he suddenly screams; it throws him into convulsions	
	to the ground. He foams at the mouth, gnashes his teeth and becomes rigid.	so that he foams at the mouth.	
		It scarcely ever leaves him and is destroying him.	
He often falls into the fire or into the water. ¹⁶I brought him to your disciples, but they	I asked	⁴⁰I begged your disciples to drive it out, but they could not."	

Matt. 17	Mark 9	Luke 9	John
	your disciples to drive out the spirit, but they		
could not heal him."	could not."		
17"O unbelieving and perverse generation," Jesus replied, "how long shall I stay with you? How long shall I put up with you? Bring the boy here to me."	19"O unbelieving generation," Jesus replied, "how long shall I stay with you? How long shall I put up with you? Bring the boy to me."	41"O unbelieving and perverse generation," Jesus replied, "how long shall I stay with you and put up with you? Bring your son here."	
	20So they brought him. When the spirit saw Jesus,	42Even	
		while the boy was coming, the demon	
	it		
	immediately threw the boy into a convulsion. He fell to the ground and rolled around, foaming at the mouth.	threw him to the ground in a convulsion.	
	21Jesus asked the boy's father, "How long has he been like this?"		
	"From childhood," he answered. 22"It has often thrown him into fire or water to kill him. But if you can do anything, take pity on us and help us."		
	23"'If you can'?" said Jesus. "Everything is possible for him who believes."		
	24Immediately the boy's father exclaimed, "I do believe; help me overcome my unbelief!"		
	25When Jesus saw that a crowd was running to the scene, he rebuked the evila spirit. "You deaf and mute spirit," he said, "I command you, come out of him and never enter him again."		
18Jesus rebuked the demon,		But Jesus rebuked the evila spirit,	
	26The spirit shrieked, convulsed him violently		
and it came out of the boy, and he was healed from that moment.	and came out.		
		healed the boy	
	The boy looked so much like a corpse that many said, "He's dead." 27But Jesus took him by the hand and lifted him to his feet, and he stood up.		
		and heb gave him back to his fa-	

a. *42* Greek *unclean*
b. The NIV omits "he." It is inserted here to improve the reading of the composite narrative.

a. *25* Greek *unclean*

Matt. 17	Mark 9	Luke 9	John
		ther. [43]And they were all amazed at the greatness of God.	
[19]Then the disciples came to Jesus in private and asked, "Why couldn't we drive it out?"	[28]After Jesus had gone indoors, his disciples asked him privately, "Why couldn't we drive it out?"		
[20]He replied, "Because you have so little faith. I tell you the truth, if you have faith as small as a mustard seed, you can say to this mountain, 'Move from here to there' and it will move. Nothing will be impossible for you.[a]"	[29]He replied,		
	"This kind can come out only by prayer.[a]"		

a. *20 Some manuscripts* you. *21 But this kind does not go out except by prayer and fasting.*

a. *29 Some manuscripts* prayer and fasting

89. Jesus' Quiet Return to Galilee

Matt. 17:22–23	Mark 9:30–32	Luke 9:43b–45	John
		[43b]While everyone was marveling at all that Jesus did,	
[22]When they came together in Galilee,	[30]They left that place and passed through Galilee. Jesus did not want anyone to know where they were, [31]because he was teaching his disciples. He said to them,	he said to his disciples,	
		[44]"Listen carefully to what I am about to tell you: The Son of Man is	
he said to them, "The Son of Man is	"The Son of Man is		
going to be betrayed into the hands of men. [23]They will kill him, and	going to be betrayed into the hands of men. They will kill him, and	going to be betrayed into the hands of men."	
on the third day he will be raised to life." And the disciples were filled with grief.	after three days he will rise."		
	[32]But they did not understand what he meant	[45]But they did not understand what this meant. It was hidden from them, so that they did not grasp it, and they were afraid to ask him about it.	
	and were afraid to ask him about it.		

90. The Temple Tax

Capernaum

Matt. 17:24–27	Mark 9:33a	Luke	John
[24]After Jesus and his disciples arrived in Capernaum, the collectors of the two-drachma tax came to Peter and asked, "Doesn't your teacher pay the temple tax[a]?"	[33]They came to Capernaum.		Mark

[24]After Jesus and his disciples arrived in Capernaum, the collectors of the two-drachma tax came to Peter and asked, "Doesn't your teacher pay the temple tax[a]?"

[25]"Yes, he does," he replied.

When Peter came into the house, Jesus was the first to speak. "What do you think, Simon?" he asked. "From whom do the kings of the earth collect duty and taxes—from their own sons or from others?"

[26]"From others," Peter answered.

"Then the sons are exempt," Jesus said to him. [27]"But so that we may not offend them, go to the lake and throw out your line. Take the first fish you catch; open its mouth and you will find a four-drachma coin. Take it and give it to them for my tax and yours."

a. *24* Greek *the two drachmas*

91. Jesus' Unbelieving Brothers

Matt.	Mark	Luke	John 7:1–9

John 7:1–9

[1]After this, Jesus went around in Galilee, purposely staying away from Judea because the Jews there were waiting to take his life. [2]But when the Jewish Feast of Tabernacles was near, [3]Jesus' brothers said to him, "You ought to leave here and go to Judea, so that your disciples may see the miracles you do. [4]No one who wants to become a public figure acts in secret. Since you are doing these things, show yourself to the world." [5]For even his own brothers did not believe in him.

[6]Therefore Jesus told them, "The right time for me has not yet come; for you any time is right. [7]The world cannot hate you, but it hates me because I testify that what it does is evil. [8]You go to the Feast. I am not yet[a] going up to this Feast, because for me the right time has not yet come." [9]Having said this, he stayed in Galilee.

a. *8* Some early manuscripts do not have *yet.*

92. The Necessity for Childlikeness, Tolerance, and Forgiveness

Capernaum

Matt. 18:1–35	Mark 9:33b–50	Luke 9:46–50	John
[1]At that time			
the disciples came to Jesus and asked, "Who is the greatest in the kingdom of heaven?"		[46]An argument started among the disciples as to which of them would be the greatest.	
	[33b]When he was in the house, he		

Matt. 18	Mark 9	Luke 9	John
	asked them, "What were you arguing about on the road?" 34But they kept quiet because on the way they had argued about who was the greatest. 35Sitting down, Jesus called the Twelve and said, "If anyone wants to be first, he must be the very last, and the servant of all."	47Jesus, knowing their thoughts,	
2He called a little child and had him stand among them. 3And he said: "I tell you the truth, unless you change and become like little children, you will never enter the kingdom of heaven. 4Therefore, whoever humbles himself like this child is the greatest in the kingdom of heaven.	36He took a little child and had him stand among them. Taking him in his arms, he said to them,	took a little child and had him stand beside him. 48Then he said to them,	
5"And whoever welcomes a little child like this in my name welcomes me.	37"Whoever welcomes one of these little children in my name welcomes me; and whoever welcomes me does not welcome me but the one who sent me."	"Whoever welcomes this little child in my name welcomes me; and whoever welcomes me welcomes the one who sent me. For he who is least among you all—he is the greatest."	
	38"Teacher," said John, "we saw a man driving out demons in your name and we told him to stop, because he was not one of us."	49"Master," said John, "we saw a man driving out demons in your name and we tried to stop him, because he is not one of us."	
	39"Do not stop him," Jesus said. "No one who does a miracle in my name can in the next moment say anything bad about me, 40for whoever is not against us is for us. 41I tell you the truth, anyone who gives you a cup of water in my name because you belong to Christ will certainly not lose his reward.	50"Do not stop him," Jesus said, "for whoever is not against you is for you."	
6But if anyone causes one of these little ones who believe in me to sin, it would be better for him to have a large millstone hung around his neck and to be	42"And if anyone causes one of these little ones who believe in me to sin, it would be better for him to be thrown into the sea with a large millstone tied around his neck.		

Matt. 18	Mark 9	Luke	John

Matt. 18

drowned in the depths of the sea.

7"Woe to the world because of the things that cause people to sin! Such things must come, but woe to the man through whom they come! 8If your hand or your foot causes you to sin cut it off and throw it away. It is better for you to enter life maimed or crippled than to have two hands

or two feet and be thrown into eternal fire. 9And if your eye causes you to sin, gouge it out and throw it away. It is better for you to

enter life with one eye than to have two eyes and be thrown into the fire of hell.

Mark 9

43If your hand causes you to sin, cut it off. It is better for you to enter life maimed than with two hands to go into hell, where the fire never goes out.a 45And if your foot causes you to sin, cut it off. It is better for you to enter life crippled than to have two feet and be thrown into hell.b 47And if your eye causes you to sin, pluck it out. It is better for you to

enter the kingdom of God with one eye than to have two eyes and be thrown into hell, 48where

"'their worm does not die,
    and the fire is not quenched.'c

49Everyone will be salted with fire.

50"Salt is good, but if it loses its saltiness, how can you make it salty again? Have salt in yourselves, and be at peace with each other."

a. *43* Some manuscripts *"out, 44 where*
'their worm does not die,
and the fire is not quenched.'"
b. *45* Some manuscripts *"hell, 46 where*
'their worm does not die,
and the fire is not quenched.'"
c. *48* Isa. 66:24

Mark

10"See that you do not look down on one of these little ones. For I tell you that their angels in heaven always see the face of my Father in heaven.a

12"What do you think? If a man owns a hundred sheep, and one of them wanders away, will he not leave the ninety-nine on the hills and go to look for the one that wandered off? 13And if he finds it, I tell you the truth, he is happier about that one sheep than about the ninety-nine that did not wander off. 14In the same way your Father in heaven is not willing that any of these little ones should be lost.

15"If your brother sins against you,b go and show him his fault, just between the two of you. If he listens to you, you have won your brother over. 16But if he will not listen, take one or two others along, so that 'every matter may be established by the testimony of two or three witnesses.'c 17If he refuses to listen to them, tell it to the church; and if he refuses to listen even to the church, treat him as you would a pagan or a tax collector.

18"I tell you the truth, whatever you bind on earth will bed bound in heaven, and whatever you loose on earth will bee loosed in heaven.

a. *10* Some manuscripts *heaven. 11 The Son of Man came to save what was lost.*
b. *15* Some manuscripts do not have *against you.*
c. *16* Deut. 19:15
d. *18* Or *have been*
e. *18* Or *have been*

	Mark	Luke	John

Matt. 18

19"Again, I tell you that if two of you on earth agree about anything you ask for, it will be done for you by my Father in heaven. 20For where two or three come together in my name, there am I with them."

21Then Peter came to Jesus and asked, "Lord, how many times shall I forgive my brother when he sins against me? Up to seven times?"

22Jesus answered, "I tell you, not seven times, but seventy-seven times.a

23"Therefore, the kingdom of heaven is like a king who wanted to settle accounts with his servants. 24As he began the settlement, a man who owed him ten thousand talentsb was brought to him. 25Since he was not able to pay, the master ordered that he and his wife and his children and all that he had be sold to repay the debt.

26"The servant fell on his knees before him. 'Be patient with me,' he begged, 'and I will pay back everything.' 27The servant's master took pity on him, canceled the debt and let him go.

28"But when that servant went out, he found one of his fellow servants who owed him a hundred denarii.c He grabbed him and began to choke him. 'Pay back what you owe me!' he demanded.

29"His fellow servant fell to his knees and begged him, 'Be patient with me, and I will pay you back.'

30"But he refused. Instead, he went off and had the man thrown into prison until he could pay the debt. 31When the other servants saw what had happened, they were greatly distressed and went and told their master everything that had happened.

32"Then the master called the servant in. 'You wicked servant,' he said, 'I canceled all that debt of yours because you begged me to. 33Shouldn't you have had mercy on your fellow servant just as I had on you?' 34In anger his master turned him over to the jailers to be tortured, until he should pay back all he owed.

35"This is how my heavenly Father will treat each of you unless you forgive your brother from your heart."

a. 22 Or seventy times seven
b. 24 That is, millions of dollars
c. 28 That is, a few dollars

93. The Mistaken Zeal of James and John

Matt.	Mark	Luke 9:51–56	John 7:10
		51As the time approached for him to be taken up to heaven, Jesus resolutely set out for Jerusalem. 52And he sent messengers on ahead, who went into a Samaritan village to get things ready for him; 53but the people there did not welcome him, because he was heading for Jerusalem. 54When the disciples James and John saw this, they asked, "Lord, do you want us to call fire	10However, after his brothers had left for the Feast, he went also, not publicly, but in secret.

Matt.	Mark	Luke 9	John

down from heaven to destroy them[a]?" [55]But Jesus turned and rebuked them, [56]and[b] they went to another village.

---

a. *54* Some manuscripts *them, even as Elijah did*
b. *55, 56* Some manuscripts *them. And he said, "You do not know what kind of spirit you are of, for the Son of Man did not come to destroy men's lives, but to save them." 56 And*

94. Would-Be Followers

Samaria or Judea

Matt. 8:19–22	Mark	Luke 9:57–62	John

Matt. 8:19–22

[19]Then
a teacher of the law came to him and said, "Teacher, I will follow you wherever you go." [20]Jesus replied, "Foxes have holes and birds of the air have nests, but the Son of Man has no place to lay his head."

[21]Another disciple

said to him, "Lord, first let me go and bury my father." [22]But Jesus told him, "Follow me, and let the dead bury their own dead."

Luke 9:57–62

[57]As they were walking along the road, a man said to him, "I will follow you wherever you go." [58]Jesus replied, "Foxes have holes and birds of the air have nests, but the Son of Man has no place to lay his head." [59]He said to another man,

"Follow me."
But the man replied, "Lord, first let me go and bury my father." [60]Jesus said to him, "Let the dead bury their own dead, but you go and proclaim the kingdom of God." [61]Still another said, "I will follow you, Lord; but first let me go back and say good-by to my family." [62]Jesus replied, "No one who puts his hand to the plow and looks back is fit for service in the kingdom of God."

PART 8

Christ's Later Judean Ministry

October to December, A.D. *29*

95. Jesus at the Festival of Tabernacles

The temple, Jerusalem

Matt.	Mark	Luke	John 7:11–52

John 7:11–52

[11]Now at the Feast the Jews were watching for him and asking, "Where is that man?"

[12]Among the crowds there was widespread whispering about him. Some said, "He is a good man."

Others replied, "No, he deceives the people." [13]But no one would say anything publicly about him for fear of the Jews.

[14]Not until halfway through the Feast did Jesus go up to the temple courts and begin to teach. [15]The Jews were amazed and asked, "How did this man get such learning without having studied?"

[16]Jesus answered, "My teaching is not my own. It comes from him who sent me. [17]If anyone chooses to do God's will, he will find out whether my teaching comes from God or whether I speak on my own. [18]He who speaks on his own does so to gain honor for himself, but he who works for the honor of the one who sent him is a man of truth; there is nothing false about him. [19]Has not Moses given you the law? Yet not one of you keeps the law. Why are you trying to kill me?"

[20]"You are demon-possessed," the crowd answered. "Who is trying to kill you?"

[21]Jesus said to them, "I did one miracle, and you are all astonished. [22]Yet, because Moses gave you circumcision (though actually it did not come from Moses, but from the patriarchs), you circumcise a child on the Sabbath. [23]Now if a child can be circumcised on the Sabbath so that the law of Moses may not be broken, why are you angry with me for healing the whole man on the Sabbath? [24]Stop judging by mere appearances, and make a right judgment."

[25]At that point some of the people of Jerusalem began to ask, "Isn't this the man they are trying to kill? [26]Here he is, speaking publicly, and they are not saying a word to him. Have the authorities really concluded that he is the Christ[a]? [27]But we know where this man is from; when the Christ comes, no one will know where he is from."

a. *26* Or *Messiah;* also in verses 27, 31, 41 and 42

Matt.	Mark	Luke

John 7

[28]Then Jesus, still teaching in the temple courts, cried out, "Yes, you know me, and you know where I am from. I am not here on my own, but he who sent me is true. You do not know him, [29]but I know him because I am from him and he sent me."

[30]At this they tried to seize him, but no one laid a hand on him, because his time had not yet come. [31]Still, many in the crowd put their faith in him. They said, "When the Christ comes, will he do more miraculous signs than this man?"

[32]The Pharisees heard the crowd whispering such things about him. Then the chief priests and the Pharisees sent temple guards to arrest him.

[33]Jesus said, "I am with you for only a short time, and then I go to the one who sent me. [34]You will look for me, but you will not find me; and where I am, you cannot come."

[35]The Jews said to one another, "Where does this man intend to go that we cannot find him? Will he go where our people live scattered among the Greeks, and teach the Greeks? [36]What did he mean when he said, 'You will look for me, but you will not find me,' and 'Where I am, you cannot come'?"

[37]On the last and greatest day of the Feast, Jesus stood and said in a loud voice, "If anyone is thirsty, let him come to me and drink. [38]Whoever believes in me, as[a] the Scripture has said, streams of living water will flow from within him." [39]By this he meant the Spirit, whom those who believed in him were later to receive. Up to that time the Spirit had not been given, since Jesus had not yet been glorified.

[40]On hearing his words, some of the people said, "Surely this man is the Prophet."

[41]Others said, "He is the Christ."

Still others asked, "How can the Christ come from Galilee? [42]Does not the Scripture say that the Christ will come from David's family[b] and from Bethlehem, the town where David lived?" [43]Thus the people were divided because of Jesus. [44]Some wanted to seize him, but no one laid a hand on him.

[45]Finally the temple guards went back to the chief priests and Pharisees, who asked them, "Why didn't you bring him in?"

[46]"No one ever spoke the way this man does," the guards declared.

[47]"You mean he has deceived you also?" the Pharisees retorted. [48]"Has any of the rulers or of the Pharisees believed in him? [49]No! But this mob that knows nothing of the law—there is a curse on them."

[50]Nicodemus, who had gone to Jesus earlier and who was one of their own number, asked, [51]"Does our law condemn anyone without first hearing him to find out what he is doing?"

[52]They replied, "Are you from Galilee, too? Look into it, and you will find that a prophet[c] does not come out of Galilee."

---

a. *37, 38* Or *if anyone is thirsty, let him come to me. And let him drink, 38 who believes in me. As*
b. *42* Greek *seed*
c. *52* Two early manuscripts *the Prophet*

96. Christ and the Adulteress

The temple, Jerusalem

Matt.	Mark	Luke	John 7:53–8:11

John 7:53–8:11

53a Then each went to his own home.

1But Jesus went to the Mount of Olives. 2At dawn he appeared again in the temple courts, where all the people gathered around him, and he sat down to teach them. 3The teachers of the law and the Pharisees brought in a woman caught in adultery. They made her stand before the group 4and said to Jesus, "Teacher, this woman was caught in the act of adultery. 5In the Law Moses commanded us to stone such women. Now what do you say?" 6They were using this question as a trap, in order to have a basis for accusing him.

But Jesus bent down and started to write on the ground with his finger. 7When they kept on questioning him, he straightened up and said to them, "If any one of you is without sin, let him be the first to throw a stone at her." 8Again he stooped down and wrote on the ground.

9At this, those who heard began to go away one at a time, the older ones first, until only Jesus was left, with the woman still standing there. 10Jesus straightened up and asked her, "Woman, where are they? Has no one condemned you?"

11"No one, sir," she said.

"Then neither do I condemn you," Jesus declared. "Go now and leave your life of sin."b

---

a. The earliest and most reliable manuscripts and other ancient witnesses do not have John 7:53–8:11.

b. The earliest and most reliable Greek manuscript do not have John 7:53–8:11.

97. The Hostility of the Religious Leaders

The temple, Jerusalem

Matt.	Mark	Luke	John 8:12–59

John 8:12–59

12When Jesus spoke again to the people, he said, "I am the light of the world. Whoever follows me will never walk in darkness, but will have the light of life."

13The Pharisees challenged him, "Here you are, appearing as your own witness; your testimony is not valid."

14Jesus answered, "Even if I testify on my own behalf, my testimony is valid, for I know where I came from and where I am going. But you have no idea where I come from or where I am going. 15You judge by human standards; I pass judgment on no one. 16But if I do judge, my decisions are right, because I am not alone. I stand with the Father, who sent me. 17In your own Law it is written that the testimony of two men is valid. 18I am one who testifies for myself; my other witness is the Father, who sent me."

19Then they asked him, "Where is your father?"

"You do not know me or my Father," Jesus replied. "If you knew me, you would know my Father also." 20He spoke these words while teaching in the temple area near the place where the offerings were put. Yet no one seized him, because his time had not yet come.

21Once more Jesus said to them, "I am going away, and you will look for me, and you will die in your sin. Where I go, you cannot come."

Matt.	Mark	Luke

John 8

[22]This made the Jews ask, "Will he kill himself? Is that why he says, 'Where I go, you cannot come'?"

[23]But he continued, "You are from below; I am from above. You are of this world; I am not of this world. [24]I told you that you would die in your sins; if you do not believe that I am the one I claim to be,[a] you will indeed die in your sins."

[25]"Who are you?" they asked.

"Just what I have been claiming all along," Jesus replied. [26]"I have much to say in judgment of you. But he who sent me is reliable, and what I have heard from him I tell the world."

[27]They did not understand that he was telling them about his Father. [28]So Jesus said, "When you have lifted up the Son of Man, then you will know that I am the one I claim to be and that I do nothing on my own but speak just what the Father has taught me. [29]The one who sent me is with me; he has not left me alone, for I always do what pleases him." [30]Even as he spoke, many put their faith in him.

[31]To the Jews who had believed him, Jesus said, "If you hold to my teaching, you are really my disciples. [32]Then you will know the truth, and the truth will set you free."

[33]They answered him, "We are Abraham's descendants[b] and have never been slaves of anyone. How can you say that we shall be set free?"

[34]Jesus replied, "I tell you the truth, everyone who sins is a slave to sin. [35]Now a slave has no permanent place in the family, but a son belongs to it forever. [36]So if the Son sets you free, you will be free indeed. [37]I know you are Abraham's descendants. Yet you are ready to kill me, because you have no room for my word. [38]I am telling you what I have seen in the Father's presence, and you do what you have heard from your father.[c]"

[39]"Abraham is our father," they answered.

"If you were Abraham's children," said Jesus, "then you would[d] do the things Abraham did. [40]As it is, you are determined to kill me, a man who has told you the truth that I heard from God. Abraham did not do such things. [41]You are doing the things your own father does."

"We are not illegitimate children," they protested. "The only Father we have is God himself."

[42]Jesus said to them, "If God were your Father, you would love me, for I came from God and now am here. I have not come on my own; but he sent me. [43]Why is my language not clear to you? Because you are unable to hear what I say. [44]You belong to your father, the devil, and you want to carry out your father's desire. He was a murderer from the beginning, not holding to the truth, for there is no truth in him. When he lies, he speaks his native language, for he is a liar and the father of lies. [45]Yet because I tell the truth, you do not believe me! [46]Can any of you prove me guilty of sin? If I am telling the truth, why don't you believe me? [47]He who belongs to God hears what God says. The reason you do not hear is that you do not belong to God."

[48]The Jews answered him, "Aren't we right in saying that you are a Samaritan and demon-possessed?"

[49]"I am not possessed by a demon," said Jesus, "but I honor my Father and you dishonor me. [50]I am not seeking glory for myself; but there is one who seeks it, and he is the judge. [51]I tell you the truth, if anyone keeps my word, he will never see death."

---

a. *24* Or *I am he;* also in verse 28
b. *33* Greek *seed;* also in verse 37
c. *38* Or *presence. Therefore do what you have heard from the Father.*
d. *39* Some early manuscripts *"If you are Abraham's children," said Jesus, "then*

Matt.	Mark	Luke

John 8

⁵²At this the Jews exclaimed, "Now we know that you are demon-possessed! Abraham died and so did the prophets, yet you say that if anyone keeps your word, he will never taste death. ⁵³Are you greater than our father Abraham? He died, and so did the prophets. Who do you think you are?"

⁵⁴Jesus replied, "If I glorify myself, my glory means nothing. My Father, whom you claim as your God, is the one who glorifies me. ⁵⁵Though you do not know him, I know him. If I said I did not, I would be a liar like you, but I do know him and keep his word. ⁵⁶Your father Abraham rejoiced at the thought of seeing my day; he saw it and was glad."

⁵⁷"You are not yet fifty years old," the Jews said to him, "and you have seen Abraham!"

⁵⁸"I tell you the truth," Jesus answered, "before Abraham was born, I am!" ⁵⁹At this, they picked up stones to stone him, but Jesus hid himself, slipping away from the temple grounds.

98. The Healing of a Man Born Blind

Jerusalem

Matt.	Mark	Luke

John 9:1–10:21

¹As he went along, he saw a man blind from birth. ²His disciples asked him, "Rabbi, who sinned, this man or his parents, that he was born blind?"

³"Neither this man nor his parents sinned," said Jesus, "but this happened so that the work of God might be displayed in his life. ⁴As long as it is day, we must do the work of him who sent me. Night is coming, when no one can work. ⁵While I am in the world, I am the light of the world."

⁶Having said this, he spit on the ground, made some mud with the saliva, and put it on the man's eyes. ⁷"Go," he told him, "wash in the Pool of Siloam" (this word means Sent). So the man went and washed, and came home seeing.

⁸His neighbors and those who had formerly seen him begging asked, "Isn't this the same man who used to sit and beg?" ⁹Some claimed that he was.

Others said, "No, he only looks like him."

But he himself insisted, "I am the man."

¹⁰"How then were your eyes opened?" they demanded.

¹¹He replied, "The man they call Jesus made some mud and put it on my eyes. He told me to go to Siloam and wash. So I went and washed, and then I could see."

¹²"Where is this man?" they asked him.

"I don't know," he said.

¹³They brought to the Pharisees the man who had been blind. ¹⁴Now the day on which Jesus had made the mud and opened the man's eyes was a Sabbath. ¹⁵Therefore the Pharisees also asked him how he had received his sight. "He put mud on my eyes," the man replied, "and I washed, and now I see."

¹⁶Some of the Pharisees said, "This man is not from God, for he does not keep the Sabbath."

But others asked, "How can a sinner do such miraculous signs?" So they were divided.

¹⁷Finally they turned again to the blind man, "What have you to say about him? It was your eyes he opened."

The man replied, "He is a prophet."

Matt.	Mark	Luke

John 9

[18]The Jews still did not believe that he had been blind and had received his sight until they sent for the man's parents. [19]"Is this your son?" they asked. "Is this the one you say was born blind? How is it that now he can see?"

[20]"We know he is our son," the parents answered, "and we know he was born blind. [21]But how he can see now, or who opened his eyes, we don't know. Ask him. He is of age; he will speak for himself." [22]His parents said this because they were afraid of the Jews, for already the Jews had decided that anyone who acknowledged that Jesus was the Christ[a] would be put out of the synagogue. [23]That was why his parents said, "He is of age; ask him."

[24]A second time they summoned the man who had been blind. "Give glory to God,[b]" they said. "We know this man is a sinner."

[25]He replied, "Whether he is a sinner or not, I don't know. One thing I do know. I was blind but now I see!"

[26]Then they asked him, "What did he do to you? How did he open your eyes?"

[27]He answered, "I have told you already and you did not listen. Why do you want to hear it again? Do you want to become his disciples, too?"

[28]Then they hurled insults at him and said, "You are this fellow's disciple! We are disciples of Moses! [29]We know that God spoke to Moses, but as for this fellow, we don't even know where he comes from."

[30]The man answered, "Now that is remarkable! You don't know where he comes from, yet he opened my eyes. [31]We know that God does not listen to sinners. He listens to the godly man who does his will. [32]Nobody has ever heard of opening the eyes of a man born blind. [33]If this man were not from God, he could do nothing."

[34]To this they replied, "You were steeped in sin at birth; how dare you lecture us!" And they threw him out.

[35]Jesus heard that they had thrown him out, and when he found him, he said, "Do you believe in the Son of Man?"

[36]"Who is he, sir?" the man asked. "Tell me so that I may believe in him."

[37]Jesus said, "You have now seen him; in fact, he is the one speaking with you."

[38]Then the man said, "Lord, I believe," and he worshiped him.

[39]Jesus said, "For judgment I have come into this world, so that the blind will see and those who see will become blind."

[40]Some Pharisees who were with him heard him say this and asked, "What? Are we blind too?"

[41]Jesus said, "If you were blind, you would not be guilty of sin; but now that you claim you can see, your guilt remains.

[1]"I tell you the truth, the man who does not enter the sheep pen by the gate, but climbs in by some other way, is a thief and a robber. [2]The man who enters by the gate is the shepherd of his sheep. [3]The watchman opens the gate for him, and the sheep listen to his voice. He calls his own sheep by name and leads them out. [4]When he has brought out all his own, he goes on ahead of them, and his sheep follow him because they know his voice. [5]But they will never follow a stranger; in fact, they will run away from him because they do not recognize a stranger's voice." [6]Jesus used this figure of speech, but they did not understand what he was telling them.

[7]Therefore Jesus said again, "I tell you the truth, I am the gate for the sheep. [8]All who ever came before me were thieves and robbers, but the sheep did not listen to them. [9]I am

a. *22* Or *Messiah*
b. *24* A solemn charge to tell the truth (see Josh. 7:19)

Matt.	Mark	Luke

John 10

the gate; whoever enters through me will be saved.[a] He will come in and go out, and find pasture. [10]The thief comes only to steal and kill and destroy; I have come that they may have life, and have it to the full.

[11]"I am the good shepherd. The good shepherd lays down his life for the sheep. [12]The hired hand is not the shepherd who owns the sheep. So when he sees the wolf coming, he abandons the sheep and runs away. Then the wolf attacks the flock and scatters it. [13]The man runs away because he is a hired hand and cares nothing for the sheep.

[14]"I am the good shepherd; I know my sheep and my sheep know me—[15]just as the Father knows me and I know the Father—and I lay down my life for the sheep. [16]I have other sheep that are not of this sheep pen. I must bring them also. They too will listen to my voice, and there shall be one flock and one shepherd. [17]The reason my Father loves me is that I lay down my life—only to take it up again. [18]No one takes it from me, but I lay it down of my own accord. I have authority to lay it down and authority to take it up again. This command I received from my Father."

[19]At these words the Jews were again divided. [20]Many of them said, "He is demon-possessed and raving mad. Why listen to him?"

[21]But others said, "These are not the sayings of a man possessed by a demon. Can a demon open the eyes of the blind?"

---

a. *9* Or *kept safe*

99. The Mission of the Seventy-Two

Probably in Judea[a]

Matt.	Mark

Luke 10:1–24

John

[1]After this the Lord appointed seventy-two[b] others and sent them two by two ahead of him to every town and place where he was about to go. [2]He told them, "The harvest is plentiful, but the workers are few. Ask the Lord of the harvest, therefore, to send out workers into his harvest field. [3]Go! I am sending you out like lambs among wolves. [4]Do not take a purse or bag or sandals; and do not greet anyone on the road.

[5]"When you enter a house, first say, 'Peace to this house.' [6]If a man of peace is there, your peace will rest on him; if not, it will return to you. [7]Stay in that house, eating and drinking whatever they give you, for the worker deserves his wages. Do not move around from house to house.

[8]"When you enter a town and are welcomed, eat what is set before you. [9]Heal the sick who are there and tell them, 'The kingdom of God is near you.' [10]But when you enter a town and are not welcomed, go into its streets and say, [11]'Even the dust of your town that sticks to our feet we wipe off against you. Yet be sure of this: The kingdom of God is near.' [12]I tell you, it will be more bearable on that day for Sodom than for that town.

[13]"Woe to you, Korazin! Woe to you, Bethsaida! For if the miracles that were performed in you had been performed in Tyre and Sidon, they would have repented long ago, sitting

---

a. New Testament scholars hold different opinions about the time and place of events recorded in a large part of Luke's Gospel. Strong arguments support the probability that the events described in Luke 10:1–13:21 occurred in Judea during the three-month interval between Christ's appearances in Jerusalem at the Festival of Tabernacles and the Festival of Dedication.

b. *1* Some manuscripts *seventy;* also in verse 17

Matt.	Mark	Luke 10	John

in sackcloth and ashes. [14]But it will be more bearable for Tyre and Sidon at the judgment than for you. [15]And you, Capernaum, will you be lifted up to the skies? No, you will go down to the depths.[a]

[16]"He who listens to you listens to me; he who rejects you rejects me; but he who rejects me rejects him who sent me."

[17]The seventy-two returned with joy and said, "Lord, even the demons submit to us in your name."

[18]He replied, "I saw Satan fall like lightning from heaven. [19]I have given you authority to trample on snakes and scorpions and to overcome all the power of the enemy; nothing will harm you. [20]However, do not rejoice that the spirits submit to you, but rejoice that your names are written in heaven."

[21]At that time Jesus, full of joy through the Holy Spirit, said, "I praise you, Father, Lord of heaven and earth, because you have hidden these things from the wise and learned, and revealed them to little children. Yes, Father, for this was your good pleasure.

[22]"All things have been committed to me by my Father. No one knows who the Son is except the Father, and no one knows who the Father is except the Son and those to whom the Son chooses to reveal him."

[23]Then he turned to his disciples and said privately, "Blessed are the eyes that see what you see. [24]For I tell you that many prophets and kings wanted to see what you see but did not see it, and to hear what you hear but did not hear it."

a. *15* Greek *Hades*

100. A Test Question

Matt.	Mark	Luke 10:25–37	John

[25]On one occasion an expert in the law stood up to test Jesus. "Teacher," he asked, "what must I do to inherit eternal life?"

[26]"What is written in the Law?" he replied. "How do you read it?"

[27]He answered: "'Love the Lord your God with all your heart and with all your soul and with all your strength and with all your mind'[b]; and, 'Love your neighbor as yourself.'[c]"

[28]"You have answered correctly," Jesus replied. "Do this and you will live."

[29]But he wanted to justify himself, so he asked Jesus, "And who is my neighbor?"

[30]In reply Jesus said: "A man was going down from Jerusalem to Jericho, when he fell into the hands of robbers. They stripped him of his clothes, beat him and went away, leaving him half dead. [31]A priest happened to be going down the same road, and when he saw the man, he passed by on the other side. [32]So too, a Levite, when he came to the place and saw him, passed by on the other side. [33]But a Samaritan, as he traveled, came where the man was; and when he saw him, he took pity on him. [34]He went to him and bandaged his wounds, pouring on oil and wine. Then he put the man on his own donkey, took him to an inn and took care of him. [35]The next day he took out two silver coins[d] and gave them to the innkeeper. 'Look after him,' he said, 'and when I return, I will reimburse you for any extra expense you may have.'

b. *27* Deut. 6:5
c. *27* Lev. 19:18
d. *35* Greek *two denarii*

Matt.	Mark	Luke 10	John

³⁶"Which of these three do you think was a neighbor to the man who fell into the hands of robbers?"

³⁷The expert in the law replied, "The one who had mercy on him."

Jesus told him, "Go and do likewise."

101. Jesus at the Home of Martha and Mary

Bethany, near Jerusalem

Matt.	Mark	Luke 10:38–42	John

³⁸As Jesus and his disciples were on their way, he came to a village where a woman named Martha opened her home to him. ³⁹She had a sister called Mary, who sat at the Lord's feet listening to what he said. ⁴⁰But Martha was distracted by all the preparations that had to be made. She came to him and asked, "Lord, don't you care that my sister has left me to do the work by myself? Tell her to help me!"

⁴¹"Martha, Martha," the Lord answered, "you are worried and upset about many things, ⁴²but only one thing is needed.^a Mary has chosen what is better, and it will not be taken away from her."

---

a. *42* Some manuscripts *but few things are needed—or only one*

102. A Discourse on Prayer

Matt.	Mark	Luke 11:1–13	John

¹One day Jesus was praying in a certain place. When he finished, one of his disciples said to him, "Lord, teach us to pray, just as John taught his disciples."

²He said to them, "When you pray, say:

"'Father,^b
hallowed be your name,
your kingdom come.^c
³Give us each day our daily bread.
⁴Forgive us our sins,
  for we also forgive everyone who sins against us.^d
And lead us not into temptation.^e'"

⁵Then he said to them, "Suppose one of you has a friend, and he goes to him at midnight and says, 'Friend, lend me three loaves of bread, ⁶because a friend of mine on a journey has come to me, and I have nothing to set before him.'

⁷"Then the one inside answers, 'Don't bother me. The door is already locked, and my children are with me in bed. I can't get up and give you anything.' ⁸I tell you, though he will not get up and give him the bread because he is his friend, yet because of the man's boldness^f he will get up and give him as much as he needs.

---

b. *2* Some manuscripts *Our Father in heaven*
c. *2* Some manuscripts *come. May your will be done on earth as it is in heaven.*
d. *4* Greek *everyone who is indebted to us*
e. *4* Some manuscripts *temptation but deliver us from the evil one*
f. *8* Or *persistence*

Matt.	Mark	Luke 11	John

⁹"So I say to you: Ask and it will be given to you; seek and you will find; knock and the door will be opened to you. ¹⁰For everyone who asks receives; he who seeks finds; and to him who knocks, the door will be opened.

¹¹"Which of you fathers, if your son asks for ͣ a fish, will give him a snake instead? ¹²Or if he asks for an egg, will give him a scorpion? ¹³If you then, though you are evil, know how to give good gifts to your children, how much more will your Father in heaven give the Holy Spirit to those who ask him!"

a. *11* Some manuscripts *for bread, will give him a stone; or if he asks for*

103. The Healing of a Dumb Demoniac

Matt.	Mark	Luke 11:14–36	John

¹⁴Jesus was driving out a demon that was mute. When the demon left, the man who had been mute spoke, and the crowd was amazed. ¹⁵But some of them said, "By Beelzebub,ᵇ the prince of demons, he is driving out demons." ¹⁶Others tested him by asking for a sign from heaven.

¹⁷Jesus knew their thoughts and said to them: "Any kingdom divided against itself will be ruined, and a house divided against itself will fall. ¹⁸If Satan is divided against himself, how can his kingdom stand? I say this because you claim that I drive out demons by Beelzebub. ¹⁹Now if I drive out demons by Beelzebub, by whom do your followers drive them out? So then, they will be your judges. ²⁰But if I drive out demons by the finger of God, then the kingdom of God has come to you.

²¹"When a strong man, fully armed, guards his own house, his possessions are safe. ²²But when someone stronger attacks and overpowers him, he takes away the armor in which the man trusted and divides up the spoils.

²³"He who is not with me is against me, and he who does not gather with me, scatters.

²⁴"When an evilᶜ spirit comes out of a man, it goes through arid places seeking rest and does not find it. Then it says, 'I will return to the house I left.' ²⁵When it arrives, it finds the house swept clean and put in order. ²⁶Then it goes and takes seven other spirits more wicked than itself, and they go in and live there. And the final condition of that man is worse than the first."

²⁷As Jesus was saying these things, a woman in the crowd called out, "Blessed is the mother who gave you birth and nursed you."

²⁸He replied, "Blessed rather are those who hear the word of God and obey it."

²⁹As the crowds increased, Jesus said, "This is a wicked generation. It asks for a miraculous sign, but none will be given it except the sign of Jonah. ³⁰For as Jonah was a sign to the Ninevites, so also will the Son of Man be to this generation. ³¹The Queen of the South will rise at the judgment with the men of this generation and condemn them; for she came from the ends of the earth to listen to Solomon's wisdom, and now oneᵈ greater than Solomon is here. ³²The men of Nineveh will stand up at the judgment with this generation and condemn it; for they repented at the preaching of Jonah, and now one greater than Jonah is here.

b. *15* Greek *Beezeboul* or *Beelzeboul*; also in verses 18 and 19
c. *24* Greek *unclean*
d. *31* Or *something;* also in verse 32

Matt.	Mark	<div align="center">Luke 11</div>	John

33"No one lights a lamp and puts it in a place where it will be hidden, or under a bowl. Instead he puts it on its stand, so that those who come in may see the light. 34Your eye is the lamp of your body. When your eyes are good, your whole body also is full of light. But when they are bad, your body also is full of darkness. 35See to it, then, that the light within you is not darkness. 36Therefore, if your whole body is full of light, and no part of it dark, it will be completely lighted, as when the light of a lamp shines on you."

104. A Denunciation of Religious Hypocrisy

Matt.	Mark	<div align="center">Luke 11:37–12:12</div>	John

37When Jesus had finished speaking, a Pharisee invited him to eat with him; so he went in and reclined at the table. 38But the Pharisee, noticing that Jesus did not first wash before the meal, was surprised.

39Then the Lord said to him, "Now then, you Pharisees clean the outside of the cup and dish, but inside you are full of greed and wickedness. 40You foolish people! Did not the one who made the outside make the inside also? 41But give what is inside [the dish]a to the poor, and everything will be clean for you.

42"Woe to you Pharisees, because you give God a tenth of your mint, rue and all other kinds of garden herbs, but you neglect justice and the love of God. You should have practiced the latter without leaving the former undone.

43"Woe to you Pharisees, because you love the most important seats in the synagogues and greetings in the marketplaces.

44"Woe to you, because you are like unmarked graves, which men walk over without knowing it."

45One of the experts in the law answered him, "Teacher, when you say these things, you insult us also."

46Jesus replied, "And you experts in the law, woe to you, because you load people down with burdens they can hardly carry, and you yourselves will not lift one finger to help them.

47"Woe to you, because you build tombs for the prophets, and it was your forefathers who killed them. 48So you testify that you approve of what your forefathers did; they killed the prophets, and you build their tombs. 49Because of this, God in his wisdom said, 'I will send them prophets and apostles, some of whom they will kill and others they will persecute.' 50Therefore this generation will be held responsible for the blood of all the prophets that has been shed since the beginning of the world, 51from the blood of Abel to the blood of Zechariah, who was killed between the altar and the sanctuary. Yes, I tell you, this generation will be held responsible for it all.

52"Woe to you experts in the law, because you have taken away the key to knowledge. You yourselves have not entered, and you have hindered those who were entering."

53When Jesus left there, the Pharisees and the teachers of the law began to oppose him fiercely and to besiege him with questions, 54waiting to catch him in something he might say.

1Meanwhile, when a crowd of many thousands had gathered, so that they were trampling on one another, Jesus began to speak first to his disciples, saying: "Be on your guard against the yeast of the Pharisees, which is hypocrisy. 2There is nothing concealed that will not be

---

a. *41* Or *what you have*

Matt.	Mark	Luke 12	John

disclosed, or hidden that will not be made known. ³What you have said in the dark will be heard in the daylight, and what you have whispered in the ear in the inner rooms will be proclaimed from the roofs.

⁴"I tell you, my friends, do not be afraid of those who kill the body and after that can do no more. ⁵But I will show you whom you should fear: Fear him who, after the killing of the body, has power to throw you into hell. Yes, I tell you, fear him. ⁶Are not five sparrows sold for two pennies[a]? Yet not one of them is forgotten by God. ⁷Indeed, the very hairs of your head are all numbered. Don't be afraid; you are worth more than many sparrows.

⁸"I tell you, whoever acknowledges me before men, the Son of Man will also acknowledge him before the angels of God. ⁹But he who disowns me before men will be disowned before the angels of God. ¹⁰And everyone who speaks a word against the Son of Man will be forgiven, but anyone who blasphemes against the Holy Spirit will not be forgiven.

¹¹"When you are brought before synagogues, rulers and authorities, do not worry about how you will defend yourselves or what you will say, ¹²for the Holy Spirit will teach you at that time what you should say."

---

a. *6* Greek *two assaria*

105. Parables about Worldliness and Spiritual Alertness

Matt.	Mark	Luke 12:13–59	John

¹³Someone in the crowd said to him, "Teacher, tell my brother to divide the inheritance with me."

¹⁴Jesus replied, "Man, who appointed me a judge or an arbiter between you?" ¹⁵Then he said to them, "Watch out! Be on your guard against all kinds of greed; a man's life does not consist in the abundance of his possessions."

¹⁶And he told them this parable: "The ground of a certain rich man produced a good crop. ¹⁷He thought to himself, 'What shall I do? I have no place to store my crops.'

¹⁸"Then he said, 'This is what I'll do. I will tear down my barns and build bigger ones, and there I will store all my grain and my goods. ¹⁹And I'll say to myself, "You have plenty of good things laid up for many years. Take life easy; eat, drink and be merry."'

²⁰"But God said to him, 'You fool! This very night your life will be demanded from you. Then who will get what you have prepared for yourself?'

²¹"This is how it will be with anyone who stores up things for himself but is not rich toward God."

²²Then Jesus said to his disciples: "Therefore I tell you, do not worry about your life, what you will eat; or about your body, what you will wear. ²³Life is more than food, and the body more than clothes. ²⁴Consider the ravens: They do not sow or reap, they have no storeroom or barn; yet God feeds them. And how much more valuable you are than birds! ²⁵Who of you by worrying can add a single hour to his life[b]? ²⁶Since you cannot do this very little thing, why do you worry about the rest?

²⁷"Consider how the lilies grow. They do not labor or spin. Yet I tell you, not even Solomon in all his splendor was dressed like one of these. ²⁸If that is how God clothes the grass of the field, which is here today, and tomorrow is thrown into the fire, how much

---

b. *25* Or *single cubit to his height*

more will he clothe you, O you of little faith! [29]And do not set your heart on what you will eat or drink; do not worry about it. [30]For the pagan world runs after all such things, and your Father knows that you need them. [31]But seek his kingdom, and these things will be given to you as well.

[32]"Do not be afraid, little flock, for your Father has been pleased to give you the kingdom. [33]Sell your possessions and give to the poor. Provide purses for yourselves that will not wear out, a treasure in heaven that will not be exhausted, where no thief comes near and no moth destroys. [34]For where your treasure is, there your heart will be also.

[35]"Be dressed ready for service and keep your lamps burning, [36]like men waiting for their master to return from a wedding banquet, so that when he comes and knocks they can immediately open the door for him. [37]It will be good for those servants whose master finds them watching when he comes. I tell you the truth, he will dress himself to serve, will have them recline at the table and will come and wait on them. [38]It will be good for those servants whose master finds them ready, even if he comes in the second or third watch of the night. [39]But understand this: If the owner of the house had known at what hour the thief was coming, he would not have let his house be broken into. [40]You also must be ready, because the Son of Man will come at an hour when you do not expect him."

[41]Peter asked, "Lord, are you telling this parable to us, or to everyone?"

[42]The Lord answered, "Who then is the faithful and wise manager, whom the master puts in charge of his servants to give them their food allowance at the proper time? [43]It will be good for that servant whom the master finds doing so when he returns. [44]I tell you the truth, he will put him in charge of all his possessions. [45]But suppose the servant says to himself, 'My master is taking a long time in coming,' and he then begins to beat the menservants and maidservants and to eat and drink and get drunk. [46]The master of that servant will come on a day when he does not expect him and at an hour he is not aware of. He will cut him to pieces and assign him a place with the unbelievers.

[47]"That servant who knows his master's will and does not get ready or does not do what his master wants will be beaten with many blows. [48]But the one who does not know and does things deserving punishment will be beaten with few blows. From everyone who has been given much, much will be demanded; and from the one who has been entrusted with much, much more will be asked.

[49]"I have come to bring fire on the earth, and how I wish it were already kindled! [50]But I have a baptism to undergo, and how distressed I am until it is completed! [51]Do you think I came to bring peace on earth? No, I tell you, but division. [52]From now on there will be five in one family divided against each other, three against two and two against three. [53]They will be divided, father against son and son against father, mother against daughter and daughter against mother, mother-in-law against daughter-in-law and daughter-in-law against mother-in-law."

[54]He said to the crowd: "When you see a cloud rising in the west, immediately you say, 'It's going to rain,' and it does. [55]And when the south wind blows, you say, 'It's going to be hot,' and it is. [56]Hypocrites! You know how to interpret the appearance of the earth and the sky. How is it that you don't know how to interpret this present time?

[57]"Why don't you judge for yourselves what is right? [58]As you are going with your adversary to the magistrate, try hard to be reconciled to him on the way, or he may drag you off to the judge, and the judge turn you over to the officer, and the officer throw you into prison. [59]I tell you, you will not get out until you have paid the last penny.[a]"

---

a. *59* Greek *lepton*

106. The Imperativeness of Repentance

Matt.	Mark	Luke 13:1–9	John

¹Now there were some present at that time who told Jesus about the Galileans whose blood Pilate had mixed with their sacrifices. ²Jesus answered, "Do you think that these Galileans were worse sinners than all the other Galileans because they suffered this way? ³I tell you, no! But unless you repent, you too will all perish. ⁴Or those eighteen who died when the tower in Siloam fell on them—do you think they were more guilty than all the others living in Jerusalem? ⁵I tell you, no! But unless you repent, you too will all perish."

⁶Then he told this parable: "A man had a fig tree, planted in his vineyard, and he went to look for fruit on it, but did not find any. ⁷So he said to the man who took care of the vineyard, 'For three years now I've been coming to look for fruit on this fig tree and haven't found any. Cut it down! Why should it use up the soil?'

⁸"'Sir,' the man replied, 'leave it alone for one more year, and I'll dig around it and fertilize it. ⁹If it bears fruit next year, fine! If not, then cut it down.'"

107. The Healing of a Crippled Woman

Matt.	Mark	Luke 13:10–21	John

¹⁰On a Sabbath Jesus was teaching in one of the synagogues, ¹¹and a woman was there who had been crippled by a spirit for eighteen years. She was bent over and could not straighten up at all. ¹²When Jesus saw her, he called her forward and said to her, "Woman, you are set free from your infirmity." ¹³Then he put his hands on her, and immediately she straightened up and praised God.

¹⁴Indignant because Jesus had healed on the Sabbath, the synagogue ruler said to the people, "There are six days for work. So come and be healed on those days, not on the Sabbath."

¹⁵The Lord answered him, "You hypocrites! Doesn't each of you on the Sabbath untie his ox or donkey from the stall and lead it out to give it water? ¹⁶Then should not this woman, a daughter of Abraham, whom Satan has kept bound for eighteen long years, be set free on the Sabbath day from what bound her?"

¹⁷When he said this, all his opponents were humiliated, but the people were delighted with all the wonderful things he was doing.

¹⁸Then Jesus asked, "What is the kingdom of God like? What shall I compare it to? ¹⁹It is like a mustard seed, which a man took and planted in his garden. It grew and became a tree, and the birds of the air perched in its branches."

²⁰Again he asked, "What shall I compare the kingdom of God to? ²¹It is like yeast that a woman took and mixed into a large amount[a] of flour until it worked all through the dough."

a. *21* Greek *three satas* (probably about ½ bushel or 22 liters)

108. Jesus at the Festival of Dedication

The temple, Jerusalem

Matt.	Mark	Luke

John 10:22–39

22Then came the Feast of Dedication[a] at Jerusalem. It was winter, 23and Jesus was in the temple area walking in Solomon's Colonnade. 24The Jews gathered around him, saying, "How long will you keep us in suspense? If you are the Christ,[b] tell us plainly."

25Jesus answered, "I did tell you, but you do not believe. The miracles I do in my Father's name speak for me, 26but you do not believe because you are not my sheep. 27My sheep listen to my voice; I know them, and they follow me. 28I give them eternal life, and they shall never perish; no one can snatch them out of my hand. 29My Father, who has given them to me, is greater than all[c]; no one can snatch them out of my Father's hand. 30I and the Father are one."

31Again the Jews picked up stones to stone him, 32but Jesus said to them, "I have shown you many great miracles from the Father. For which of these do you stone me?"

33"We are not stoning you for any of these," replied the Jews, "but for blasphemy, because you, a mere man, claim to be God."

34Jesus answered them, "Is it not written in your Law, 'I have said you are gods'[d]? 35If he called them 'gods,' to whom the word of God came—and the Scripture cannot be broken—36what about the one whom the Father set apart as his very own and sent into the world? Why then do you accuse me of blasphemy because I said, 'I am God's Son'? 37Do not believe me unless I do what my Father does. 38But if I do it, even though you do not believe me, believe the miracles, that you may know and understand that the Father is in me, and I in the Father." 39Again they tried to seize him, but he escaped their grasp.

---

a. *22* That is, Hanukkah
b. *24* Or *Messiah*
c. *29* Many early manuscripts *What my Father has given me is greater than all*
d. *34* Ps. 82:6

PART 9

Christ's Perean Ministry

January to March, A.D. 30

A. The First Perean Tour

109. Jesus' Move into Perea

Matt.	Mark	Luke	John 10:40–42
			40Then Jesus went back across the Jordan to the place where John had been baptizing in the early days. Here he stayed 41and many people came to him. They said, "Though John never performed a miraculous sign, all that John said about this man was true." 42And in that place many believed in Jesus.

110. An Outline of the First Perean Tour

Matt.	Mark	Luke 13:22	John
		22Then Jesus went through the towns and villages, teaching as he made his way to Jerusalem.a	

a. This tour through Perea seems to have been a circular one. After preaching in many towns and villages as he journeyed northward, Jesus apparently turned southward. From then on, his listeners probably included people traveling toward Jerusalem by the Perean route; it was the route commonly used by Jews from northern regions, who preferred not to pass through Samaria.

111. A Question Whether Few Will Be Saved

Probably in Pereab

Matt.	Mark	Luke 13:23–30	John
		23Someone asked him, "Lord, are only a few people going to be saved?"	

b. In relation to Christ's later Judean ministry it was noted that New Testament scholars are divided in their opinions about the time and location of events recorded in a large section of Luke's Gospel (see the footnote on page 119). Strong arguments support the probability that the events described in Luke 13:22–17:10 occurred in Perea during the early part of A.D. 30.

Matt.	Mark	Luke 13	John

He said to them, [24]"Make every effort to enter through the narrow door, because many, I tell you, will try to enter and will not be able to. [25]Once the owner of the house gets up and closes the door, you will stand outside knocking and pleading, 'Sir, open the door for us.'

"But he will answer, 'I don't know you or where you come from.'

[26]"Then you will say, 'We ate and drank with you, and you taught in our streets.'

[27]"But he will reply, 'I don't know you or where you come from. Away from me, all you evildoers!'

[28]"There will be weeping there, and gnashing of teeth, when you see Abraham, Isaac and Jacob and all the prophets in the kingdom of God, but you yourselves thrown out. [29]People will come from east and west and north and south, and will take their places at the feast in the kingdom of God. [30]Indeed there are those who are last who will be first, and first who will be last."

112. A Warning about Herod Antipas

Matt.	Mark	Luke 13:31–35	John

[31]At that time some Pharisees came to Jesus and said to him, "Leave this place and go somewhere else. Herod wants to kill you."

[32]He replied, "Go tell that fox, 'I will drive out demons and heal people today and tomorrow, and on the third day I will reach my goal.' [33]In any case, I must keep going today and tomorrow and the next day—for surely no prophet can die outside Jerusalem!

[34]"O Jerusalem, Jerusalem, you who kill the prophets and stone those sent to you, how often I have longed to gather your children together, as a hen gathers her chicks under her wings, but you were not willing! [35]Look, your house is left to you desolate. I tell you, you will not see me again until you say, 'Blessed is he who comes in the name of the Lord.'[a]"

a. *35* Ps. 118:26

113. The Healing of a Man with Dropsy

Matt.	Mark	Luke 14:1–24	John

[1]One Sabbath, when Jesus went to eat in the house of a prominent Pharisee, he was being carefully watched. [2]There in front of him was a man suffering from dropsy. [3]Jesus asked the Pharisees and experts in the law, "Is it lawful to heal on the Sabbath or not?" [4]But they remained silent. So taking hold of the man, he healed him and sent him away.

[5]Then he asked them, "If one of you has a son[b] or an ox that falls into a well on the Sabbath day, will you not immediately pull him out?" [6]And they had nothing to say.

[7]When he noticed how the guests picked the places of honor at the table, he told them this parable: [8]"When someone invites you to a wedding feast, do not take the place of honor, for a person more distinguished than you may have been invited. [9]If so, the host who invited both of you will come and say to you, 'Give this man your seat.' Then, humiliated,

b. *5* Some manuscripts *donkey*

Matt.	Mark	Luke 14	John

you will have to take the least important place. ¹⁰But when you are invited, take the lowest place, so that when your host comes, he will say to you, 'Friend, move up to a better place.' Then you will be honored in the presence of all your fellow guests. ¹¹For everyone who exalts himself will be humbled, and he who humbles himself will be exalted."

¹²Then Jesus said to his host, "When you give a luncheon or dinner, do not invite your friends, your brothers or relatives, or your rich neighbors; if you do, they may invite you back and so you will be repaid. ¹³But when you give a banquet, invite the poor, the crippled, the lame, the blind, ¹⁴and you will be blessed. Although they cannot repay you, you will be repaid at the resurrection of the righteous."

¹⁵When one of those at the table with him heard this, he said to Jesus, "Blessed is the man who will eat at the feast in the kingdom of God."

¹⁶Jesus replied: "A certain man was preparing a great banquet and invited many guests. ¹⁷At the time of the banquet he sent his servant to tell those who had been invited, 'Come, for everything is now ready.'

¹⁸"But they all alike began to make excuses. The first said, 'I have just bought a field, and I must go and see it. Please excuse me.'

¹⁹"Another said, 'I have just bought five yoke of oxen, and I'm on my way to try them out. Please excuse me.'

²⁰"Still another said, 'I just got married, so I can't come.'

²¹"The servant came back and reported this to his master. Then the owner of the house became angry and ordered his servant, 'Go out quickly into the streets and alleys of the town and bring in the poor, the crippled, the blind and the lame.'

²²"'Sir,' the servant said, 'what you ordered has been done, but there is still room.'

²³"Then the master told his servant, 'Go out to the roads and country lanes and make them come in, so that my house will be full. ²⁴I tell you, not one of those men who were invited will get a taste of my banquet.'"

114. Parables about the Demands of True Discipleship

Matt.	Mark	Luke 14:25–35	John

²⁵Large crowds were traveling with Jesus, and turning to them he said: ²⁶"If anyone comes to me and does not hate his father and mother, his wife and children, his brothers and sisters—yes, even his own life—he cannot be my disciple. ²⁷And anyone who does not carry his cross and follow me cannot be my disciple.

²⁸"Suppose one of you wants to build a tower. Will he not first sit down and estimate the cost to see if he has enough money to complete it? ²⁹For if he lays the foundation and is not able to finish it, everyone who sees it will ridicule him, ³⁰saying, 'This fellow began to build and was not able to finish.'

³¹"Or suppose a king is about to go to war against another king. Will he not first sit down and consider whether he is able with ten thousand men to oppose the one coming against him with twenty thousand? ³²If he is not able, he will send a delegation while the other is still a long way off and will ask for terms of peace. ³³In the same way, any of you who does not give up everything he has cannot be my disciple.

³⁴"Salt is good, but if it loses its saltiness, how can it be made salty again? ³⁵It is fit neither for the soil nor for the manure pile; it is thrown out.

"He who has ears to hear, let him hear."

115. Parables about a Lost Sheep, a Lost Coin, and a Wayward Son

| Matt. | Mark | Luke 15:1–32 | John |

Luke 15:1–32

[1]Now the tax collectors and "sinners" were all gathering around to hear him. [2]But the Pharisees and the teachers of the law muttered, "This man welcomes sinners and eats with them."

[3]Then Jesus told them this parable: [4]"Suppose one of you has a hundred sheep and loses one of them. Does he not leave the ninety-nine in the open country and go after the lost sheep until he finds it? [5]And when he finds it, he joyfully puts it on his shoulders [6]and goes home. Then he calls his friends and neighbors together and says, 'Rejoice with me; I have found my lost sheep.' [7]I tell you that in the same way there will be more rejoicing in heaven over one sinner who repents than over ninety-nine righteous persons who do not need to repent.

[8]"Or suppose a woman has ten silver coins[a] and loses one. Does she not light a lamp, sweep the house and search carefully until she finds it? [9]And when she finds it, she calls her friends and neighbors together and says, 'Rejoice with me; I have found my lost coin.' [10]In the same way, I tell you, there is rejoicing in the presence of the angels of God over one sinner who repents."

[11]Jesus continued: "There was a man who had two sons. [12]The younger one said to his father, 'Father, give me my share of the estate.' So he divided his property between them.

[13]"Not long after that, the younger son got together all he had, set off for a distant country and there squandered his wealth in wild living. [14]After he had spent everything, there was a severe famine in that whole country, and he began to be in need. [15]So he went and hired himself out to a citizen of that country, who sent him to his fields to feed pigs. [16]He longed to fill his stomach with the pods that the pigs were eating, but no one gave him anything.

[17]"When he came to his senses, he said, 'How many of my father's hired men have food to spare, and here I am starving to death! [18]I will set out and go back to my father and say to him: Father, I have sinned against heaven and against you. [19]I am no longer worthy to be called your son; make me like one of your hired men.' [20]So he got up and went to his father.

"But while he was still a long way off, his father saw him and was filled with compassion for him; he ran to his son, threw his arms around him and kissed him.

[21]"The son said to him, 'Father, I have sinned against heaven and against you. I am no longer worthy to be called your son.[b]'

[22]"But the father said to his servants, 'Quick! Bring the best robe and put it on him. Put a ring on his finger and sandals on his feet. [23]Bring the fattened calf and kill it. Let's have a feast and celebrate. [24]For this son of mine was dead and is alive again; he was lost and is found.' So they began to celebrate.

[25]"Meanwhile, the older son was in the field. When he came near the house, he heard music and dancing. [26]So he called one of the servants and asked him what was going on. [27]'Your brother has come,' he replied, 'and your father has killed the fattened calf because he has him back safe and sound.'

[28]"The older brother became angry and refused to go in. So his father went out and pleaded with him. [29]But he answered his father, 'Look! All these years I've been slaving for

a. *8* Greek *ten drachmas,* each worth about a day's wages
b. *21* Some early manuscripts *son. Make me like one of your hired men.*

Matt.	Mark	Luke 15	John

you and never disobeyed your orders. Yet you never gave me even a young goat so I could celebrate with my friends. ³⁰But when this son of yours who has squandered your property with prostitutes comes home, you kill the fattened calf for him!'

³¹"'My son,' the father said, 'you are always with me, and everything I have is yours. ³²But we had to celebrate and be glad, because this brother of yours was dead and is alive again; he was lost and is found.'"

116. Parables about the Advantageous Use of Money

Matt.	Mark	Luke 16:1–31	John

¹Jesus told his disciples: "There was a rich man whose manager was accused of wasting his possessions. ²So he called him in and asked him, 'What is this I hear about you? Give an account of your management, because you cannot be manager any longer.'

³"The manager said to himself, 'What shall I do now? My master is taking away my job. I'm not strong enough to dig, and I'm ashamed to beg—⁴I know what I'll do so that, when I lose my job here, people will welcome me into their houses.'

⁵"So he called in each one of his master's debtors. He asked the first, 'How much do you owe my master?'

⁶"'Eight hundred gallonsª of olive oil,' he replied.

"The manager told him, 'Take your bill, sit down quickly, and make it four hundred.'

⁷"Then he asked the second, 'And how much do you owe?'

"'A thousand bushelsᵇ of wheat,' he replied.

"He told him, 'Take your bill and make it eight hundred.'

⁸"The master commended the dishonest manager because he had acted shrewdly. For the people of this world are more shrewd in dealing with their own kind than are the people of the light. ⁹I tell you, use worldly wealth to gain friends for yourselves, so that when it is gone, you will be welcomed into eternal dwellings.

¹⁰"Whoever can be trusted with very little can also be trusted with much, and whoever is dishonest with very little will also be dishonest with much. ¹¹So if you have not been trustworthy in handling worldly wealth, who will trust you with true riches? ¹²And if you have not been trustworthy with someone else's property, who will give you property of your own?

¹³"No servant can serve two masters. Either he will hate the one and love the other, or he will be devoted to the one and despise the other. You cannot serve both God and Money."

¹⁴The Pharisees, who loved money, heard all this and were sneering at Jesus. ¹⁵He said to them, "You are the ones who justify yourselves in the eyes of men, but God knows your hearts. What is highly valued among men is detestable in God's sight.

¹⁶"The Law and the Prophets were proclaimed until John. Since that time, the good news of the kingdom of God is being preached, and everyone is forcing his way into it. ¹⁷It is easier for heaven and earth to disappear than for the least stroke of a pen to drop out of the Law.

a. *6* Greek *one hundred batous* (probably about 3 kiloliters)
b. *7* Greek *one hundred korous* (probably about 35 kiloliters)

Matt.	Mark	Luke 16	John

18"Anyone who divorces his wife and marries another woman commits adultery, and the man who marries a divorced woman commits adultery.

19"There was a rich man who was dressed in purple and fine linen and lived in luxury every day. 20At his gate was laid a beggar named Lazarus, covered with sores 21and longing to eat what fell from the rich man's table. Even the dogs came and licked his sores.

22"The time came when the beggar died and the angels carried him to Abraham's side. The rich man also died and was buried. 23In hell,a where he was in torment, he looked up and saw Abraham far away, with Lazarus by his side. 24So he called to him, 'Father Abraham, have pity on me and send Lazarus to dip the tip of his finger in water and cool my tongue, because I am in agony in this fire.'

25"But Abraham replied, 'Son, remember that in your lifetime you received your good things, while Lazarus received bad things, but now he is comforted here and you are in agony. 26And besides all this, between us and you a great chasm has been fixed, so that those who want to go from here to you cannot, nor can anyone cross over from there to us.'

27"He answered, 'Then I beg you, father, send Lazarus to my father's house, 28for I have five brothers. Let him warn them, so that they will not also come to this place of torment.'

29"Abraham replied, 'They have Moses and the Prophets; let them listen to them.'

30"'No, father Abraham,' he said, 'but if someone from the dead goes to them, they will repent.'

31"He said to him, 'If they do not listen to Moses and the Prophets, they will not be convinced even if someone rises from the dead.'"

---

a. 23 Greek *Hades*

117. Teaching about Forgiveness, Faith, and Service

Matt.	Mark	Luke 17:1–10	John

1Jesus said to his disciples: "Things that cause people to sin are bound to come, but woe to that person through whom they come. 2It would be better for him to be thrown into the sea with a millstone tied around his neck than for him to cause one of these little ones to sin. 3So watch yourselves.

"If your brother sins, rebuke him, and if he repents, forgive him. 4If he sins against you seven times in a day, and seven times comes back to you and says, 'I repent,' forgive him."

5The apostles said to the Lord, "Increase our faith!"

6He replied, "If you have faith as small as a mustard seed, you can say to this mulberry tree, 'Be uprooted and planted in the sea,' and it will obey you.

7"Suppose one of you had a servant plowing or looking after the sheep. Would he say to the servant when he comes in from the field, 'Come along now and sit down to eat'? 8Would he not rather say, 'Prepare my supper, get yourself ready and wait on me while I eat and drink; after that you may eat and drink'? 9Would he thank the servant because he did what he was told to do? 10So you also, when you have done everything you were told to do, should say, 'We are unworthy servants; we have only done our duty.'"

B. An Interlude in Judea, Samaria, and Galilee

118. Jesus' Raising of Lazarus

Bethany, near Jerusalem

Matt.	Mark	Luke	John 11:1–44

John 11:1–44

[1]Now a man named Lazarus was sick. He was from Bethany, the village of Mary and her sister Martha. [2]This Mary, whose brother Lazarus now lay sick, was the same one who poured perfume on the Lord and wiped his feet with her hair. [3]So the sisters sent word to Jesus, "Lord, the one you love is sick."

[4]When he heard this, Jesus said, "This sickness will not end in death. No, it is for God's glory so that God's Son may be glorified through it." [5]Jesus loved Martha and her sister and Lazarus. [6]Yet when he heard that Lazarus was sick, he stayed where he was two more days.

[7]Then he said to his disciples, "Let us go back to Judea."

[8]"But Rabbi," they said, "a short while ago the Jews tried to stone you, and yet you are going back there?"

[9]Jesus answered, "Are there not twelve hours of daylight? A man who walks by day will not stumble, for he sees by this world's light. [10]It is when he walks by night that he stumbles, for he has no light."

[11]After he had said this, he went on to tell them, "Our friend Lazarus has fallen asleep; but I am going there to wake him up."

[12]His disciples replied, "Lord, if he sleeps, he will get better." [13]Jesus had been speaking of his death, but his disciples thought he meant natural sleep.

[14]So then he told them plainly, "Lazarus is dead, [15]and for your sake I am glad I was not there, so that you may believe. But let us go to him."

[16]Then Thomas (called Didymus) said to the rest of the disciples, "Let us also go, that we may die with him."

[17]On his arrival, Jesus found that Lazarus had already been in the tomb for four days. [18]Bethany was less than two miles[a] from Jerusalem, [19]and many Jews had come to Martha and Mary to comfort them in the loss of their brother. [20]When Martha heard that Jesus was coming, she went out to meet him, but Mary stayed at home.

[21]"Lord," Martha said to Jesus, "if you had been here, my brother would not have died. [22]But I know that even now God will give you whatever you ask."

[23]Jesus said to her, "Your brother will rise again."

[24]Martha answered, "I know he will rise again in the resurrection at the last day."

[25]Jesus said to her, "I am the resurrection and the life. He who believes in me will live, even though he dies; [26]and whoever lives and believes in me will never die. Do you believe this?"

[27]"Yes, Lord," she told him, "I believe that you are the Christ,[b] the Son of God, who was to come into the world."

[28]And after she had said this, she went back and called her sister Mary aside. "The Teacher is here," she said, "and is asking for you." [29]When Mary heard this, she got up quickly and went to him. [30]Now Jesus had not yet entered the village, but was still at the

---

a. *18* Greek *fifteen stadia* (about 3 kilometers)
b. *27* Or *Messiah*

Matt.	Mark	Luke

John 11

place where Martha had met him. [31]When the Jews who had been with Mary in the house, comforting her, noticed how quickly she got up and went out, they followed her, supposing she was going to the tomb to mourn there.

[32]When Mary reached the place where Jesus was and saw him, she fell at his feet and said, "Lord, if you had been here, my brother would not have died."

[33]When Jesus saw her weeping, and the Jews who had come along with her also weeping, he was deeply moved in spirit and troubled. [34]"Where have you laid him?" he asked.

"Come and see, Lord," they replied.

[35]Jesus wept.

[36]Then the Jews said, "See how he loved him!"

[37]But some of them said, "Could not he who opened the eyes of the blind man have kept this man from dying?"

[38]Jesus, once more deeply moved, came to the tomb. It was a cave with a stone laid across the entrance. [39]"Take away the stone," he said.

"But, Lord," said Martha, the sister of the dead man, "by this time there is a bad odor, for he has been there four days."

[40]Then Jesus said, "Did I not tell you that if you believed, you would see the glory of God?"

[41]So they took away the stone. Then Jesus looked up and said, "Father, I thank you that you have heard me. [42]I knew that you always hear me, but I said this for the benefit of the people standing here, that they may believe that you sent me."

[43]When he had said this, Jesus called in a loud voice, "Lazarus, come out!" [44]The dead man came out, his hands and feet wrapped with strips of linen, and a cloth around his face. Jesus said to them, "Take off the grave clothes and let him go."

119. Consequences of Jesus' Raising of Lazarus

Matt.	Mark	Luke

John 11:45–54

[45]Therefore many of the Jews who had come to visit Mary, and had seen what Jesus did, put their faith in him. [46]But some of them went to the Pharisees and told them what Jesus had done. [47]Then the chief priests and the Pharisees called a meeting of the Sanhedrin.

"What are we accomplishing?" they asked. "Here is this man performing many miraculous signs. [48]If we let him go on like this, everyone will believe in him, and then the Romans will come and take away both our place[a] and our nation."

[49]Then one of them, named Caiaphas, who was high priest that year, spoke up, "You know nothing at all! [50]You do not realize that it is better for you that one man die for the people than that the whole nation perish."

[51]He did not say this on his own, but as high priest that year he prophesied that Jesus would die for the Jewish nation, [52]and not only for that nation but also for the scattered children of God, to bring them together and make them one. [53]So from that day on they plotted to take his life.

[54]Therefore Jesus no longer moved about publicly among the Jews. Instead he withdrew to a region near the desert, to a village called Ephraim, where he stayed with his disciples.

---

a. *48* Or *temple*

120. The Healing of Ten Lepers

Probably in Galilee, near the northeastern border of Samaria

Matt.	Mark	Luke 17:11–19	John

Luke 17:11–19

[11]Now on his way to Jerusalem, Jesus traveled along the border between Samaria and Galilee.[a] [12]As he was going into a village, ten men who had leprosy[b] met him. They stood at a distance [13]and called out in a loud voice, "Jesus, Master, have pity on us!"

[14]When he saw them, he said, "Go, show yourselves to the priests." And as they went, they were cleansed.

[15]One of them, when he saw he was healed, came back, praising God in a loud voice. [16]He threw himself at Jesus' feet and thanked him—and he was a Samaritan.

[17]Jesus asked, "Were not all ten cleansed? Where are the other nine? [18]Was no one found to return and give praise to God except this foreigner?" [19]Then he said to him, "Rise and go; your faith has made you well."

a. On his departure from Ephraim (sec. 119), Jesus apparently continued northward through Samaria and Galilee, probably with the intention of meeting the Passover crowds in northern Perea. He could teach them as they journeyed slowly southward through Perea on their way to Jerusalem.
b. *12* The Greek word was used for various diseases affecting the skin—not necessarily leprosy.

121. A Question about the Coming of God's Kingdom

Probably in southeastern Galilee

Matt.	Mark	Luke 17:20–37	John

Luke 17:20–37

[20]Once, having been asked by the Pharisees when the kingdom of God would come, Jesus replied, "The kingdom of God does not come with your careful observation, [21]nor will people say, 'Here it is,' or 'There it is,' because the kingdom of God is within[c] you."

[22]Then he said to his disciples, "The time is coming when you will long to see one of the days of the Son of Man, but you will not see it. [23]Men will tell you, 'There he is!' or 'Here he is!' Do not go running off after them. [24]For the Son of Man in his day[d] will be like the lightning, which flashes and lights up the sky from one end to the other. [25]But first he must suffer many things and be rejected by this generation.

[26]"Just as it was in the days of Noah, so also will it be in the days of the Son of Man. [27]People were eating, drinking, marrying and being given in marriage up to the day Noah entered the ark. Then the flood came and destroyed them all.

[28]"It was the same in the days of Lot. People were eating and drinking, buying and selling, planting and building. [29]But the day Lot left Sodom, fire and sulfur rained down from heaven and destroyed them all.

[30]"It will be just like this on the day the Son of Man is revealed. [31]On that day no one who is on the roof of his house, with his goods inside, should go down to get them. Likewise, no one in the field should go back for anything. [32]Remember Lot's wife! [33]Whoever tries to keep his life will lose it, and whoever loses his life will preserve it. [34]I tell you, on

c. *21* Or *among*
d. *24* Some manuscripts do not have *in his day*.

Matt.	Mark	Luke 17	John

that night two people will be in one bed; one will be taken and the other left. ³⁵Two women will be grinding grain together; one will be taken and the other left.ᵃ”

³⁷“Where, Lord?” they asked.

He replied, “Where there is a dead body, there the vultures will gather.”

a. *35* Some manuscripts *left.* *36* *Two men will be in the field; one will be taken and the other left.*

122. Parabolic Teaching on Prayer

Probably in southeastern Galilee

Matt.	Mark	Luke 18:1–14	John

¹Then Jesus told his disciples a parable to show them that they should always pray and not give up. ²He said: “In a certain town there was a judge who neither feared God nor cared about men. ³And there was a widow in that town who kept coming to him with the plea, ‘Grant me justice against my adversary.’

⁴“For some time he refused. But finally he said to himself, ‘Even though I don’t fear God or care about men, ⁵yet because this widow keeps bothering me, I will see that she gets justice, so that she won’t eventually wear me out with her coming!’”

⁶And the Lord said, “Listen to what the unjust judge says. ⁷And will not God bring about justice for his chosen ones, who cry out to him day and night? Will he keep putting them off? ⁸I tell you, he will see that they get justice, and quickly. However, when the Son of Man comes, will he find faith on the earth?”

⁹To some who were confident of their own righteousness and looked down on everybody else, Jesus told this parable: ¹⁰“Two men went up to the temple to pray, one a Pharisee and the other a tax collector. ¹¹The Pharisee stood up and prayed aboutᵇ himself: ‘God, I thank you that I am not like other men—robbers, evildoers, adulterers—or even like this tax collector. ¹²I fast twice a week and give a tenth of all I get.’

¹³“But the tax collector stood at a distance. He would not even look up to heaven, but beat his breast and said, ‘God, have mercy on me, a sinner.’

¹⁴“I tell you that this man, rather than the other, went home justified before God. For everyone who exalts himself will be humbled, and he who humbles himself will be exalted.”

b. *11* Or *to*

C. The Second Perean Tour

123. Christ's Healing and Teaching Ministry

Matt. 19:1–2	Mark 10:1	Luke	John

¹When Jesus had finished saying these things, he left Galilee and went into the region of Judea

¹Jesus then left that place and went into the region of Judea and across the Jordan. Again crowds

Matt. 19	Mark 10	Luke	John
to the other side of the Jordan.[a] ²Large crowds followed him, and he healed them there.	of people came to him, and as was his custom, he taught them.		

a. The Perean route was commonly used by Jews traveling from Galilee to Judea (see the footnote on page 129).

124. Teaching Concerning Divorce

Matt. 19:3–12	Mark 10:2–12	Luke	John
³Some Pharisees came to him to test him. They asked, "Is it lawful for a man to divorce his wife for any and every reason?" ⁴"Haven't you read," he replied, "that at the beginning the Creator 'made them male and female,'[b] ⁵and said, 'For this reason a man will leave his father and mother and be united to his wife, and the two will become one flesh'[c]? ⁶So they are no longer two, but one. Therefore what God has joined together, let man not separate." ⁷"Why then," they asked, "did Moses command that a man give his wife a certificate of divorce and send her away?" ⁸Jesus replied, "Moses permitted you to divorce your wives because your hearts were hard. But it was not this way from the beginning.	²Some Pharisees came and tested him by asking, "Is it lawful for a man to divorce his wife?" ³"What did Moses command you?" he replied. ⁴They said, "Moses permitted a man to write a certificate of divorce and send her away." ⁵"It was because your hearts were hard that Moses wrote you this law," Jesus replied. ⁶"But at the beginning of creation God 'made them male and female.'[a] ⁷'For this reason a man will leave his father and mother and be united to his wife,[b] ⁸and the two will become one flesh.'[c] So they are no longer two, but one. ⁹Therefore what God has joined together, let man not separate."		
⁹I tell you that anyone who divorces his wife, except for marital unfaithfulness, and marries another woman commits adultery."	¹⁰When they were in the house again, the disciples asked Jesus about this. ¹¹He answered, "Anyone who divorces his wife and marries another woman commits adultery against her. ¹²And if she divorces her husband and marries another man, she commits adultery."		
¹⁰The disciples said to him, "If this is the situation between a husband and wife, it is better not to marry." ¹¹Jesus replied, "Not everyone can accept this word, but only those to whom it has been given. ¹²For some are eunuchs because they were born that way; others were made that way by men; and others have renounced marriage[d] because of the kingdom of heaven. The one who can accept this should accept it."			

b. 4 Gen. 1:27
c. 5 Gen. 2:24
d. 12 Or have made themselves eunuchs

a. 6 Gen. 1:27
b. 7 Some early manuscripts do not have and be united to his wife.
c. 8 Gen. 2:24

125. The Blessing of Little Children

Matt. 19:13–15	Mark 10:13–16	Luke 18:15–17	John
13Then little children were brought to Jesus for him to place his hands on them and pray for them.	13People were bringing little children to Jesus		
But the disciples rebuked those who brought them.	to have him touch them, but the disciples rebuked them.	15People were also bringing babies to Jesus to have him touch them. When the disciples saw this, they rebuked them.	
	14When Jesus saw this, he was indignant. He	16But Jesus	
14Jesus said, "Let the little children come to me, and do not hinder them, for the kingdom of heaven belongs to such as these."	said to them, "Let the little children come to me, and do not hinder them, for the kingdom of God belongs to such as these. 15I tell you the truth, anyone who will not receive the kingdom of God like a little child will never enter it." 16And he took the children in his arms, put his hands on them and blessed them.	called the children to him and said, "Let the little children come to me, and do not hinder them, for the kingdom of God belongs to such as these. 17I tell you the truth, anyone who will not receive the kingdom of God like a little child will never enter it."	
15When he had placed his hands on them, he went on from there.			

126. A Rich Young Ruler's Faltering Faith

Matt. 19:16–20:16	Mark 10:17–31	Luke 18:18–30	John
16Now a man came up to Jesus and asked, "Teacher, what good thing must I do to get eternal life?" 17"Why do you ask me about what is good?" Jesus replied.	17As Jesus started on his way, a man ran up to him and fell on his knees before him. "Good teacher," he asked, "what must I do to inherit eternal life?"	18A certain ruler asked him, "Good teacher, what must I do to inherit eternal life?"	
"There is only One who is good. If you want to enter life, obey the commandments."	18"Why do you call me good?" Jesus answered. "No one is good—except God alone.	19"Why do you call me good?" Jesus answered. "No one is good—except God alone.	

Matt. 19	Mark 10	Luke 18	John

Matt. 19

[18]"Which ones?" the man inquired.

Jesus replied,

"'Do not murder, do not commit adultery, do not steal, do not give false testimony, [19]honor your father and mother,'[a] and 'love your neighbor as yourself.'[b]"

[20]"All these I have kept," the young man said.

"What do I still lack?"

[21]Jesus answered,

"If you want to be perfect, go, sell your possessions and give to the poor, and you will have treasure in heaven. Then come, follow me."

[22]When the young man heard this, he went away sad, because he had great wealth.

[23]Then Jesus said to his disciples, "I tell you the truth, it is hard for a rich man to enter the kingdom of heaven.

[24]Again I tell you, it is easier for a camel to go through the eye of a needle than for a rich man to enter the kingdom of God."

Mark 10

[19]You know the commandments: 'Do not murder, do not commit adultery, do not steal, do not give false testimony, do not defraud, honor your father and mother.'[a]"

[20]"Teacher," he declared, "all these I have kept since I was a boy."

[21]Jesus looked at him and loved him. "One thing you lack," he said. "Go, sell everything you have and give to the poor, and you will have treasure in heaven. Then come, follow me."

[22]At this the man's face fell.[b] He went away sad, because he had great wealth. [23]Jesus looked around and said to his disciples, "How hard it is for the rich to enter the kingdom of God!"

[24]The disciples were amazed at his words. But Jesus said again, "Children, how hard it is[c] to enter the kingdom of God! [25]It is easier for a camel to go through the eye of a needle than for a rich man to enter the kingdom of God."

Luke 18

[20]You know the commandments: 'Do not commit adultery, do not murder, do not steal, do not give false testimony, honor your father and mother.'[a]"

[21]"All these I have kept since I was a boy," he said.

[22]When Jesus heard this, he said to him, "You still lack one thing. Sell everything you have and give to the poor, and you will have treasure in heaven. Then come, follow me."

[23]When he heard this, he became very sad, because he was a man of great wealth. [24]Jesus looked at him and said, "How hard it is for the rich to enter the kingdom of God!

[25]Indeed, it is easier for a camel to go through the eye of a needle than for a rich man to enter the kingdom of God."

Mark notes:

a. *19* Exod. 20:12–16; Deut. 5:16–20
b. The NIV correctly reads "the man's face fell." The pronoun has been substituted to make the composite narrative run smoothly.
c. *24* Some manuscripts *is for those who trust in riches*

Matt. notes:

a. *19* Exod. 20:12–16; Deut. 5:16–20
b. *19* Lev. 19:18

Luke notes:

a. *20* Exod. 20:12–16; Deut. 5:16–20

Matt. 19	Mark 10	Luke 18	John
[25]When the disciples heard this, they were greatly astonished and	[26]The disciples were even more amazed, and		
asked, "Who then can be saved?"	said to each other, "Who then can be saved?"	[26]Those who heard this asked, "Who then can be saved?"	
[26]Jesus looked at them and said, "With man this is impossible, but with God all things are possible."	[27]Jesus looked at them and said, "With man this is impossible, but not with God; all things are possible with God."	[27]Jesus replied, "What is impossible with men is possible with God."	
[27]Peter answered him, "We have left everything to follow you! What then will there be for us?"	[28]Peter said to him, "We have left everything to follow you!"	[28]Peter said to him, "We have left all we had to follow you!"	
[28]Jesus said to them, "I tell you the truth, at the renewal of all things, when the Son of Man sits on his glorious throne, you who have followed me will also sit on twelve thrones, judging the twelve tribes of Israel. [29]And everyone who has left houses or brothers or sisters or father or mother[a] or children or fields for my sake will receive a hundred times as much and will inherit eternal life.	[29]"I tell you the truth," Jesus replied, "no one who has left home or brothers or sisters or mother or father or children or fields for me and the gospel [30]will fail to receive a hundred times as much in this present age (homes, brothers, sisters, mothers, children and fields—and with them, persecutions) and in the age to come, eternal life. [31]But many who are first will be last, and	[29]"I tell you the truth," Jesus said to them, "no one who has left home or wife or brothers or parents or children for the sake of the kingdom of God [30]will fail to receive many times as much in this age and, in the age to come, eternal life."	
[30]But many who are first will be last, and			
many who are last will be first.	the last first."		

a. [29] Some manuscripts *mother or wife*

[1]"For the kingdom of heaven is like a landowner who went out early in the morning to hire men to work in his vineyard. [2]He agreed to pay them a denarius for the day and sent them into his vineyard.

[3]"About the third hour he went out and saw others standing in the marketplace doing nothing. [4]He told them, 'You also go and work in my vineyard, and I will pay you whatever is right.' [5]So they went.

"He went out again about the sixth hour and the ninth hour and did the same thing. [6]About the eleventh hour he went out and found still others standing around. He asked them, 'Why have you been standing here all day long doing nothing?'

[7]"'Because no one has hired us,' they answered.

"He said to them, 'You also go and work in my vineyard.'

Mark	Luke

Matt. 20

| | Mark | Luke | John |

8"When evening came, the owner of the vineyard said to his foreman, 'Call the workers and pay them their wages, beginning with the last ones hired and going on to the first.'

9"The workers who were hired about the eleventh hour came and each received a denarius. 10So when those came who were hired first, they expected to receive more. But each one of them also received a denarius. 11When they received it, they began to grumble against the landowner. 12'These men who were hired last worked only one hour,' they said, 'and you have made them equal to us who have borne the burden of the work and the heat of the day.'

13"But he answered one of them, 'Friend, I am not being unfair to you. Didn't you agree to work for a denarius? 14Take your pay and go. I want to give the man who was hired last the same as I gave you. 15Don't I have the right to do what I want with my own money? Or are you envious because I am generous?'

16"So the last will be first, and the first will be last."

127. Jesus' Prediction of His Approaching Death and Resurrection

Matt. 20:17–19	Mark 10:32–34	Luke 18:31–34	John
17Now as Jesus was going up to Jerusalem,	32They were on their way up to Jerusalem, with Jesus leading the way, and the disciples were astonished, while those who followed were afraid. Again he took the Twelve aside and told them what was going to happen to him. 33"We are going up to Jerusalem," he said, "and		
he took the twelve disciples aside and said to them, 18"We are going up to Jerusalem,		31Jesus took the Twelve aside and told them, "We are going up to Jerusalem, and	
		everything that is written by the prophets about the Son of Man will be fulfilled. 32He will	
and the Son of Man will be betrayed to the chief	the Son of Man will		
	be betrayed to the chief		
priests and the teachers of the law. They will condemn him to death 19and will turn him over to the Gentiles to be mocked	priests and teachers of the law. They will condemn him to death and will hand him over to the Gentiles, 34who will mock him and spit on	be handed over to the Gentiles. They will mock him, insult him, spit on him, flog him and kill him. 33On	
and flogged and crucified. On the third day he will be raised to life!"a	him, flog him and kill him. Three days later he will rise."	the third day he will rise again."	

| | Mark | 34The disciples did not understand any of this. Its meaning was hidden from them, and they did not know what he was talking about. |

a. Twice previously (sec. 85 and sec. 89) Jesus had foretold his death and resurrection, but this was the first time that he disclosed precise details. With reference to the resurrection, on all three occasions Mark says "after three days," while Matthew and Luke say "the third day." As Matthew elsewhere (27:63) also uses the expression "after three days," it seems obvious that these words are not to be interpreted in a strictly literal sense.

128. Humble, Unselfish Service

Matt. 20:20–28	Mark 10:35–45	Luke	John

Matt. 20:20–28

²⁰Then the mother of Zebedee's sons came to Jesus with her sons

and, kneeling down, asked a favor of him.

²¹"What is it you want?" he asked.

She said, "Grant that one of these two sons of mine may sit at your right and the other at your left in your kingdom."

²²"You don't know what you are asking," Jesus said to them. "Can you drink the cup I am going to drink?"

"We can," they answered.
²³Jesus said to them, "You will indeed drink from my cup,

but to sit at my right or left is not for me to grant. These places belong to those for whom they have been prepared by my Father."

²⁴When the ten heard about this, they were indignant with the two brothers. ²⁵Jesus called them together and said, "You know that the rulers of the Gentiles lord it over them, and their high officials exercise authority over them. ²⁶Not so with you. Instead, whoever wants to become great among you must be your servant, ²⁷and whoever wants to be first must be your slave—²⁸just as the Son of Man did not come to be served, but to serve, and to give his life as a ransom for many."

Mark 10:35–45

³⁵Then

James and John, the sons of Zebedee, came to him. "Teacher," they said, "we want you to do for us whatever we ask."
³⁶"What do you want me to do for you?" he asked.
³⁷They replied, "Let one of us sit at your right and the other at your left in your glory."

³⁸"You don't know what you are asking," Jesus said. "Can you drink the cup I

drink or be baptized with the baptism I am baptized with?"
³⁹"We can," they answered.

Jesus said to them, "You will drink the cup I drink and be baptized with the baptism I am baptized with, ⁴⁰but to sit at my right or left is not for me to grant. These places belong to those for whom they have been prepared."

⁴¹When the ten heard about this, they became indignant with James and John. ⁴²Jesus called them together and said, "You know that those who are regarded as rulers of the Gentiles lord it over them, and their high officials exercise authority over them. ⁴³Not so with you. Instead, whoever wants to become great among you must be your servant, ⁴⁴and whoever wants to be first must be slave of all. ⁴⁵For even the Son of Man did not come to be served, but to serve, and to give his life as a ransom for many."

D. A Postlude

129. The Healing of Blind Bartimaeus

Probably on the way out of Old Jericho

Matt. 20:29–34	Mark 10:46–52	Luke 18:35–43	John
29As Jesus and his disciples were leaving Jericho, a large crowd followed him. 30Two blind men were sitting by the roadside,	46Then they came to Jericho. As Jesus and his disciples, together with a large crowd, were leaving the city, a blind man,a Bartimaeus (that is, the Son of Timaeus), was sitting by the roadside begging.	35As Jesus approached Jericho,a a blind man was sitting by the roadside begging. 36When he heard the crowd going by, he asked what was happening. 37They told him, "Jesus of Nazareth is passing by."	
and when they heard that Jesus was going by, they shouted, "Lord, Son of David, have mercy on us!"	47When he heard that it was Jesus of Nazareth, he began to shout, "Jesus, Son of David, have mercy on me!"	38He called out, "Jesus, Son of David, have mercy on me!"	
31The crowd rebuked them and told them to be quiet, but they shouted all the louder, "Lord, Son of David, have mercy on us!"	48Many rebuked him and told him to be quiet, but he shouted all the more, "Son of David, have mercy on me!"	39Those who led the way rebuked him and told him to be quiet, but he shouted all the more, "Son of David, have mercy on me!"	
32Jesus stopped and called them.	49Jesus stopped and said, "Call him." So they called to the blind man, "Cheer up! On your feet! He's calling you." 50Throwing his cloak aside, he jumped to his feet and came to Jesus.	40Jesus stopped and ordered the man to be brought to him.	
"What do you want me to do for you?" he asked. 33"Lord," they answered, "we want our sight."	51"What do you want me to do for you?" Jesus asked him. The blind man said, "Rabbi, I want to see."	When he came near, Jesus asked him, 41"What do you want me to do for you?" "Lord, I want to see," he replied.	

a. Matthew mentions two blind men. Probably the one described by Mark and Luke was the more prominent one (cf. sec. 64).

a. Luke's statement seems to contradict the two other Gospel accounts. Matthew and Mark say that Jesus was leaving Jericho, but Luke says that Jesus was approaching Jericho. Apparently he was leaving Old Jericho and was on his way to the new city built by Herod the Great.

Matt. 20	Mark 10	Luke 18	John
34Jesus had compassion on them and touched their eyes.a Immediately they received their sight and followed him.	52"Go," said Jesus, "your faith has healed you." Immediately he received his sight and followed Jesus along the road.	42Jesus said to him, "Receive your sight; your faith has healed you." 43Immediately he received his sight and followed Jesus, praising God. When all the people saw it, they also praised God.	

a. Unfortunately, because of the plural pronouns this sentence in Matthew's account could not be included in the boldfaced composite narrative.

130. Jesus and Zacchaeus

Probably New Jericho

Matt.	Mark	Luke 19:1–10	John

1Jesus entered Jericho and was passing through. 2A man was there by the name of Zacchaeus; he was a chief tax collector and was wealthy. 3He wanted to see who Jesus was, but being a short man he could not, because of the crowd. 4So he ran ahead and climbed a sycamore-fig tree to see him, since Jesus was coming that way.

5When Jesus reached the spot, he looked up and said to him, "Zacchaeus, come down immediately. I must stay at your house today." 6So he came down at once and welcomed him gladly.

7All the people saw this and began to mutter, "He has gone to be the guest of a 'sinner.'"

8But Zacchaeus stood up and said to the Lord, "Look, Lord! Here and now I give half of my possessions to the poor, and if I have cheated anybody out of anything, I will pay back four times the amount."

9Jesus said to him, "Today salvation has come to this house, because this man, too, is a son of Abraham. 10For the Son of Man came to seek and to save what was lost."

131. The Parable of the Ten Minas

Matt.	Mark	Luke 19:11–28	John

11While they were listening to this, he went on to tell them a parable, because he was near Jerusalem and the people thought that the kingdom of God was going to appear at once. 12He said: "A man of noble birth went to a distant country to have himself appointed king and then to return. 13So he called ten of his servants and gave them ten minas.a 'Put this money to work,' he said, 'until I come back.'

14"But his subjects hated him and sent a delegation after him to say, 'We don't want this man to be our king.'

15"He was made king, however, and returned home. Then he sent for the servants to whom he had given the money, in order to find out what they had gained with it.

16"The first one came and said, 'Sir, your mina has earned ten more.'

a. *13* A mina was about three months' wages.

Matt.	Mark	Luke 19	John

17"'Well done, my good servant!' his master replied. 'Because you have been trustworthy in a very small matter, take charge of ten cities.'

18"The second came and said, 'Sir, your mina has earned five more.'

19"His master answered, 'You take charge of five cities.'

20"Then another servant came and said, 'Sir, here is your mina; I have kept it laid away in a piece of cloth. 21I was afraid of you, because you are a hard man. You take out what you did not put in and reap what you did not sow.'

22"His master replied, 'I will judge you by your own words, you wicked servant! You knew, did you, that I am a hard man, taking out what I did not put in, and reaping what I did not sow? 23Why then didn't you put my money on deposit, so that when I came back, I could have collected it with interest?'

24"Then he said to those standing by, 'Take his mina away from him and give it to the one who has ten minas.'

25"'Sir,' they said, 'he already has ten!'

26"He replied, 'I tell you that to everyone who has, more will be given, but as for the one who has nothing, even what he has will be taken away. 27But those enemies of mine who did not want me to be king over them—bring them here and kill them in front of me.'"

28After Jesus had said this, he went on ahead, going up to Jerusalem.

132. The Hostility of the Sanhedrin

Matt.	Mark	Luke	John 11:55–57

55When it was almost time for the Jewish Passover, many went up from the country to Jerusalem for their ceremonial cleansing before the Passover. 56They kept looking for Jesus, and as they stood in the temple area they asked one another, "What do you think? Isn't he coming to the Feast at all?" 57But the chief priests and Pharisees had given orders that if anyone found out where Jesus was, he should report it so that they might arrest him.

133. Popular Interest and Priestly Plots

Matt.	Mark	Luke	John 12:1, 9–11

1Six days before the Passover, Jesus arrived at Bethany, where Lazarus lived, whom Jesus had raised from the dead. 9Meanwhile a large crowd of Jews found out that Jesus was there and came, not only because of him but also to see Lazarus, whom he had raised from the dead. 10So the chief priests made plans to kill Lazarus as well, 11for on account of him many of the Jews were going over to Jesus and putting their faith in him.

PART 10

Christ's Final Ministry in Jerusalem

Sunday to Wednesday Morning, April 2–5, A.D. 30

134. Jesus and Popular Support

Sunday, April 2

Matt. 21:1–11	Mark 11:1–11	Luke 19:29–44	John 12:12–19
			¹²The next day

Matt. 21:1–11

¹As they approached Jerusalem and came to Bethphage on the Mount of Olives, Jesus sent two disciples, ²saying to them, "Go to the village ahead of you, and at

once you will find a donkey tied there, with her colt
by her.

Untie them and bring them to me. ³If anyone says anything to you, tell him that the Lord needs them, and he will send them right away."
⁶The disciples went and did as Jesus had instructed them.

Mark 11:1–11

¹As they approached **Jerusalem and came to Bethphage and Bethany at the Mount of Olives, Jesus sent two of his disciples, ²saying to them, "Go to the village ahead of you, and just as you enter it,** you will find a colt tied there,

which no one has ever ridden.

Untie it and bring it here. ³If anyone asks you, 'Why are you doing this?' tell him, 'The Lord needs it and will send it back here shortly.'"

⁴They went and found a colt outside in the street, tied at a doorway.
As they untied it, ⁵some people

Luke 19:29–44

²⁹As he approached Bethphage and Bethany at the hill called the Mount of Olives, he sent two of his disciples, saying to them, ³⁰"Go to the village ahead of you, and as you enter it, you will find a colt tied there, which no one has ever ridden.

Untie it and bring it here. ³¹If anyone asks you, 'Why are you untying it?' tell him, 'The Lord needs it.'"

³²Those who were sent ahead went and found it just as he had told them. ³³As they were untying the colt, its owners

Matt. 21	Mark 11	Luke 19	John 12
	standing there asked, "What are you doing, untying that colt?" 6They answered as Jesus had told them to,	asked them, "Why are you untying the colt?" 34They replied,	
		"The Lord needs it."	
	and the people let them go.		
7They brought the donkey and the	7When they brought the	35They brought it to Jesus,	
colt, placed their cloaks on them, and Jesus sat on them. 8A very large crowd spread their cloaks on the road, while others cut branches from the trees and spread them on the road.	colt to Jesus and threw their cloaks over it, he sat on it. 8Many people spread their cloaks on the road, while others spread branches they had cut in the fields.	threw their cloaks on the colt and put Jesus on it. 36As he went along, people spread their cloaks on the road. 37When he came near the place where the road goes down the Mount of Olives,	
			the great crowd that had come for the Feast heard that Jesus was on his way to Jerusalem. 13They took palm branches and went out to meet him, shouting,
			"Hosanna!a" "Blessed is he who comes in the name of the Lord!"b "Blessed is the King of Israel!"
9The crowds that went ahead of him and those that followed shouted,	9Those who went ahead and those who followed shouted,	the whole crowd of disciples began joyfully to praise God in loud voices for all the miracles they had seen:	
	"Hosanna!a"		
"Hosannaa to the Son of David!" "Blessed is he who	"Blessed is he who	38"Blessed is the king	

---

a. *9* A Hebrew expression meaning "Save!" which became an exclamation of praise; also in verse 15

a. *9* A Hebrew expression meaning "Save!" which became an exclamation of praise; also in verse 10

a. *13* A Hebrew expression meaning "Save!" which became an exclamation of praise
b. *13* Ps. 118:25, 26

Matt. 21	Mark 11	Luke 19	John 12
comes in the name of the Lord!"[a]	comes in the name of the Lord!"[a]	who comes in the name of the Lord!"[a]	
	10"Blessed is the coming kingdom of our father David!"		
"Hosanna[b] in the highest!"	"Hosanna in the highest!"		
		"Peace in heaven and glory in the highest!"	

<table>
<tr><td>a. 9 Ps. 118:26
b. 9 A Hebrew expression meaning "Save!" which became an exclamation of praise; also in verse 15</td><td>a. 9 Ps. 118:25,26</td><td>a. 38 Ps. 118:26</td><td></td></tr>
</table>

Mark

17Now the crowd that was with him when he called Lazarus from the tomb and raised him from the dead continued to spread the word. 18Many people, because they had heard that he had given this miraculous sign, went out to meet him. 19So the Pharisees said to one another, "See, this is getting us nowhere. Look how the whole world has gone after him!"

39Some of the Pharisees in the crowd said to Jesus, "Teacher, rebuke your disciples!"

40"I tell you," he replied, "if they keep quiet, the stones will cry out."

4This took place to fulfill what was spoken through the prophet:

5"Say to the Daughter of Zion,

14Jesus found a young donkey and sat upon it, as it is written,

'See, your king
　comes to you,
gentle and riding on a donkey,
　on a colt, the foal of a donkey.'"[c]

15"Do not be afraid, O
　Daughter of Zion;
see, your king
　is coming,
　seated on a donkey's colt."[a]

16At first his disciples did not understand all this. Only after Jesus was glorified did they realize that these things had been

---

c. 5 Zech. 9:9

a. 15 Zech. 9:9

Matt. 21	Mark 11	Luke 19	John 12
			written about him and that they had done these things to him.
		⁴¹As he approached Jerusalem and saw the city, he wept over it ⁴²and said, "If you, even you, had only known on this day what would bring you peace—but now it is hidden from your eyes. ⁴³The days will come upon you when your enemies will build an embankment against you and encircle you and hem you in on every side. ⁴⁴They will dash you to the ground, you and the children within your walls. They will not leave one stone on another, because you did not recognize the time of God's coming to you."	**John**
¹⁰When Jesus entered Jerusalem,	¹¹Jesus entered Jerusalem		
	and went to the temple.		
the whole city was stirred and asked, "Who is this?" ¹¹The crowds answered, "This is Jesus, the prophet from Nazareth in Galilee."			
	He looked around at everything, but since it was already late, he went out to Bethany with the Twelve.		

135. A Fruitless Fig Tree

Monday, April 3

Matt. 21:18–19	Mark 11:12–14	Luke	John
	¹²The next day		
¹⁸Early in the morning, as he was	as they were leaving Bethany,		
on his way back to the city, he was hungry. ¹⁹Seeing	Jesus was hungry. ¹³Seeing		
a fig tree by the road,	in the distance a fig tree		
he went up to it but found nothing on it except leaves. Then he said to it, "May you never bear fruit again!"	in leaf, he went to find out if it had any fruit. When he reached it, he found nothing but leaves, because it was not the season for figs.		

Matthew 21	Mark 11	Luke	John
	[14]Then he said to the tree, "May no one ever eat fruit from you again." And his disciples heard him say it.		
Immediately the tree withered.			

136. The Second[a] Cleansing of the Temple

Monday, April 3

Matthew 21:12–16	Mark 11:15–18[a]	Luke 19:45–48	John
[12]Jesus entered the temple area and drove out	[15]On reaching Jerusalem, Jesus entered the temple area and began driving out	[45]Then he entered the temple area and began driving out those who were selling.	
all who were buying and selling there. He overturned the tables of the money changers	those who were buying and selling there. He overturned the tables of the money changers		
and the benches of those selling doves.	and the benches of those selling doves, [16]and would not allow anyone to carry merchandise through the temple courts. [17]And as he taught them, he said, "Is it not written:		
[13]"It is written," he said to them,		[46]"It is written," he said to them,	
"'My house will be called a house of prayer,'[a]	"'My house will be called a house of prayer for all nations'[b]?	"'My house will be a house of prayer'[a];	
but you are making it a 'den of robbers.'[b]"	But you have made it 'a den of robbers.'[c]"	but you have made it 'a den of robbers.'[b]"	
[14]The blind and the lame came to him at the temple, and he healed them. [15]But when the chief priests and the teachers of the law saw the wonderful things he did and the children shouting in the temple area, "Hosanna to the Son of David," they were indignant.			
[16]"Do you hear what these children are saying?" they asked him.			
"Yes," replied Jesus, "have you never read,			
"'From the lips of children and infants			

a. See sec. 31, especially the footnote.

a. *13* Isa. 56:7
b. *13* Jer. 7:11

b. *17* Isa. 56:7
c. *17* Jer. 7:11

a. *46* Isa. 56:7
b. *46* Jer. 7:11

Matt. 21	Mark 11	Luke 19	John
you have ordained praise'ᵃ?"			
	18The chief priests and the teachers of the law	47Every day he was teaching at the temple. But the chief priests, the teachers of the law and the leaders among the people	
	heard this and began looking for a way to kill him, for they feared him, because the whole crowd was amazed at his teaching.	were trying to kill him.	
		48Yet they could not find any way to do it, because all the people hung on his words.	

a. *16* Ps. 8:2

137. The Significance of Jesus' Approaching Death

Monday, April 3

Matt.	Mark	Luke	John 12:20–50

John 12:20–50

20Now there were some Greeks among those who went up to worship at the Feast. 21They came to Philip, who was from Bethsaida in Galilee, with a request. "Sir," they said, "we would like to see Jesus." 22Philip went to tell Andrew; Andrew and Philip in turn told Jesus.

23Jesus replied, "The hour has come for the Son of Man to be glorified. 24I tell you the truth, unless a kernel of wheat falls to the ground and dies, it remains only a single seed. But if it dies, it produces many seeds. 25The man who loves his life will lose it, while the man who hates his life in this world will keep it for eternal life. 26Whoever serves me must follow me; and where I am, my servant also will be. My Father will honor the one who serves me.

27"Now my heart is troubled, and what shall I say? 'Father, save me from this hour'? No, it was for this very reason I came to this hour. 28Father, glorify your name!"

Then a voice came from heaven, "I have glorified it, and will glorify it again." 29The crowd that was there and heard it said it had thundered; others said an angel had spoken to him.

30Jesus said, "This voice was for your benefit, not mine. 31Now is the time for judgment on this world; now the prince of this world will be driven out. 32But I, when I am lifted up from the earth, will draw all men to myself." 33He said this to show the kind of death he was going to die.

34The crowd spoke up, "We have heard from the Law that the Christᵃ will remain forever, so how can you say, 'The Son of Man must be lifted up'? Who is this 'Son of Man'?"

35Then Jesus told them, "You are going to have the light just a little while longer. Walk while you have the light, before darkness overtakes you. The man who walks in the dark does not know where he is going. 36Put your trust in the light while you have it, so that you may become sons of light." When he had finished speaking, Jesus left and hid himself from them.

a. *34* Or *Messiah*

Matt.	Mark	Luke

John 12

37Even after Jesus had done all these miraculous signs in their presence, they still would not believe in him. 38This was to fulfill the word of Isaiah the prophet:

> "Lord, who has believed our message
>   and to whom has the arm of the Lord been revealed?"[a]

39For this reason they could not believe, because, as Isaiah says elsewhere:

> 40"He has blinded their eyes
>   and deadened their hearts,
> so they can neither see with their eyes,
>   nor understand with their hearts,
>   nor turn—and I would heal them."[b]

41Isaiah said this because he saw Jesus' glory and spoke about him.

42Yet at the same time many even among the leaders believed in him. But because of the Pharisees they would not confess their faith for fear they would be put out of the synagogue; 43for they loved praise from men more than praise from God.

44Then Jesus cried out, "When a man believes in me, he does not believe in me only, but in the one who sent me. 45When he looks at me, he sees the one who sent me. 46I have come into the world as a light, so that no one who believes in me should stay in darkness.

47"As for the person who hears my words but does not keep them, I do not judge him. For I did not come to judge the world, but to save it. 48There is a judge for the one who rejects me and does not accept my words; that very word which I spoke will condemn him at the last day. 49For I did not speak of my own accord, but the Father who sent me commanded me what to say and how to say it. 50I know that his command leads to eternal life. So whatever I say is just what the Father has told me to say."

a. *38* Isa. 53:1
b. *40* Isa. 6:10

Matt. 21:17	**Mark 11:19**	Luke	John

Matt. 21:17

17And

he left them and went out of the city to Bethany, where he spent the night.

Mark 11:19

19When evening came, they[a] went out of the city.

a. *19* Some early manuscripts *he*

138. A Lesson on Faith

Tuesday, April 4

Matt. 21:20–22	**Mark 11:20–25**	Luke	John

Matt. 21:20–22

20When the disciples saw this, they were amazed. "How did the fig tree wither so quickly?" they asked.

21Jesus replied,

"I tell you the truth, if you have faith and do not doubt, not only can you do what was done to the

Mark 11:20–25

20In the morning, as they went along, they saw the fig tree withered from the roots. 21Peter remembered and said to Jesus, "Rabbi, look! The fig tree you cursed has withered!" 22"Have[b] faith in God," Jesus answered. 23"I tell you the truth,

b. *22* Some early manuscripts *If you have*

Matt. 21	Mark 11	Luke	John
fig tree, but also			

fig tree, but also
you can say to this mountain, 'Go, throw yourself into the sea,' and it will be done. ²²If you believe, you will receive whatever you ask for in prayer." | if anyone says to this mountain, 'Go, throw yourself into the sea,' and does not doubt in his heart but believes that what he says will happen, it will be done for him. ²⁴Therefore I tell you, whatever you ask for in prayer, believe that you have received it, and it will be yours. ²⁵And when you stand praying, if you hold anything against anyone, forgive him, so that your Father in heaven may forgive you your sins.ᵃ"

---

a. 25Some manuscripts *sins. 26 But if you do not forgive, neither will your Father who is in heaven forgive your sins.*

139. A Shrewd Question and Pertinent Parables

Tuesday, April 4

Matt. 21:23–22:14	Mark 11:27–12:12	Luke 20:1–19	John
²³Jesus entered the temple courts, and, while he was teaching, the chief priests and the elders of the people came to him. "By what authority are you doing these things?" they asked. "And who gave you this authority?"	²⁷They arrived again in Jerusalem, and while Jesus was walking in the temple courts, the chief priests, the teachers of the law and the elders came to him.	¹One day as he was teaching the people in the temple courts and preaching the gospel, the chief priests and the teachers of the law, together with the elders, came up to him.	
	²⁸"By what authority are you doing these things?" they asked. "And who gave you authority to do this?"	²"Tell us by what authority you are doing these things," they said. "Who gave you this authority?"	
²⁴Jesus replied, "I will also ask you one question. If you answer me, I will tell you by what authority I am doing these things. ²⁵John's baptism—where did it come from? Was it from heaven, or from men?"	²⁹Jesus replied, "I will ask you one question. Answer me, and I will tell you by what authority I am doing these things. ³⁰John's baptism—was it from heaven, or from men? Tell me!"	³He replied, "I will also ask you a question. Tell me, ⁴John's baptism— was it from heaven, or from men?"	
They discussed it among themselves and said, "If we say, 'From heaven,' he will ask, 'Then why didn't you believe him?' ²⁶But if we say, 'From men'—we are afraid of the people, for they all hold that John was a prophet." ²⁷So they answered Jesus, "We don't know."	³¹They discussed it among themselves and said, "If we say, 'From heaven,' he will ask, 'Then why didn't you believe him?' ³²But if we say, 'From men'. . . ." (They feared the people, for everyone held that John really was a prophet.)	⁵They discussed it among themselves and said, "If we say, 'From heaven,' he will ask, 'Why didn't you believe him?' ⁶But if we say, 'From men,' all the people will stone us, because they are	

Matt. 21	Mark 11	Luke 20	John

Then he said, "Neither will I tell you by what authority I am doing these things.

33So they answered Jesus, "We don't know."

Jesus said, "Neither will I tell you by what authority I am doing these things."

persuaded that John was a prophet."

7So they answered, "We don't know where it was from."

8Jesus said, "Neither will I tell you by what authority I am doing these things."

1He then began to speak to them in parables:

9He went on to tell the people this parable:

	Mark	Luke

28"What do you think? There was a man who had two sons. He went to the first and said, 'Son, go and work today in the vineyard.'

29"'I will not,' he answered, but later he changed his mind and went.

30"Then the father went to the other son and said the same thing. He answered, 'I will, sir,' but he did not go.

31"Which of the two did what his father wanted?"

"The first," they answered.

Jesus said to them, "I tell you the truth, the tax collectors and the prostitutes are entering the kingdom of God ahead of you. **32**For John came to you to show you the way of righteousness, and you did not believe him, but the tax collectors and the prostitutes did. And even after you saw this, you did not repent and believe him.

33"Listen to another parable: There was a landowner who planted a vineyard. He put a wall around it, dug a winepress in it and built a watchtower. Then he rented the vineyard to some farmers and went away on a journey. **34**When the harvest time approached, he sent his servants to the tenants to collect his fruit.

35"The tenants seized his servants; they beat one,

killed another,

and stoned a third. **36**Then he sent other servants to them, more than the first time, and the tenants treated them the same way.

37Last of all, he sent his son to them. 'They will respect my son,' he said.

"A man planted a vineyard. He put a wall around it, dug a pit for the winepress and built a watchtower. Then he rented the vineyard to some farmers and went away on a journey. **2**At harvest time he sent a servant to the tenants to collect from them some of the fruit of the vineyard. **3**But they seized him, beat him and sent him away empty-handed. **4**Then he sent another servant to them; they struck this man on the head and treated him shamefully.

5He sent still another, and that one they killed. He sent many others; some of them they beat, others they killed.

6"He had one left to send, a son, whom he loved. He sent him last of

"A man planted a vineyard, rented it to some farmers and went away for a long time. **10**At harvest time he sent a servant to the tenants so they would give him some of the fruit of the vineyard. But the tenants beat him and sent him away empty-handed. **11**He sent another servant, but that one also they beat and treated shamefully and sent away empty-handed. **12**He sent still a third, and they wounded him and threw him out.

13"Then the owner of the vineyard said, 'What shall I do? I will

Matt. 21–22	Mark 12	Luke 20	John
	all, saying, 'They will respect my son.'	send my son, whom I love; perhaps they will respect him.'	
38"But when the tenants saw the son, they said to each other, 'This is the heir. Come, let's kill him and take his inheritance.'	7"But the tenants said to one another, 'This is the heir.	14"But when the tenants saw him, they talked the matter over. 'This is the heir,' they said.	
	Come, let's kill him, and the inheritance will be ours.'	'Let's kill him, and the inheritance will be ours.'	
39So they took him and threw him out of the vineyard and killed him.	8So they took him and killed him, and threw him out of the vineyard.	15So they threw him out of the vineyard and killed him.	
40"Therefore, when the owner of the vineyard comes, what will he do to those tenants?"	9"What then will the owner of the vineyard do?	"What then will the owner of the vineyard do to them?	
41"He will bring those wretches to a wretched end," they replied, "and he will rent the vineyard to other tenants, who will give him his share of the crop at harvest time."	He will come and kill those tenants and give the vineyard to others.	16He will come and kill those tenants and give the vineyard to others."	
		When the people heard this, they said, "May this never be!" 17Jesus looked directly at them and asked, "Then what is the meaning of that which is written:	
42Jesus said to them, "Have you never read in the Scriptures:	10Haven't you read this scripture:		

Matt. 21–22	Mark 12	Luke 20

"'The stone the builders rejected
  has become the capstone[a];
the Lord has done this,
  and it is marvelous in our
    eyes'[b]?
	"'The stone the builders rejected
	  has become the capstone[a];
	11the Lord has done this,
	  and it is marvelous in our
	    eyes'[b]?"
		"'The stone the builders rejected
		  has become the capstone[a][b]?

| a. 42 Or cornerstone
b. 42 Ps. 118:22, 23 | a. 10 Or cornerstone
b. 11 Ps. 118:22, 23 | a. 17 Or cornerstone
b. 17 Ps. 118:22 |

43"Therefore I tell you that the kingdom of God will be taken away from you and given to a people who will produce its fruit. 44He who falls on this stone will be broken to pieces, but he on whom it falls will be crushed."[c]

Mark

18Everyone who falls on that stone will be broken to pieces, but he on whom it falls will be crushed."

c. 44 Some manuscripts do not have verse 44.

45When the chief priests and the Pharisees heard Jesus' parables, they knew he was talking about them. 46They looked for a way to arrest him, but they were afraid of the crowd because the people held that he was a prophet.   **Mark** **Luke**
1Jesus spoke to them again in parables, saying: 2"The kingdom of heaven is like a king who prepared a wedding banquet for his son. 3He sent his servants to those who had been invited to the banquet to tell them to come, but they refused to come.

Matt. 22			Mark	Luke	John

4"Then he sent some more servants and said, 'Tell those who have been invited that I have prepared my dinner: My oxen and fattened cattle have been butchered, and everything is ready. Come to the wedding banquet.'

5"But they paid no attention and went off—one to his field, another to his business. 6The rest seized his servants, mistreated them and killed them. 7The king was enraged. He sent his army and destroyed those murderers and burned their city.

8"Then he said to his servants, 'The wedding banquet is ready, but those I invited did not deserve to come. 9Go to the street corners and invite to the banquet anyone you find.' 10So the servants went out into the streets and gathered all the people they could find, both good and bad, and the wedding hall was filled with guests.

11"But when the king came in to see the guests, he noticed a man there who was not wearing wedding clothes. 12'Friend,' he asked, 'how did you get in here without wedding clothes?' The man was speechless.

13"Then the king told the attendants, 'Tie him hand and foot, and throw him outside, into the darkness, where there will be weeping and gnashing of teeth.'

14"For many are invited, but few are chosen."

Matt.		
	12Then they looked for a way to arrest him because they knew he had spoken the parable against them. But they were afraid of the crowd; so they left him and went away.	19The teachers of the law and the chief priests looked for a way to arrest him immediately, because they knew he had spoken this parable against them. But they were afraid of the people.

140. A Question about Paying Taxes to Caesar

Tuesday, April 4

Matt. 22:15–22	Mark 12:13–17	Luke 20:20–26	John
15Then the Pharisees went out and laid plans to trap him in his words.			
16They sent	13Later they sent some of	20Keeping a close watch on him, they	
their disciples to him along with the Herodians.	the Pharisees and Herodians	sent spies,	
	to Jesus to catch him in his words. 14They	who pretended to be honest. They hoped to catch Jesus in something he said so that they might hand him over to the power and authority of the governor. 21So the spies	
"Teacher," they said, "we know you are a man of integrity and that you teach the way of God in accordance with the truth.	came to him and said, "Teacher, we know you are a man of integrity. You aren't swayed by men,	questioned him: "Teacher, we know that	

Matt. 22	Mark 12	Luke 20	John
You aren't swayed by men, because you pay no attention to who they are.	because you pay no attention to who they are; but		
	you teach the way of God in accordance with the truth.	you speak and teach what is right, and that you do not show partiality but teach the way of God in accordance with the truth. ²²Is it right for us to pay taxes to Caesar or not?"	
¹⁷Tell us then, what is your opinion? Is it right to pay taxes to Caesar or not?"	Is it right to pay taxes to Caesar or not? ¹⁵Should we pay or shouldn't we?"		
¹⁸But Jesus, knowing their evil intent, said, "You hypocrites, why are you trying to trap me? ¹⁹Show me the coin used for paying the tax." They brought him a denarius, ²⁰and he asked them, "Whose portrait is this? And whose inscription?"	But Jesus knew their hypocrisy. "Why are you trying to trap me?" he asked. "Bring me a denarius and let me look at it." ¹⁶They brought the coin, and he asked them, "Whose portrait is this? And whose inscription?"	²³He saw through their duplicity and said to them, ²⁴"Show me a denarius. Whose portrait and inscription are on it?"	
²¹"Caesar's," they replied.	"Caesar's," they replied.	²⁵"Caesar's," they replied.	
Then he said to them, "Give to Caesar what is Caesar's, and to God what is God's."	¹⁷Then Jesus said to them, "Give to Caesar what is Caesar's and to God what is God's."	He said to them, "Then give to Caesar what is Caesar's, and to God what is God's."	
²²When they heard this, they were amazed.	And they were amazed at him.		
		²⁶They were unable to trap him in what he had said there in public. And astonished by his answer, they became silent.	
So they left him and went away.			

141. A Skeptical Question about the Resurrection

Tuesday, April 4

Matt. 22:23–33	Mark 12:18–27	Luke 20:27–40	John
²³That same day the Sadducees, who say there is no resurrection, came to him with a question. ²⁴"Teacher," they said, "Moses told us that if a man dies without having children, his brother must marry the widow and have children for him. ²⁵Now there were seven	¹⁸Then the Sadducees, who say there is no resurrection, came to him with a question. ¹⁹"Teacher," they said, "Moses wrote for us that if a man's brother dies and leaves a wife but no children, the man must marry the widow and have children for his brother. ²⁰Now there were seven	²⁷Some of the Sadducees, who say there is no resurrection, came to Jesus with a question. ²⁸"Teacher," they said, "Moses wrote for us that if a man's brother dies and leaves a wife but no children, the man must marry the widow and have children for his brother. ²⁹Now there were seven brothers.	

Matt. 22	Mark 12	Luke 20	John
brothers among us. The first one married and died, and since he had no children, he left his wife to his brother.	brothers. The first one married and died without leaving any children.	The first one married a woman and died childless.	

brothers among us. The first one married and died, and since he had no children, he left his wife to his brother.

26The same thing happened to the second and

third brother, right on down to the seventh.

27Finally, the woman died.

28Now then, at the resurrection, whose wife will she be of the seven, since all of them were married to
her?"

29Jesus replied, "You are in error because you do not know the Scriptures or the power of God.

30At the resurrection people will neither marry nor be given in marriage; they will be like the angels in heaven.

31But about the resurrection of the dead—have you not read what God said to you, 32'I am the God of Abraham, the God of Isaac, and the God of Jacob'a? He is not the God of the dead but of the living."

---

brothers. The first one married and died without leaving any children.

21The second one married the widow, but he also died, leaving no child. It was the same with the third.

22In fact, none of the seven left any children. Last of all, the woman died too.

23At the resurrectiona whose wife will she be, since the seven were married to

her?"

24Jesus replied, "Are you not in error because you do not know the Scriptures or the power of God?

25When the dead rise, they will neither marry nor be given in marriage; they will be like the angels in heaven.

26Now about the dead rising— have you not read in the book of Moses, in the account of the bush, how

God said to him, 'I am the God of Abraham, the God of Isaac, and the God of Jacob'b? 27He is not the God of the dead, but
of the living.
You are badly mistaken!"

The first one married a woman and died childless.

30The second

31and then the third married her, and in the same way the seven died, leaving no children.
32Finally, the woman died too.
33Now then, at the resurrection whose wife will she be, since the seven were married to her?"
    34Jesus replied,

"The people of this age marry and are given in marriage. 35But those who are considered worthy of taking part in that age and in the resurrection from the dead will neither marry nor be given in marriage, 36and they can no longer die; for they are like the angels. They are God's children, since they are children of the resurrection.
37But in the account of the bush,

even Moses showed that the dead rise, for he calls the Lord 'the God of Abraham, and the God of Isaac, and the God of Jacob.'a 38He is not the God of the dead, but
of the living, for to him all are alive."

---

a. *23* Some manuscripts *resurrection, when men rise from the dead,*

a. *32* Exod. 3:6

b. *26* Exod. 3:6

a. *37* Exod. 3:6

Matt. 22	Mark	Luke 20	John

³³When the crowds heard this, they were astonished at his teaching.

³⁹Some of the teachers of the law responded, "Well said, teacher!" ⁴⁰And no one dared to ask him any more questions.

142. A Question about the Greatest Commandment

Tuesday afternoon, April 4

Matt. 22:34–40	Mark 12:28–34	Luke	John

³⁴Hearing that Jesus had silenced the Sadducees, the Pharisees got together. ³⁵One of them, an expert in
the law,
tested him with this question: ³⁶"Teacher, which is the greatest commandment in the Law?"

³⁷Jesus replied: "'Love the Lord your God with all your heart and with all your soul and with all your mind.'ᵃ
³⁸This is the first and greatest commandment. ³⁹And the second is like it: 'Love your neighbor as yourself.'ᵇ ⁴⁰All the Law and the Prophets hang on these two commandments."

²⁸One of the teachers of
the law came and heard them debating. Noticing that Jesus had given them a good answer, he asked him, "Of all the commandments, which is the most important?"

²⁹"The most important one," answered Jesus, "is this: 'Hear, O Israel, the Lord our God, the Lord is one.ᵃ ³⁰Love the Lord your God with all your heart and with all your soul and with all your mind and with all your strength.'ᵇ ³¹The second is this: 'Love your neighbor as yourself.'ᶜ

There is no commandment greater than these."
³²"Well said, teacher," the man replied. "You are right in saying that God is one and there is no other but him. ³³To love him with all your heart, with all your understanding and with all your strength, and to love your neighbor as yourself is more important than all burnt offerings and sacrifices."
³⁴When Jesus saw that he had answered wisely, he said to him, "You are not far from the kingdom of God." And from then on no one dared ask him any more questions.

---

a. *37* Deut. 6:5
b. *39* Lev. 19:18

a. *29* Or *the Lord our God is one Lord*
b. *30* Deut. 6:4,5
c. *31* Lev. 19:18

Matt.	Mark	Luke 21:37	

³⁷Each day Jesus was teaching at the temple, and each evening he went out to spend the night on the hill called the Mount of Olives,

143. A Question about the Messiah

Wednesday,[a] April 5

Matt. 22:41–46	Mark 12:35–37a	Luke 21:38; 20:41–44	John
		[b]38and all the people came early in the morning to hear him at the temple.	
41While the Pharisees were gathered together, Jesus asked them, 42"What do you think about the Christ[a]? Whose son is he?" "The son of David," they replied. 43He said to them, "How is it then that David, speaking by the Spirit, calls him 'Lord'? For he says,	35While Jesus was teaching in the temple courts, he asked, "How is it that the teachers of the law say that the Christ[a] is the son of David? 36David himself, speaking by the Holy Spirit, declared:	20:41Then Jesus said to them, "How is it that they say the Christ[c] is the Son of David? 42David himself declares in the Book of Psalms:	

44"'The Lord said to my Lord:
  "Sit at my right hand
until I put your enemies
  under your feet."'[b]
	"'The Lord said to my Lord:
	  "Sit at my right hand
	until I put your enemies
	  under your feet."'[b]
		"'The Lord said to my Lord:
		  "Sit at my right hand
		43until I make your enemies
		  a footstool for your feet."'[d]	

45If then David calls him 'Lord,' how can he be his son?"	37aDavid himself calls him 'Lord.' How then can he be his son?"	44David calls him 'Lord.' How then can he be his son?"	
46No one could say a word in reply, and from that day on no one dared to ask him any more questions.			

a. According to some Harmonies of the Gospels, all the events recorded in secs. 138–149 of this Harmony took place on Tuesday, with nothing said about Wednesday; presumably Jesus rested in Bethany on that day.

Instead of thus overcrowding Tuesday, it seems better to adopt the alternative advanced by Moffatt and some other New Testament scholars. In Moffatt's view the language of Matt. 22:41 and Mark 12:35 suggests the occurrence of an interval after Tuesday's incident described in sec. 142 of this Harmony. If so, Jesus probably concluded his final ministry in Jerusalem on Wednesday morning with the events recorded in secs. 143–145.

b. The NIV begins Luke 21:38 with "and" (a small "a"), after a comma at the end of verse 37.

a. *42* Or *Messiah*
b. *44* Ps. 110:1

a. *35* Or *Messiah*
b. *36* Ps. 110:1

c. *41* Or *Messiah*
d. *43* Ps. 110:1

144. A Public Denunciation of the Teachers of the Law and the Pharisees

Wednesday, April 5

Matt. 23:1–39	Mark 12:37b–40	Luke 20:45–47	John
	37bThe large crowd listened to him with delight.	45While all the people were listening, Jesus said to his disciples,	
1Then Jesus said to the crowds and to his disciples: 2"The teachers of the law	38As he taught, Jesus said, "Watch out for the teachers of the law. They	46"Beware of the teachers of the law.	

and the Pharisees sit in Moses' seat. 3So you must obey them and do everything they tell **Mark** **Luke**
you. But do not do what they do, for they do not practice what they preach. 4They tie up
heavy loads and put them on men's shoulders, but they themselves are not willing to lift a
finger to move them.

5"Everything they do is done for men to see: They make their phylacteries[a] wide and the
tassels on their garments long; 6they

	like to walk around in flowing robes and	They like to walk around in flowing robes and love to be greeted in the
love the place of honor at banquets and the most important seats in the synagogues; 7they love to be greeted in the marketplaces and to have men call them 'Rabbi.'	be greeted in the marketplaces, 39and have the most important seats in the synagogues and the places of honor at banquets.	marketplaces and have the most important seats in the synagogues and the places of honor at banquets.
	40They devour widows' houses and for a show make lengthy prayers. Such men will be punished most severely."	47They devour widows' houses and for a show make lengthy prayers. Such men will be punished most severely."

a. *5 That is, boxes containing Scripture verses, worn on forehead and arm*

8"But you are not to be called 'Rabbi,' for you have only one Master and you are all broth- **Mark** **Luke**
ers. 9And do not call anyone on earth 'father,' for you have one Father, and he is in heaven.
10Nor are you to be called 'teacher,' for you have one Teacher, the Christ.[b] 11The greatest
among you will be your servant. 12For whoever exalts himself will be humbled, and whoever humbles himself will be exalted.

13"Woe to you, teachers of the law and Pharisees, you hypocrites! You shut the kingdom
of heaven in men's faces. You yourselves do not enter, nor will you let those enter who are
trying to.[c]

15"Woe to you, teachers of the law and Pharisees, you hypocrites! You travel over land
and sea to win a single convert, and when he becomes one, you make him twice as much
a son of hell as you are.

16"Woe to you, blind guides! You say, 'If anyone swears by the temple, it means nothing;
but if anyone swears by the gold of the temple, he is bound by his oath.' 17You blind fools!

b. *10 Or Messiah*
c. *13 Some manuscripts* to. *14 Woe to you, teachers of the law and Pharisees, you hypocrites! You devour widows'
houses and for a show make lengthy prayers. Therefore you will be punished more severely.*

Matt. 23

| | Mark | Luke | John |

Which is greater: the gold, or the temple that makes the gold sacred? [18]You also say, 'If anyone swears by the altar, it means nothing; but if anyone swears by the gift on it, he is bound by his oath.' [19]You blind men! Which is greater: the gift, or the altar that makes the gift sacred? [20]Therefore, he who swears by the altar swears by it and by everything on it. [21]And he who swears by the temple swears by it and by the one who dwells in it. [22]And he who swears by heaven swears by God's throne and by the one who sits on it.

[23]"Woe to you, teachers of the law and Pharisees, you hypocrites! You give a tenth of your spices—mint, dill and cummin. But you have neglected the more important matters of the law—justice, mercy and faithfulness. You should have practiced the latter, without neglecting the former. [24]You blind guides! You strain out a gnat but swallow a camel.

[25]"Woe to you, teachers of the law and Pharisees, you hypocrites! You clean the outside of the cup and dish, but inside they are full of greed and self-indulgence. [26]Blind Pharisee! First clean the inside of the cup and dish, and then the outside also will be clean.

[27]"Woe to you, teachers of the law and Pharisees, you hypocrites! You are like whitewashed tombs, which look beautiful on the outside but on the inside are full of dead men's bones and everything unclean. [28]In the same way, on the outside you appear to people as righteous but on the inside you are full of hypocrisy and wickedness.

[29]"Woe to you, teachers of the law and Pharisees, you hypocrites! You build tombs for the prophets and decorate the graves of the righteous. [30]And you say, 'If we had lived in the days of our forefathers, we would not have taken part with them in shedding the blood of the prophets.' [31]So you testify against yourselves that you are the descendants of those who murdered the prophets. [32]Fill up, then, the measure of the sin of your forefathers!

[33]"You snakes! You brood of vipers! How will you escape being condemned to hell? [34]Therefore I am sending you prophets and wise men and teachers. Some of them you will kill and crucify; others you will flog in your synagogues and pursue from town to town. [35]And so upon you will come all the righteous blood that has been shed on earth, from the blood of righteous Abel to the blood of Zechariah son of Berekiah, whom you murdered between the temple and the altar. [36]I tell you the truth, all this will come upon this generation.

[37]"O Jerusalem, Jerusalem, you who kill the prophets and stone those sent to you, how often I have longed to gather your children together, as a hen gathers her chicks under her wings, but you were not willing. [38]Look, your house is left to you desolate. [39]For I tell you, you will not see me again until you say, 'Blessed is he who comes in the name of the Lord.'[a]"

a. *39* Psalm 118:26

145. A Widow's Two Small Coins

Wednesday, April 5

Matt.	Mark 12:41–44	Luke 21:1–4	John
	[41]Jesus sat down opposite the place where the offerings were put and watched the crowd putting their money into the temple treasury. Many rich people threw in large amounts. [42]But a poor widow came and put in two very small copper coins,[a] worth only a fraction of a penny.[b]	[1]As he looked up, Jesus saw the rich putting their gifts into the temple treasury. [2]He also saw a poor widow put in two very small copper coins.[a]	

a. *42* Greek *two lepta*   b. *42* Greek *kodrantes*

a. *2* Greek *two lepta*

Matt.	Mark 12	Luke 21	John

Mark 12

⁴³Calling his disciples to him, Jesus said, "I tell you the truth, this poor widow has put more into the treasury than all the others.

⁴⁴They all gave out of their wealth;

but she, out of her poverty, put in everything—all she had to live on."

Luke 21

³"I tell you the truth," he said, "this poor widow has put in more than all the others.

⁴All these people gave their gifts out of their wealth;

but she out of her poverty put in all she had to live on."

PART 11

Jesus with the Twelve in the Shadow of the Cross

Wednesday Afternoon to Thursday Night, April 5–6, A.D. 30

146. A Discourse on the Destruction of Jerusalem and the End of the World

Wednesday afternoon,[a] April 5, on the Mount of Olives

Matt. 24–25	Mark 13:1–37	Luke 21:5–36	John
¹Jesus left the temple and was walking away when his disciples came up to him to call his attention to	¹As he was leaving the temple, one of his disciples said to him,	⁵Some of his disciples were remarking about	
its buildings. ²"Do you see all these things?" he asked. "I tell you the truth, not one stone here will be left on another; every one will be thrown down."	"Look, Teacher! What massive stones! What magnificent buildings!" ²"Do you see all these great buildings?" replied Jesus. "Not one stone here will be left on another; every one will be thrown down."	how the temple was adorned with beautiful stones and with gifts dedicated to God. But Jesus said, ⁶"As for what you see here, the time will come when not one stone will be left on another; every one of them will be thrown down."	
³As Jesus was sitting on the Mount of Olives, the disciples came to him privately. "Tell us," they said, "when will this happen,	³As Jesus was sitting on the Mount of Olives opposite the temple, Peter, James, John and Andrew asked him privately, ⁴"Tell us, when will these things happen? And what will be the sign that they are all about to be fulfilled?"	⁷"Teacher," they asked, "when will these things happen? And what will be the sign that they are about to take place?"	
and what will be the sign of your coming and of the end of the age?"			

a. According to some Harmonies of the Gospels, the events recorded in secs. 146–149 of this Harmony occurred on Tuesday. See footnote a, col. 3, page 163.

Matt. 24–25	Mark 13	Luke 21	John
4Jesus answered: "Watch out that no one deceives you. **5**For many will come in my name, claiming, 'I am the Christ,ᵃ' and will deceive many.	**5**Jesus said to them: "Watch out that no one deceives you. **6**Many will come in my name, claiming, 'I am he,' and will deceive many.	**8**He replied: "Watch out that you are not deceived. For many will come in my name, claiming, 'I am he,' and, 'The time is near.' Do not follow them.	
6You will hear of wars and rumors of wars, but see to it that you are not alarmed. Such things must happen, but the end is still to come.	**7**When you hear of wars and rumors of wars, do not be alarmed. Such things must happen, but the end is still to come.	**9**When you hear of wars and revolutions, do not be frightened. These things must happen first, but the end will not come right away."	
7Nation will rise against nation, and kingdom against kingdom. There will be famines and earthquakes in various places.	**8**Nation will rise against nation, and kingdom against kingdom. There will be earthquakes in various places, and famines.	**10**Then he said to them: "Nation will rise against nation, and kingdom against kingdom. **11**There will be great earthquakes, famines and pestilences in various places, and fearful events and great signs from heaven. **12**"But before all this, they will lay hands on you and persecute you.	
8All these are the beginning of birth pains.	These are the beginning of birth pains. **9**"You must be on your guard. You will be handed over to the local councils and flogged in the synagogues. On account of me you will stand before		
9"Then you will be handed over		They will deliver you to	
	governors and kings	synagogues and prisons, and you will be brought before	
to be persecuted and put to death,	as witnesses to them.	kings and governors, and all on account of my name. **13**This will result in your being witnesses to them.	
	11Whenever you are arrested and brought to trial, do not worry beforehand about what to say.	**14**But make up your mind not to worry beforehand how you will defend yourselves.	
	Just say whatever is given you at the time, for it is not you speaking, but the Holy Spirit.	**15**For I will give you words and wisdom that none of your adversaries will be able to resist or contradict.	

a. *5* Or *Messiah;* also in verse 23

Matt. 24–25	Mark 13	Luke 21	John
and you will be hated by all nations because of me. [10]At that time many will turn away from the faith and will betray and hate each other, [11]and many false prophets will appear and deceive many people.	[13]All men will hate you because of me,	[17]All men will hate you because of me.	
	[12]"Brother will betray brother to death, and a father his child.		
	Children will rebel against their parents and have them put to death.	[16]You will be betrayed even by parents, brothers, relatives and friends, and they will put some of you to death. [18]But not a hair of your head will perish.	
[12]Because of the increase of wickedness, the love of most will grow cold, [13]but he who stands firm to the end will be saved. [14]And this gospel of the kingdom will be preached in the whole world as a testimony to all nations, and then the end will come.	[13b]but he who stands firm to the end will be saved. [10]And the gospel must first be preached to all nations.	[19]By standing firm you will gain life.	
		[20]"When you see Jerusalem being surrounded by armies, you will know that its desolation is near.	
[15]"So when you see standing in the holy place 'the abomination that causes desolation,'[a] spoken of through the prophet Daniel—let the reader understand—[16]then let those who are in Judea flee to the mountains.	[14]"When you see 'the abomination that causes desolation'[a] standing where it[b] does not belong—let the reader understand—then let those who are in Judea flee to the mountains.	[21]Then let those who are in Judea flee to the mountains, let those in the city get out, and let those in the country not enter the city.	
[17]Let no one on the roof of his house go down to take anything out of the house. [18]Let no one in the field go back to get his cloak.	[15]Let no one on the roof of his house go down or enter the house to take anything out. [16]Let no one in the field go back to get his cloak.		
		[22]For this is the time of punishment in fulfillment of all that has been written. [23]How dreadful it will be in those days for pregnant women and nursing mothers!	
[19]How dreadful it will be in those days for pregnant women and nursing mothers!	[17]How dreadful it will be in those days for pregnant women and nurs-	There will be great distress in the land and wrath against this peo-	

a. *15* Dan. 9:27; 11:31; 12:11

a. *14* Dan. 9:27; 11:31; 12:11
b. *14* Or *he;* also in verse 29

Matt. 24–25	Mark 13	Luke 21	John

ing mothers!

ple. [24]They will fall by the sword and will be taken as prisoners to all the nations. Jerusalem will be trampled on by the Gentiles until the times of the Gentiles are fulfilled.

Matt. 24–25

[20]Pray that your flight will not take place in winter or on the Sabbath. [21]For then there will be great distress, unequaled from the beginning of the world until now—and never to be equaled again.

[22]If those days had not been cut short, no one would survive, but for the sake of the elect those days will be shortened.

[23]At that time if anyone says to you, 'Look, here is the Christ!' or, 'There he is!' do not believe it.

[24]For false Christs and false prophets will appear and perform

great signs and miracles to deceive even the elect—if that were

possible. [25]See, I have told you ahead of time.

Mark 13

[18]Pray that this will not take place in winter, [19]because those

will be days of distress unequaled from the beginning, when God created the world, until now—and never to be equaled again. [20]If the Lord had not cut short those days, no one would survive. But for the sake of the elect, whom he has chosen, he has shortened them. [21]At that time if anyone says to you, 'Look, here is the Christ[a]!' or, 'Look, there he is!' do not believe it. [22]For false Christs and false prophets will appear and perform

signs and miracles to deceive the elect—if that were

possible. [23]So be on your guard; I have told you everything ahead of time.

a. *21* Or *Messiah*

[Mark]

[26]"So if anyone tells you, 'There he is, out in the desert,' do not go out; or, 'Here he is, in the inner rooms,' do not believe it. [27]For as lightning that comes from the east is visible even in the west, so will be the coming of the Son of Man. [28]Wherever there is a carcass, there the vultures will gather.

Matt. 24–25	Mark 13	Luke 21
[29]"Immediately after the distress of those days	[24]"But in those days, following that distress,	
		[25]"There will be signs in the sun, moon and stars.
"'the sun will be darkened, and the moon will not give its light; the stars will fall from the sky,	"'the sun will be darkened, and the moon will not give its light; [25]the stars will fall from the sky,	
		On the earth, nations will be in anguish and perplexity at the roaring and tossing of the sea. [26]Men will faint from terror, apprehensive of what is coming on the world, for the heavenly bodies will be shaken.
and the heavenly bodies will be shaken.'[a]	and the heavenly bodies will be shaken.'[b]	

a. *29* Isa. 13:10; 34:4

b. *25* Isa. 13:10; 34:4

Matt. 24–25	Mark 13	Luke 21	John
30"At that time the sign of the Son of Man will appear in the sky, and all the nations of the earth will mourn. They will see the Son of Man coming on the clouds of the sky, with power and great glory. 31And he will send his angels with a loud trumpet call, and they will gather his elect from the four winds,	26"At that time		
from one end of the heavens to the other.	men will see the Son of Man coming in clouds with great power and glory. 27And he will send his angels and gather his elect from the four winds,	27At that time they will see the Son of Man coming in a cloud with power and great glory.	
	from the ends of the earth to the ends of the heavens.		
		28When these things begin to take place, stand up and lift up your heads, because your redemption is drawing near." 29He told them this parable:	
32"Now learn this lesson from the fig tree: As soon as its twigs get tender and its leaves come out,	28"Now learn this lesson from the fig tree: As soon as its twigs get tender and its leaves come out,	"Look at the fig tree and all the trees. 30When they sprout leaves,	
you know that summer is near. 33Even so, when you see all these things, you know that it[a] is near, right at the door. 34I tell you the truth, this generation[b] will certainly not pass away until all these things have happened. 35Heaven and earth will pass away, but my words will never pass away.	you know that summer is near. 29Even so, when you see these things happening, you know that it is near, right at the door. 30I tell you the truth, this generation[a] will certainly not pass away until all these things have happened. 31Heaven and earth will pass away, but my words will never pass away.	you can see for yourselves and know that summer is near. 31Even so, when you see these things happening, you know that the kingdom of God is near. 32"I tell you the truth, this generation[a] will certainly not pass away until all these things have happened. 33Heaven and earth will pass away, but my words will never pass away.	
36"No one knows about that day or hour, not even the angels in heaven, nor the Son,[c] but only	32"No one knows about that day or hour, not even the angels in heaven, nor the Son, but only the Father.		

a. 33 Or *he*
b. 34 Or *race*
c. 36 Some manuscripts do not have *nor the Son.*

a. 30 Or *race*

a. 32 Or *race*

the Father. 37As it was in the days of Noah, so it will be at the coming of the Son of Man. | Mark | Luke |
38For in the days before the flood, people were eating and drinking, marrying and giving in marriage, up to the day Noah entered the ark; 39and they knew nothing about what would happen until the flood came and took them all away. That is how it will be at the coming of the Son of Man. 40Two men will be in the field; one will be taken and the other left. 41Two women will be grinding with a hand mill; one will be taken and the other left.

Matt. 24–25	**Mark 13**	**Luke 21**	John

---

a. 33 Some manuscripts alert and pray

Matt.	Mark

34"Be careful, or your hearts will be weighed down with dissipation, drunkenness and the anxieties of life, and that day will close on you unexpectedly like a trap. 35For it will come upon all those who live on the face of the whole earth. 36Be always on the watch, and pray that you may be able to escape all that is about to happen, and that you may be able to stand before the Son of Man."

42"Therefore keep watch, because you do not know on what day your Lord will come.

You do not know when that time will come. 34It's like a man going away: He leaves his

Luke

Matt. house and puts his servants in charge, each with his assigned task, and tells the one at the door to keep watch.

35"Therefore keep watch because you do not know when the owner of the house will come back—whether in the evening, or at midnight, or when the rooster crows, or at dawn. 36If he comes suddenly, do not let him find you sleeping. 37What I say to you, I say to everyone: 'Watch!'"

43But understand this: If the owner of the house had known at what time of night the thief | Mark |
was coming, he would have kept watch and would not have let his house be broken into. 44So you also must be ready, because the Son of Man will come at an hour when you do not expect him.

45"Who then is the faithful and wise servant, whom the master has put in charge of the servants in his household to give them their food at the proper time? 46It will be good for that servant whose master finds him doing so when he returns. 47I tell you the truth, he will put him in charge of all his possessions. 48But suppose that servant is wicked and says to himself, 'My master is staying away a long time,' 49and he then begins to beat his fellow servants and to eat and drink with drunkards. 50The master of that servant will come on a day when he does not expect him and at an hour he is not aware of. 51He will cut him to pieces and assign him a place with the hypocrites, where there will be weeping and gnashing of teeth.

1"At that time the kingdom of heaven will be like ten virgins who took their lamps and went out to meet the bridegroom. 2Five of them were foolish and five were wise. 3The foolish ones took their lamps but did not take any oil with them. 4The wise, however, took oil in jars along with their lamps. 5The bridegroom was a long time in coming, and they all became drowsy and fell asleep.

6"At midnight the cry rang out: 'Here's the bridegroom! Come out to meet him!'

7"Then all the virgins woke up and trimmed their lamps. 8The foolish ones said to the wise, 'Give us some of your oil; our lamps are going out.'

9"'No,' they replied, 'there may not be enough for both us and you. Instead, go to those who sell oil and buy some for yourselves.'

10"But while they were on their way to buy the oil, the bridegroom arrived. The virgins who were ready went in with him to the wedding banquet. And the door was shut.

11"Later the others also came. 'Sir! Sir!' they said. 'Open the door for us!'

12"But he replied, 'I tell you the truth, I don't know you.'

13"Therefore keep watch, because you do not know the day or the hour.

14"Again, it will be like a man going on a journey, who called his servants and entrusted

Matt. 24–25

| | Mark | Luke | John |

his property to them. [15]To one he gave five talents[a] of money, to another two talents, and to another one talent, each according to his ability. Then he went on his journey. [16]The man who had received the five talents went at once and put his money to work and gained five more. [17]So also, the one with the two talents gained two more. [18]But the man who had received the one talent went off, dug a hole in the ground and hid his master's money.

[19]"After a long time the master of those servants returned and settled accounts with them. [20]The man who had received the five talents brought the other five. 'Master,' he said, 'you entrusted me with five talents. See, I have gained five more.'

[21]"His master replied, 'Well done, good and faithful servant! You have been faithful with a few things; I will put you in charge of many things. Come and share your master's happiness!'

[22]"The man with the two talents also came. 'Master,' he said, 'you entrusted me with two talents; see, I have gained two more.'

[23]"His master replied, 'Well done, good and faithful servant! You have been faithful with a few things; I will put you in charge of many things. Come and share your master's happiness!'

[24]"Then the man who had received the one talent came. 'Master,' he said, 'I knew that you are a hard man, harvesting where you have not sown and gathering where you have not scattered seed. [25]So I was afraid and went out and hid your talent in the ground. See, here is what belongs to you.'

[26]"His master replied, 'You wicked, lazy servant! So you knew that I harvest where I have not sown and gather where I have not scattered seed? [27]Well then, you should have put my money on deposit with the bankers, so that when I returned I would have received it back with interest.

[28]"'Take the talent from him and give it to the one who has the ten talents. [29]For everyone who has will be given more, and he will have an abundance. Whoever does not have, even what he has will be taken from him. [30]And throw that worthless servant outside, into the darkness, where there will be weeping and gnashing of teeth.'

[31]"When the Son of Man comes in his glory, and all the angels with him, he will sit on his throne in heavenly glory. [32]All the nations will be gathered before him, and he will separate the people one from another as a shepherd separates the sheep from the goats. [33]He will put the sheep on his right and the goats on his left.

[34]"Then the King will say to those on his right, 'Come, you who are blessed by my Father; take your inheritance, the kingdom prepared for you since the creation of the world. [35]For I was hungry and you gave me something to eat, I was thirsty and you gave me something to drink, I was a stranger and you invited me in, [36]I needed clothes and you clothed me, I was sick and you looked after me, I was in prison and you came to visit me.'

[37]"Then the righteous will answer him, 'Lord, when did we see you hungry and feed you, or thirsty and give you something to drink? [38]When did we see you a stranger and invite you in, or needing clothes and clothe you? [39]When did we see you sick or in prison and go to visit you?'

[40]"The King will reply, 'I tell you the truth, whatever you did for one of the least of these brothers of mine, you did for me.'

[41]"Then he will say to those on his left, 'Depart from me, you who are cursed, into the eternal fire prepared for the devil and his angels. [42]For I was hungry and you gave me nothing to eat, I was thirsty and you gave me nothing to drink, [43]I was a stranger and you did

---

a. *15* A talent was worth more than a thousand dollars.

Matt. 24–25	Mark	Luke	John
not invite me in, I needed clothes and you did not clothe me, I was sick and in prison and you did not look after me.' ⁴⁴"They also will answer, 'Lord, when did we see you hungry or thirsty or a stranger or needing clothes or sick or in prison, and did not help you?' ⁴⁵"He will reply, 'I tell you the truth, whatever you did not do for one of the least of these, you did not do for me.' ⁴⁶"Then they will go away to eternal punishment, but the righteous to eternal life."			

147. Impending Crucifixion and a Death-Plot

Wednesday afternoon, April 5

Matt. 26:1–5	Mark 14:1–2	Luke 22:1–2	John
¹When Jesus had finished saying all these things, he said to his disciples, ²"As you know, the Passover is two days away—and the Son of Man will be handed over to be crucified." ³Then the chief priests and the elders of the people assembled in the palace of the high priest, whose name was Caiaphas, ⁴and they plotted to arrest Jesus in some sly way and kill him. ⁵"But not during the Feast," they said, "or there may be a riot among the people."	¹Now the Passover and the Feast of Unleavened Bread were only two days away, and the chief priests and the teachers of the law were looking for some sly way to arrest Jesus and kill him. ²"But not during the Feast," they said, "or the people may riot."	¹Now the Feast of Unleavened Bread, called the Passover, was approaching, ²and the chief priests and the teachers of the law were looking for some way to get rid of Jesus, for they were afraid of the people.	

148. Mary's Expression of Devotion

Wednesday evening, April 5

Matt. 26:6–13	Mark 14:3–9	Luke	John 12:2–8
⁶While Jesus was in Bethany in the home of a man known as Simon the Leper, ⁷a woman came to him with an alabaster jar	³While he was in Bethany, reclining at the table in the home of a man known as Simon the Leper, a woman came with	²Here	a dinner was given in Jesus' honor. Martha served, while Lazarus was among those reclining at the table with him. ³Then Mary took

Matt. 26	**Mark 14**	Luke	**John 12**
	an alabaster jar containing[a]		
of very expensive perfume,	very expensive perfume, made of pure nard. She broke the jar and poured the perfume on		about a pint[a] of pure nard, an expensive perfume; she poured it on
which she poured			
on his head as he was reclining at the table.	his head.		Jesus' feet[b] and wiped his feet with her hair. And the house was filled with the fragrance of the perfume.
8When the disciples saw this, they were indignant. "Why this waste?" they asked.	**4**Some of those present were saying indignantly to one another, "Why this waste of perfume?		**4**But one of his disciples,
			Judas Iscariot, who was later to betray him, objected,
	5bAnd they rebuked her harshly.		**5**"Why wasn't this perfume sold and the money given to the poor? It was worth a year's wages.[c]" **6**He did not say this because he cared about the poor but because he was a thief; as keeper of the money bag, he used to help himself to what was put into it.
9"This perfume could have been sold at a high price and the money given to the poor."	**5a**It could have been sold for more than a year's wages[b] and the money given to the poor."		
10Aware of this, Jesus said to them,	**6**"Leave her alone," said Jesus. "Why are you bothering her?		**7**"Leave her alone," Jesus replied. "It was intended that she should save this perfume for the day of my burial.
"Why are you bothering this woman? She has done a beautiful thing to me. **11**The poor you will always have with you, but you will not always have me.	She has done a beautiful thing to me. **7**The poor you will always have with you, and you can help them any time you want. But you will not always have me. **8**She did what she could.		**8**You will always have the poor among you, but you will not always have me."
12When she poured this perfume on my body, she did it to prepare me for burial. **13**I tell you the truth, wherever this gospel is preached throughout the world, what she has done will also be told, in memory of her."	She poured perfume on my body beforehand to prepare for my burial. **9**I tell you the truth, wherever the gospel is preached throughout the world, what she has done will also be told, in memory of her."		

a. The NIV reads "of." By substituting the word "containing," which conveys the same meaning, the composite narrative is improved.
b. *5* Greek *than three hundred denarii*

a. *3* Greek *a litra* (probably about 0.5 liter)
b. Matthew and Mark state that Mary poured the perfume on Jesus' head also.
c. *5* Greek *three hundred denarii*

149. Judas's Bargain with the Jewish Leaders

Jerusalem; Wednesday night, April 5

Matt. 26:14–16	Mark 14:10–11	Luke 22:3–6	John
14Then one of the Twelve—the one called Judas Iscariot—went to the chief priests 15and	10Then Judas Iscariot, one of the Twelve, went to the chief priests to	3Then Satan entered Judas, called Iscariot, one of the Twelve. 4And Judas went to the chief priests and the officers of the temple guard and discussed with them how he might	
asked, "What are you willing to give me if I hand him over to you?" So they counted out for him thirty silver coins.	betray Jesus to them. 11They were delighted to hear this and promised to give him money. So he	betray Jesus. 5They were delighted and agreed to give him money.	
16From then on Judas watched for an opportunity to hand him over.	watched for an opportunity to hand him over.	6He consented, and watched for an opportunity to hand Jesus over to them when no crowd was present.	

150. Preparation for the Passover

Jerusalem; Thursday, April 6

Matt. 26:17–19	Mark 14:12–16	Luke 22:7–13	John
17On the first day of the Feast of Unleavened Bread,	12On the first day of the Feast of Unleavened Bread, when it was customary to sacrifice the Passover lamb,	7Then came the day of Unleavened Bread on which the Passover lamb had to be sacrificed.	
		8Jesus sent Peter and John, saying, "Go and make preparations for us to eat the Passover."	
the disciples came to Jesus and asked, "Where do you want us to make preparations for you to eat the Passover?"	Jesus' disciples asked him, "Where do you want us to go and make preparations for you to eat the Passover?"	9"Where do you want us to prepare for it?" they asked.	
18He replied, "Go into the city to a certain man and tell him, 'The Teacher	13So he sent two of his disciples, telling them, "Go into the city, and a man carrying a jar of water will meet you. Follow him. 14Say to the owner of the house he enters, 'The Teacher asks:	10He replied, "As you enter the city, a man carrying a jar of water will meet you. Follow him to the house that he enters, 11and say to the owner of the house, 'The Teacher	
says: My appointed time is near.	**Where is my guest room, where**	asks: Where is the guest room,	
I am going to celebrate the Pass-	I may eat the Passover	where I may eat the Passover with	

Matt. 26	Mark 14	Luke 22	John
over		my disciples?' [12]He will show you a	
with my disciples at your house.'"	with my disciples?' [15]He will show you a large upper room, furnished and ready. Make preparations for us there."	large upper room, all furnished. Make preparations there."	
	[16]The disciples left, went into the city and found things just as Jesus had told them. So they	[13]They left and found things just as Jesus had told them.	
[19]So the disciples			
did as Jesus had directed them and prepared the Passover.	prepared the Passover.	So they prepared the Passover.	

151. Jesus' Washing of the Disciples' Feet

Jerusalem; Thursday evening,[a] April 6

Matt. 26:20	Mark 14:17	Luke 22:14–16, 24–30	John 13:1–20
[20]When evening came,	[17]When evening came, Jesus arrived with the Twelve.	[14]When the hour came,	
			[1]It was just before the Passover Feast. Jesus knew that the time had come for him to leave this world and go to the Father. Having loved his own who were in the world, he now showed them the full extent of his love.[a]
Jesus was reclining at the table with the Twelve.	a. After 6 P.M. it was Friday by Jewish time, the 14th day of the month Nissan.	Jesus and his apostles reclined at the table.	a. 1 Or *he loved them to the last*

Matt.	Mark		
		[3]Jesus knew that the Father had put all things under his power, and that he had come from God and was returning to God;	
	[15]And he said to them, "I have eagerly desired to eat this Passover with you before I suffer. [16]For I tell you, I will not eat it again until it finds fulfillment in the kingdom of God."		
		[2]The evening meal was being served, and the devil had already prompted Judas Iscariot, son of Simon, to betray Jesus.	
	[24]Also a dispute arose among them as to which of them was considered to be greatest.		

Luke	[4]so he got up from the meal, took off his outer clothing, and wrapped a towel around his waist. [5]After that, he poured water into a basin and began to wash his disciples' feet, drying them with the towel that was wrapped around him.

Matt.	Mark	Luke

John 13

[6]He came to Simon Peter, who said to him, "Lord, are you going to wash my feet?"
[7]Jesus replied, "You do not realize now what I am doing, but later you will understand."
[8]"No," said Peter, "you shall never wash my feet."

Jesus answered, "Unless I wash you, you have no part with me."

[9]"Then, Lord," Simon Peter replied, "not just my feet but my hands and my head as well!"

[10]Jesus answered, "A person who has had a bath needs only to wash his feet; his whole body is clean. And you are clean, though not every one of you." [11]For he knew who was going to betray him, and that was why he said not every one was clean.

[12]When he had finished washing their feet, he put on his clothes and returned to his place. "Do you understand what I have done for you?" he asked them. [13]"You call me 'Teacher' and 'Lord,' and rightly so, for that is what I am. [14]Now that I, your Lord and Teacher, have washed your feet, you also should wash one another's feet. [15]I have set you an example that you should do as I have done for you. [16]I tell you the truth, no servant is greater than his master, nor is a messenger greater than the one who sent him.

[25]Jesus said to them,

"The kings of the Gentiles lord it over them; and those who exercise authority over them call themselves Benefactors. [26]But you are not to be like that. Instead, the greatest among you should be like the youngest, and the one who rules like the one who serves. | John |

Luke

[17]Now that you know these things, you will be blessed if you do them.

[27]For who is greater, the one who is at the table or the one who serves? Is it not the one who is at the table? But I am among you as one who serves. [28]You are those who have stood by me in my trials. [29]And I confer on you a kingdom, just as my Father conferred one on me, [30]so that you may eat and drink at my table in my kingdom and sit on thrones, judging the twelve tribes of Israel. | John |

Luke

[18]"I am not referring to all of you; I know those I have chosen. But this is to fulfill the scripture: 'He who shares my bread has lifted up his heel against me.'[a]

[19]"I am telling you now before it happens, so that when it does happen you will believe that I am He. [20]I tell you the truth, whoever accepts anyone I send accepts me; and whoever accepts me accepts the one who sent me."

a. *18* Ps. 41:9

152. Jesus' Final Appeal to Judas

Jerusalem; Thursday evening, April 6

Matt. 26:21–25	Mark 14:18–21	Luke	John 13:21–30
[21]And while they were eating,	[18]While they were reclining at the table eating,		[21]After he had said this,
he said, "I tell you the truth, one of you will betray me."	he said, "I tell you the truth, one of you will betray		Jesus was troubled in spirit and testified, "I tell you the truth, one of you is going to betray

Matt. 26	Mark 14	Luke 22:21–23	John 13
	me—one who is eating with me.”		me.”
24The Son of Man will go just as it is written about him. But woe to that man who betrays the Son of Man! It would be better for him if he had not been born.”	21The Son of Man will go just as it is written about him. But woe to that man who betrays the Son of Man! It would be better for him if he had not been born.”	22The Son of Man will go as it has been decreed, but woe to that man who betrays him.”	
		21But the hand of him who is going to betray me is with mine on the table.	
			22His disciples stared at one another, at a loss to know which of them he meant.
22They were very sad and	19They were saddened,	23They	
		began to question among themselves which of them it might be who would do this.	
began to say to him one after the other, “Surely not I, Lord?”	and one by one they said to him, “Surely not I?”		
23Jesus replied, “The one who has dipped his hand into the bowl with me will betray me.	20“It is one of the Twelve,” he replied, “one who dips bread into the bowl with me.		

Matt.	Mark	Luke

23One of them, the disciple whom Jesus loved, was reclining next to him. 24Simon Peter motioned to this disciple and said, “Ask him which one he means.”

25Leaning back against Jesus, he asked him, “Lord, who is it?”

26Jesus answered, “It is the one to whom I will give this piece of bread when I have dipped it in the dish.” Then, dipping the piece of bread, he gave it to Judas Iscariot, son of Simon.

25Then Judas, the one who would betray him, said, “Surely not I, Rabbi?” Jesus answered, “Yes, it is you.”a

Mark	Luke	John

a. 25 Or “You yourself have said it”

Matt.	Mark	Luke

27As soon as Judas took the bread, Satan entered into him.

“What you are about to do, do quickly,” Jesus told him, 28but no one at the meal understood why Jesus said this to him. 29Since Judas had charge of the money, some thought Jesus was telling him to buy what was needed for the Feast, or to give something to the poor. 30As soon as Judas had taken the bread, he went out. And it was night.

153. Institution of the Ordinance of the Lord's Supper

Jerusalem; Thursday night, April 6

Matt.	Mark	Luke	John 13:31–32

John 13:31–32

31When he was gone, Jesus said, "Now is the Son of Man glorified and God is glorified in him. 32If God is glorified in him,a God will glorify the Son in himself, and will glorify him at once.

a. *32* Many early manuscripts do not have *If God is glorified in him.*

Matt. 26:26–29	Mark 14:22–25	Luke 22:17–20	John
26While they were eating, Jesus took bread, gave thanks and broke it, and gave it to his disciples, saying, "Take and eat; this is my body."	22While they were eating, Jesus took bread, gave thanks and broke it, and gave it to his disciples, saying, "Take it; this is my body."	19And he took bread, gave thanks and broke it, and gave it to them, saying, "This is my body given for you; do this in remembrance of me." 20In the same way, after the supper he took the cup,	
27Then he took the cup, gave thanks and offered it to them, saying, "Drink from it, all of you.	23Then he took the cup, gave thanks and offered it to them, and they all drank from it.	17After taking the cup, he gave thanks and said, "Take this and divide it among you.	
28This is my blood of thea covenant, which is poured out for many for the forgiveness of sins. 29I tell you,	24"This is my blood of thea covenant, which is poured out for many," he said to them. 25"I tell you the truth,	20bsaying, "This cup is the new covenant in my blood, which is poured out for you.	
I will not drink of this fruit of the vine from now on until that day when I drink it anew with you in my Father's kingdom."	I will not drink again of the fruit of the vine until that day when I drink it anew in the kingdom of God."	18For I tell you I will not drink again of the fruit of the vine until the kingdom of God comes."	
a. *28* Some manuscripts *the new*	a. *24* Some manuscripts *the new*		

154. Jesus' Farewell Discourse in the Upper Room

Jerusalem; Thursday night, April 6

Matt. 26:31–35	Mark	Luke	John 13:33–14:31

Matt. 26:31–35

31Then Jesus told them,

Matt.	Mark	Luke	

33"My children, I will be with you only a little longer. You will look for me, and just as I told the Jews, so I tell you now: Where I am going, you cannot come.

Matt.	Mark	Luke

John 13

34"A new command I give you: Love one another. As I have loved you, so you must love one another. 35By this all men will know that you are my disciples, if you love one another."

36Simon Peter asked him, "Lord, where are you going?"

Jesus replied, "Where I am going, you cannot follow now, but you will follow later."

37Peter asked, "Lord, why can't I follow you now? I will lay down my life for you."

38Then Jesus answered, "Will you really lay down your life for me?

Mark 14:27–31

Luke	John

"This very night you will all fall away on account of me, for it is written:

"'I will strike the shepherd,
  and the sheep of the flock will be scattered.'a

32But after I have risen, I will go ahead of you into Galilee."

33Peter replied,

"Even if all fall away on account of you, I never will."

27"You will all fall away," Jesus told them, "for it is written:

"'I will strike the shepherd,
  and the sheep will be scattered.'a

28But after I have risen, I will go ahead of you into Galilee."

29Peter declared,

"Even if all fall away, I will not."

30"I tell you the truth," Jesus answered,

a. *31* Zech. 13:7

a. *27* Zech. 13:7

Matt.	Mark

Luke 22:31–38

31"Simon, Simon, Satan has asked to sift youa as wheat. 32But I have prayed for you, Simon, that your faith may not fail. And when you have turned back, strengthen your brothers."

33But he replied, "Lord, I am ready to go with you to prison and to death."

a. *31* The Greek is plural.

34"I tell you the truth," Jesus answered, "this very night, before the rooster crows, you will disown me three times."

35But Peter declared, "Even if I have to die with you, I will never disown you." And all the other disciples said the same.

"today—yes, tonight—before the rooster crows twiceb you yourself will disown me three times."

31But Peter insisted emphatically, "Even if I have to die with you, I will never disown you." And all the others said the same.

34Jesus answered, "I tell you, Peter, before the rooster crows today, you will

deny three times that you know me."

I tell you the truth, before the rooster crows, you will disown me three times!

b. *30* Some early manuscripts do not have *twice.*

Matt.	Mark	Luke 22	John

³⁵Then Jesus asked them, "When I sent you without purse, bag or sandals, did you lack anything?"

"Nothing," they answered.

³⁶He said to them, "But now if you have a purse, take it, and also a bag; and if you don't have a sword, sell your cloak and buy one. ³⁷It is written: 'And he was numbered with the transgressors'ᵃ; and I tell you that this must be fulfilled in me. Yes, what is written about me is reaching its fulfillment."

³⁸The disciples said, "See, Lord, here are two swords."

"That is enough," he replied.

---

a. *37* Isa. 53:12

Luke

¹"Do not let your hearts be troubled. Trust in Godᵃ; trust also in me. ²In my Father's house are many rooms; if it were not so, I would have told you. I am going there to prepare a place for you. ³And if I go and prepare a place for you, I will come back and take you to be with me that you also may be where I am. ⁴You know the way to the place where I am going."

⁵Thomas said to him, "Lord, we don't know where you are going, so how can we know the way?"

⁶Jesus answered, "I am the way and the truth and the life. No one comes to the Father except through me. ⁷If you really knew me, you would knowᵇ my Father as well. From now on, you do know him and have seen him."

⁸Philip said, "Lord, show us the Father and that will be enough for us."

⁹Jesus answered: "Don't you know me, Philip, even after I have been among you such a long time? Anyone who has seen me has seen the Father. How can you say, 'Show us the Father'? ¹⁰Don't you believe that I am in the Father, and that the Father is in me? The words I say to you are not just my own. Rather, it is the Father, living in me, who is doing his work. ¹¹Believe me when I say that I am in the Father and the Father is in me; or at least believe on the evidence of the miracles themselves. ¹²I tell you the truth, anyone who has faith in me will do what I have been doing. He will do even greater things than these, because I am going to the Father. ¹³And I will do whatever you ask in my name, so that the Son may bring glory to the Father. ¹⁴You may ask me for anything in my name, and I will do it.

¹⁵"If you love me, you will obey what I command. ¹⁶And I will ask the Father, and he will give you another Counselor to be with you forever—¹⁷the Spirit of truth. The world cannot accept him, because it neither sees him nor knows him. But you know him, for he lives with you and will beᶜ in you. ¹⁸I will not leave you as orphans; I will come to you. ¹⁹Before long, the world will not see me anymore, but you will see me. Because I live, you also will live. ²⁰On that day you will realize that I am in my Father, and you are in me, and I am in you. ²¹Whoever has my commands and obeys them, he is the one who loves me. He who loves me will be loved by my Father, and I too will love him and show myself to him."

²²Then Judas (not Judas Iscariot) said, "But, Lord, why do you intend to show yourself to us and not to the world?"

²³Jesus replied, "If anyone loves me, he will obey my teaching. My Father will love him, and we will come to him and make our home with him. ²⁴He who does not love me will

---

a. *1* Or *You trust in God*
b. *7* Some early manuscripts *If you really have known me, you will know*
c. *17* Some early manuscripts *and is*

Matt.	Mark	Luke	John 14

not obey my teaching. These words you hear are not my own; they belong to the Father who sent me.

25"All this I have spoken while still with you. 26But the Counselor, the Holy Spirit, whom the Father will send in my name, will teach you all things and will remind you of everything I have said to you. 27Peace I leave with you; my peace I give you. I do not give to you as the world gives. Do not let your hearts be troubled and do not be afraid.

28"You heard me say, 'I am going away and I am coming back to you.' If you loved me, you would be glad that I am going to the Father, for the Father is greater than I. 29I have told you now before it happens, so that when it does happen you will believe. 30I will not speak with you much longer, for the prince of this world is coming. He has no hold on me, 31but the world must learn that I love the Father and that I do exactly what my Father has commanded me.

"Come now; let us leave.

155. Jesus' Farewell Discourse on the Way to the Garden of Gethsemane

Jerusalem; Thursday night, April 6

Matt. 26:30	Mark 14:26	Luke 22:39	John 15–16
30When they had sung a hymn, they went out to the Mount of Olives.	26When they had sung a hymn, they went out to the Mount of Olives.	39Jesus went out as usual to the Mount of Olives, and his disciples followed him.	

Matt.	Mark	Luke	

1[*On the way he said to them,*a] "I am the true vine, and my Father is the gardener. 2He cuts off every branch in me that bears no fruit, while every branch that does bear fruit he prunesb so that it will be even more fruitful. 3You are already clean because of the word I have spoken to you. 4Remain in me, and I will remain in you. No branch can bear fruit by itself; it must remain in the vine. Neither can you bear fruit unless you remain in me.

5"I am the vine; you are the branches. If a man remains in me and I in him, he will bear much fruit; apart from me you can do nothing. 6If anyone does not remain in me, he is like a branch that is thrown away and withers; such branches are picked up, thrown into the fire and burned. 7If you remain in me and my words remain in you, ask whatever you wish, and it will be given you. 8This is to my Father's glory, that you bear much fruit, showing yourselves to be my disciples.

9"As the Father has loved me, so have I loved you. Now remain in my love. 10If you obey my commands, you will remain in my love, just as I have obeyed my Father's commands and remain in his love. 11I have told you this so that my joy may be in you and that your joy may be complete. 12My command is this: Love each other as I have loved you. 13Greater love has no one than this, that he lay down his life for his friends. 14You are my friends if you do what I command. 15I no longer call you servants, because a servant does not know

a. These italicized words are not in the scriptural record; they are inserted in this Harmony to provide grammatical continuity in the composite narrative.

b. 2 The Greek for *prunes* also means *cleans*.

Matt.	Mark	Luke

John 15–16

his master's business. Instead, I have called you friends, for everything that I learned from my Father I have made known to you. [16]You did not choose me, but I chose you and appointed you to go and bear fruit—fruit that will last. Then the Father will give you whatever you ask in my name. [17]This is my command: Love each other.

[18]"If the world hates you, keep in mind that it hated me first. [19]If you belonged to the world, it would love you as its own. As it is, you do not belong to the world, but I have chosen you out of the world. That is why the world hates you. [20]Remember the words I spoke to you: 'No servant is greater than his master.'[a] If they persecuted me, they will persecute you also. If they obeyed my teaching, they will obey yours also. [21]They will treat you this way because of my name, for they do not know the One who sent me. [22]If I had not come and spoken to them, they would not be guilty of sin. Now, however, they have no excuse for their sin. [23]He who hates me hates my Father as well. [24]If I had not done among them what no one else did, they would not be guilty of sin. But now they have seen these miracles, and yet they have hated both me and my Father. [25]But this is to fulfill what is written in their Law: 'They hated me without reason.'[b]

[26]"When the Counselor comes, whom I will send to you from the Father, the Spirit of truth who goes out from the Father, he will testify about me. [27]And you also must testify, for you have been with me from the beginning.

[1]"All this I have told you so that you will not go astray. [2]They will put you out of the synagogue; in fact, a time is coming when anyone who kills you will think he is offering a service to God. [3]They will do such things because they have not known the Father or me. [4]I have told you this, so that when the time comes you will remember that I warned you. I did not tell you this at first because I was with you.

[5]"Now I am going to him who sent me, yet none of you asks me, 'Where are you going?' [6]Because I have said these things, you are filled with grief. [7]But I tell you the truth: It is for your good that I am going away. Unless I go away, the Counselor will not come to you; but if I go, I will send him to you. [8]When he comes, he will convict the world of guilt[c] in regard to sin and righteousness and judgment: [9]in regard to sin, because men do not believe in me; [10]in regard to righteousness, because I am going to the Father, where you can see me no longer; [11]and in regard to judgment, because the prince of this world now stands condemned.

[12]"I have much more to say to you, more than you can now bear. [13]But when he, the Spirit of truth, comes, he will guide you into all truth. He will not speak on his own; he will speak only what he hears, and he will tell you what is yet to come. [14]He will bring glory to me by taking from what is mine and making it known to you. [15]All that belongs to the Father is mine. That is why I said the Spirit will take from what is mine and make it known to you.

[16]"In a little while you will see me no more, and then after a little while you will see me."

[17]Some of his disciples said to one another, "What does he mean by saying, 'In a little while you will see me no more, and then after a little while you will see me,' and 'Because I am going to the Father'?" [18]They kept asking, "What does he mean by 'a little while'? We don't understand what he is saying."

[19]Jesus saw that they wanted to ask him about this, so he said to them, "Are you asking one another what I meant when I said, 'In a little while you will see me no more, and then after a little while you will see me'? [20]I tell you the truth, you will weep and mourn while

a. *20* John 13:16
b. *25* Pss. 35:19; 69:4
c. *8* Or *will expose the guilt of the world*

Matt.	Mark	Luke	John 16

the world rejoices. You will grieve, but your grief will turn to joy. [21]A woman giving birth to a child has pain because her time has come; but when her baby is born she forgets the anguish because of her joy that a child is born into the world. [22]So with you: Now is your time of grief, but I will see you again and you will rejoice, and no one will take away your joy. [23]In that day you will no longer ask me anything. I tell you the truth, my Father will give you whatever you ask in my name. [24]Until now you have not asked for anything in my name. Ask and you will receive, and your joy will be complete.

[25]"Though I have been speaking figuratively, a time is coming when I will no longer use this kind of language but will tell you plainly about my Father. [26]In that day you will ask in my name. I am not saying that I will ask the Father on your behalf. [27]No, the Father himself loves you because you have loved me and have believed that I came from God. [28]I came from the Father and entered the world; now I am leaving the world and going back to the Father."

[29]Then Jesus' disciples said, "Now you are speaking clearly and without figures of speech. [30]Now we can see that you know all things and that you do not even need to have anyone ask you questions. This makes us believe that you came from God."

[31]"You believe at last!"[a] Jesus answered. [32]"But a time is coming, and has come, when you will be scattered, each to his own home. You will leave me all alone. Yet I am not alone, for my Father is with me.

[33]"I have told you these things, so that in me you may have peace. In this world you will have trouble. But take heart! I have overcome the world."

a. *31* Or *"Do you now believe?"*

156. Christ's Intercessory Prayer

Perhaps in the temple court, Jerusalem, on the way to the Garden of Gethsemane; Thursday, April 6, toward midnight

Matt.	Mark	Luke	John 17

[1]After Jesus said this, he looked toward heaven and prayed:

"Father, the time has come. Glorify your Son, that your Son may glorify you. [2]For you granted him authority over all people that he might give eternal life to all those you have given him. [3]Now this is eternal life: that they may know you, the only true God, and Jesus Christ, whom you have sent. [4]I have brought you glory on earth by completing the work you gave me to do. [5]And now, Father, glorify me in your presence with the glory I had with you before the world began.

[6]"I have revealed you[b] to those whom you gave me out of the world. They were yours; you gave them to me and they have obeyed your word. [7]Now they know that everything you have given me comes from you. [8]For I gave them the words you gave me and they accepted them. They knew with certainty that I came from you, and they believed that you sent me. [9]I pray for them. I am not praying for the world, but for those you have given me, for they are yours. [10]All I have is yours, and all you have is mine. And glory has come to me through them. [11]I will remain in the world no longer, but they are still in the world,

b. *6* Greek *your name;* also in verse 26

Matt.	Mark	Luke

John 17

and I am coming to you. Holy Father, protect them by the power of your name—the name you gave me—so that they may be one as we are one. [12]While I was with them, I protected them and kept them safe by that name you gave me. None has been lost except the one doomed to destruction so that Scripture would be fulfilled.

[13]"I am coming to you now, but I say these things while I am still in the world, so that they may have the full measure of my joy within them. [14]I have given them your word and the world has hated them, for they are not of the world any more than I am of the world. [15]My prayer is not that you take them out of the world but that you protect them from the evil one. [16]They are not of the world, even as I am not of it. [17]Sanctify[a] them by the truth; your word is truth. [18]As you sent me into the world, I have sent them into the world. [19]For them I sanctify myself, that they too may be truly sanctified.

[20]"My prayer is not for them alone. I pray also for those who will believe in me through their message, [21]that all of them may be one, Father, just as you are in me and I am in you. May they also be in us so that the world may believe that you have sent me. [22]I have given them the glory that you gave me, that they may be one as we are one: [23]I in them and you in me. May they be brought to complete unity to let the world know that you sent me and have loved them even as you have loved me.

[24]"Father, I want those you have given me to be with me where I am, and to see my glory, the glory you have given me because you loved me before the creation of the world.

[25]"Righteous Father, though the world does not know you, I know you, and they know that you have sent me. [26]I have made you known to them, and will continue to make you known in order that the love you have for me may be in them and that I myself may be in them."

---

a. *17* Greek *hagiazo (set apart for sacred use* or *make holy);* also in verse 19

157. Christ's Agony in the Garden of Gethsemane

Thursday, April 6, about midnight

Matt. 26:36–46	Mark 14:32–42	Luke 22:40–46	John 18:1
			[1]When he had finished praying, Jesus left with his disciples and crossed the Kidron Valley. On the other side there was an olive grove,
[36]Then Jesus went with his disciples to a place called Gethsemane, and he said to them, "Sit here while	[32]They went to a place called Gethsemane, and Jesus said to his disciples, "Sit here while	[40]On reaching the place, he said to them,	
I go over there and pray." [37]He took Peter and the two sons of Zebedee along with him, and he began to be	I pray." [33]He took Peter, James and John along with him, and he began to be deeply distressed and		and he and his disciples went into it.

Matt. 26	Mark 14	Luke 22	John
sorrowful and troubled. 38Then he said to them, "My soul is overwhelmed with sorrow to the point of death. Stay here and keep watch with me."	troubled. 34"My soul is overwhelmed with sorrow to the point of death," he said to them. "Stay here and keep watch."		
		"Pray that you will not fall into temptation." 41He withdrew about a stone's throw beyond them,	
39Going a little farther, he fell	35Going a little farther, he fell		
with his face to the ground and prayed, "My Father, if it is possible, may this cup be taken from me.	to the ground and prayed that if possible the hour might pass from him. 36"Abba,a Father," he said, "everything is possible for you. Take this cup from me. Yet not what I will, but what you will."	knelt down and prayed,	
Yet not as I will, but as you will."		42"Father, if you are willing, take this cup from me; yet not my will, but yours be done." 43An angel from heaven appeared to him and strengthened him. 44And being in anguish, he prayed more earnestly, and his sweat was like drops of blood falling to the ground.a	
40Then he returned to his disciples and found them sleeping.	37Then he returned to his disciples and found them sleeping. "Simon," he said to Peter, "are you asleep?	45When he rose from prayer and went back to the disciples, he found them asleep, exhausted from sorrow.	
"Could you men not keep watch with me for one hour?" he asked Peter. 41"Watch and pray so that you will not fall into temptation. The spirit is willing, but the body is weak."	Could you not keep watch for one hour? 38Watch and pray so that you will not fall into temptation. The spirit is willing, but the body is weak."	46"Why are you sleeping?" he asked them. "Get up and pray so that you will not fall into temptation."	

a. 36 Aramaic for *Father*

a. 44 Some early manuscripts do not have verses 43 and 44.

Matt. 26	Mark 14		Luke
42He went away a second time and prayed,	39Once more he went away and prayed the same thing.		
"My Father, if it is not possible for this cup to be taken away unless I drink it, may your will be done."			
43When he came back, he again found them sleeping, because their eyes were heavy.	40When he came back, he again found them sleeping, because their eyes were heavy. They did not know what to say to him.		

Matt. 26	Mark 14	Luke	John

Matt. 26

⁴⁴So he left them and went away once more and prayed the third time, saying the same thing.

⁴⁵Then he returned to the disciples

and
said to them, "Are you still sleeping and resting? Look, the hour is near, and the Son of Man is betrayed into the hands of sinners. ⁴⁶Rise, let us go! Here comes my betrayer!"

Mark 14

⁴¹Returning the third time,

he said to them, "Are you still sleeping and resting? Enough! The hour has come. Look, the Son of Man is betrayed into the hands of sinners. ⁴²Rise! Let us go! Here comes my betrayer!"

PART 12

Christ's Crowning Sacrifice

Friday and Saturday, April 7–8, A.D. 30

158. Jesus' Betrayal, Arrest, and Abandonment

The Garden of Gethsemane; Friday, April 7, just after Thursday midnight

Matt. 26:47–56	Mark 14:43–52	Luke 22:47–53	John 18:2–12a
			[2]Now Judas, who betrayed him, knew the
[47]While he was still speaking, Judas, one of the Twelve, arrived. With him was	[43]Just as he was speaking, Judas, one of the Twelve, appeared. With him was a crowd armed with swords and clubs,	[47]While he was still speaking a crowd came up, and the man who was called Judas, one of the Twelve, was leading	place, because Jesus had often met there with his disciples. [3]So Judas came to the grove,
a large crowd			guiding a detachment of soldiers and some officials
armed with swords and clubs, sent from the chief priests and the elders of the people.	sent from the chief priests, the teachers of the law, and the elders.	them.	from the chief priests and Pharisees. They were carrying torches, lanterns and weapons.
[48]Now the betrayer had arranged a signal with them: "The one I kiss is the man; arrest him." [49]Going at once to Jesus, Judas said,	[44]Now the betrayer had arranged a signal with them: "The one I kiss is the man; arrest him and lead him away under guard." [45]Going at once to Jesus, Judas said,	He approached Jesus to kiss him, [48]but	
"Greetings, Rabbi!" and kissed him.	"Rabbi!" and kissed him.		
			[4]Jesus, knowing all that was going to happen to him, went out and asked

Matt.	Mark	Luke

them, "Who is it you want?"

5"Jesus of Nazareth," they replied.

"I am he," Jesus said. 6When Jesus said, "I am he," they drew back and fell to the ground.

7Again he asked them, "Who is it you want?"

And they said, "Jesus of Nazareth."

8"I told you that I am he," Jesus answered. "If you are looking for me, then let these men go." 9This happened so that the words he had spoken would be fulfilled: "I have not lost one of those you gave me."a 5b(And Judas the traitor was standing there with them.)

Matt./Mark/Luke	Mark	Luke	John
50Jesus replied, "Friend, do what you came for."a Then the men stepped forward, seized Jesus and arrested him.	46The men seized Jesus and arrested him.	Jesus asked him, "Judas, are you betraying the Son of Man with a kiss?" 49When Jesus' followers saw what was going to happen, they said, "Lord, should we strike with our swords?" 50And	10Then
51With that, one of Jesus' companions reached for his sword, drew it out and struck the servant of the high priest, cutting off his ear.	47Then one of those standing near drew his sword and struck the servant of the high priest, cutting off his ear.	one of them struck the servant of the high priest, cutting off his right ear. 51But Jesus answered, "No more of this!" And he touched the man's ear and healed him.	Simon Peter, who had a sword, drew it and struck the high priest's servant, cutting off his right ear. (The servant's name was Malchus.) 11Jesus commanded Peter,

a. 50 Or "Friend, why have you come?"

a. 9 John 6:39

52"Put your sword back in its place," Jesus said to him, "for all who draw the sword will die by the sword. 53Do you think I cannot call on my Father, and he will at once put at my disposal more than twelve legions of angels? 54But how then would the Scriptures be fulfilled that say it must happen in this way?"

Mark	Luke

"Put your sword away!

Shall I not drink the cup the Father has given me?"

55At that time Jesus said to the crowd, "Am I leading a rebellion, that you have

48"Am I leading a rebel-

52Then Jesus said to the chief priests, the officers of the temple guard, and the elders, who had come for him, "Am I leading a

Matt. 26	Mark 14	Luke 22	John 18
come out with swords and clubs to capture me? Every day I sat in the temple courts teaching, and you did not arrest me.	lion," said Jesus, "that you have come out with swords and clubs to capture me? [49]Every day I was with you, teaching in the temple courts, and you did not arrest me.	rebellion, that you have come with swords and clubs? [53]Every day I was with you in the temple courts, and you did not lay a hand on me. But this is your hour—when darkness reigns."	
[56]This[a] has all taken place that the writings of the prophets might be fulfilled."	But the Scriptures must be fulfilled."		
			[12a]Then the detachment of soldiers with its commander and the Jewish officials arrested Jesus.
Then all the disciples deserted him and fled.	[50]Then everyone deserted him and fled. [51]A young man, wearing nothing but a linen garment, was following Jesus. When they seized him, [52]he fled naked, leaving his garment behind.		

a. The NIV reads "But this." To avoid an awkward connection in the composite narrative, the conjunction has been omitted.

159. Jesus' Examination by Annas

Jerusalem; Friday, April 7, probably before 1 A.M.

Matt.	Mark	Luke 22:54a	John
		[54a]Then seizing him, they led him away and took him into the house of the high priest.	

John 18:12b–14, 19–23

	Luke	

[12b]They bound him [13]and brought him first to Annas, who was the father-in-law of Caiaphas, the high priest that year. [14]Caiaphas was the one who had advised the Jews that it would be good if one man died for the people.

[19]Meanwhile, the high priest[a] questioned Jesus about his disciples and his teaching.

[20]"I have spoken openly to the world," Jesus replied. "I always taught in synagogues or at the temple, where all the Jews come together. I said nothing in secret. [21]Why question me? Ask those who heard me. Surely they know what I said."

[22]When Jesus said this, one of the officials nearby struck him in the face. "Is this the way you answer the high priest?" he demanded.

[23]"If I said something wrong," Jesus replied, "testify as to what is wrong. But if I spoke the truth, why did you strike me?"

a. This is a respectful reference to the former high priest, Annas, to whom Jesus was sent first, probably while Caiaphas was hastily summoning the members of the Sanhedrin.

160. Peter and Another Disciple in the Courtyard of the High Priest's Residence

Jerusalem; Friday, April 7, probably about 1 A.M.

Matt. 26:58	Mark 14:54	Luke 22:54b–55	John 18:15–18
			[15]Simon Peter and another disciple were following Jesus.
[58]But Peter followed him at a distance,	[54]Peter followed him at a distance,	[54b]Peter followed at a distance.	

	Mark	Luke	

right up to the courtyard of the high priest.		Because this disciple was known to the high priest, he went with Jesus into the high priest's courtyard, [16]but Peter had to wait outside at the door. The other disciple, who was known to the high priest, came back, spoke to the girl on duty there and brought Peter in.
		    [17]"You are not one of his disciples, are you?" the girl at the door asked Peter.
		    He replied, "I am not."	

Matt. 26:58	Mark 14:54	Luke 22:54b–55	John 18:15–18
		[55]But when they	[18]It was cold, and the servants and officials
He entered and sat down with the guards	right into the courtyard of the high priest. There he sat with	had kindled a fire in the middle of the courtyard and had sat down together, Peter sat down with	stood around a fire they had made to keep warm. Peter also
	the guards	them.	was standing with them,
to see the outcome.	and warmed himself at the fire.		warming himself.

161. Jesus' Informal Trial

The high priest's council chamber, Jerusalem; Friday, April 7, about 2–3 A.M.[a]

Matt. 26:57, 59–68	Mark 14:53, 55–65	Luke	John 18:24
[57]Those who had arrested Jesus took him to Caiaphas, the high priest, where the	[53]They took Jesus to the high priest, and all the chief priests,		[24]Then Annas sent him, still bound, to Caiaphas the high priest.[b] ――――――――― b. 24 Or *(Now Annas had sent him, still bound, to Caiaphas the high priest.)*

―――――――――

a. The mock trials and subsequent activities of the Sanhedrin were undertaken with utmost haste in the very early morning darkness and the hours of daylight on Friday, so that the execution of Jesus could be accomplished before the Sabbath began at 6 P.M. that day.

Matt. 26	Mark 14	Luke	John

Matt. 26

teachers of the law and the elders had assembled.

⁵⁹The chief priests and the whole Sanhedrin were looking for false evidence against Jesus so that they could put him to death. ⁶⁰But they did not find any, though many false witnesses came forward.

Finally two came forward ⁶¹and

declared, "This fellow said, 'I am able to destroy

the temple of God and

rebuild it in three days.'"

⁶²Then the high priest stood up and said to Jesus, "Are you not going to answer? What is this testimony that these men are bringing against you?" ⁶³But Jesus remained silent.

The high priest said to him,

"I charge you under oath by the living God: Tell us if you are the Christ,ᵃ the Son of God."

⁶⁴"Yes, it is as you say," Jesus replied. "But I say to all of you: In the future you will see the Son of Man sitting at the right hand of the Mighty One and coming on the clouds of heaven."

⁶⁵Then the high priest tore his clothes and said, "He has spoken blasphemy! Why do we need any more witnesses? Look, now you have heard the blasphemy. ⁶⁶What do you think?"

"He is worthy of death," they answered.

a. *63* Or *Messiah;* also in verse 68

Mark 14

elders and teachers of the law came together.

⁵⁵The chief priests and the whole Sanhedrin were looking for evidence against Jesus so that they could put him to death, but they did not find any. ⁵⁶Many testified falsely against him, but their statements did not agree.

⁵⁷Then some stood up and gave this false testimony against him: ⁵⁸"We heard him say, 'I will destroy this man-made temple and in three days will build another, not made by man.'" ⁵⁹Yet even then their testimony did not agree.

⁶⁰Then the high priest stood up before them and asked Jesus, "Are you not going to answer? What is this testimony that these men are bringing against you?" ⁶¹But Jesus remained silent and gave no answer.

Again the high priest asked him, "Are you the Christ,ᵃ the Son of the Blessed One?"

⁶²"I am," said Jesus. "And you will see the Son of Man sitting at the right hand of the Mighty One and coming on the clouds of heaven."

⁶³The high priest tore his clothes. "Why do we need any more witnesses?" he asked. ⁶⁴"You have heard the blasphemy.

What do you think?"

They all condemned him as worthy of death.

a. *61* Or *Messiah*

Matt. 26

⁶⁷Then they spit in his face

and struck him with their fists. Others slapped him ⁶⁸and said, "Prophesy to us, Christ. Who hit you?"

Mark 14

⁶⁵ᵇAnd the guards took him and beat him.

⁶⁵Then some began to spit at him; they blindfolded him, struck him with their fists, and said, "Prophesy!"

Luke 22:63–65

⁶³The men who were guarding Jesus began mocking and beating him.

⁶⁴They blindfolded him and demanded, "Prophesy! Who hit you?"

Matt.	Mark	Luke 22	John
		65And they said many other insulting things to him.	

162. Peter's Denial of Christ

Courtyard of the high priest's residence, Jerusalem;
Friday, April 7, about 3–4:30 A.M.

A. The First Denial

Matt. 26:69–71a	Mark 14:66–68	Luke 22:56–57	John
69Now Peter was sitting out in the courtyard, and a servant girl came to him.	66While Peter was below in the courtyard, one of the servant girls of the high priest came by. 67When she saw Peter warming himself, she looked closely at him.	56A servant girl saw him seated there in the firelight. She looked closely at him and said, "This man was with him."	
"You also were with Jesus of Galilee," she said. 70But he denied it before them all.	"You also were with that Nazarene, Jesus," she said. 68But he denied it.	 57But he denied it. "Woman, I don't know him,"	
"I don't know what you're talking about," he said. 71aThen he went out to the gateway,	"I don't know or understand what you're talking about," he said, and went out into the entryway.a	he said.	

a. *68* Some early manuscripts *entryway and the rooster crowed*

B. The Second Denial

Matt. 26:71b–72	Mark 14:69–70a	Luke 22:58	John
71bwhere another girl saw him and said to the people there, "This fellow	69When the servant girl saw him there, she said again to those standing around, "This fel-	58A little later someone else saw him and said, "You also are one of them."	

Matt. 26	Mark 14	Luke 22	John 18:25
was with Jesus of Nazareth."[a]	low is one of them."		[25]As Simon Peter stood warming himself, he was asked, "You are not one of his disciples, are you?"
[72]He denied it again, with an oath: "I don't know the man!"	[70a]Again he denied it.	"Man, I am not!" Peter replied.	He denied it, saying, "I am not."

a. It is to be noted that Matthew attributes this statement, not to the maid who first recognized Peter (Mark 14:66–69), but to another (cf. Luke 22:58). Such apparent discrepancies are only to be expected when one reflects that the remark of the first maid would naturally result in Peter being recognized and challenged by others also. This, indeed, is clearly indicated by all the Gospel narratives comprising this section.

C. The Third Denial

Matt. 26:73–75	Mark 14:70b–72	Luke 22:59–62	John 18:26–27
[73]After a little while, those standing there went up to Peter and said, "Surely you are one of them, for your accent gives you away."	[70b]After a little while, those **standing near** said to Peter, "Surely you are one of them, for you are a Galilean."	[59]About an hour later another asserted, "Certainly this fellow was with him, for he is a Galilean."	
		[60]Peter replied, "Man, I don't know what you're talking about!"	
			[26]One of the high priest's servants, a relative of the man whose ear Peter had cut off, challenged him, "Didn't I see you with him in the olive grove?"
[74]Then he began to call down curses on himself	[71]He began to call down curses on himself, and he		

Matt. 26	Mark 14	Luke 22	John 18
and he swore to them, "I don't know the man!"	swore to them, "I don't know this man you're talking about."		27Again Peter denied it, and
Immediately a rooster crowed.	72Immediately the rooster crowed the second time.a	Just as he was speaking, the rooster crowed.	at that moment a rooster began to crow.
		61The Lord turned and looked straight at Peter.	
75Then Peter remembered the word Jesus had spoken: "Before the rooster crows, you will disown me three times." And he went outside and wept bitterly.	Then Peter remembered the word Jesus had spoken to him: "Before the rooster crows twiceb you will disown me three times." And he broke down and wept.	Then Peter remembered the word the Lord had spoken to him: "Before the rooster crows today, you will disown me three times." 62And he went outside and wept bitterly.a	

a. Incidents recorded in secs. 162–163 took place about the same time. Peter's third denial occurred while the Sanhedrin was concluding the final Jewish trial of Jesus (sec. 163). Following the Sanhedrin's formal condemnation of Jesus, he was being led from the council chamber out across the courtyard just after Peter had vehemently disowned him. Passing by at that moment, to appear before Pilate, the Roman governor, Jesus "turned and looked straight at Peter" (Luke 22:61, sec. 162).

a. 72Some early manuscripts do not have *the second time.*
b. 72 Some early manuscripts do not have *twice.*

163. Christ's Formal Condemnation

Jerusalem; Friday, April 7, before 5 A.M.

Matt. 27:1–2	Mark 15:1	Luke 22:66–23:1	John
1Early in the morning, all the chief priests and the elders of the people came to	1Very early in the morning, the chief priests, with the elders, the teachers of the law and the whole Sanhedrin, reached	66At daybreak the council of the elders of the people, both the chief priests and teachers of the law, met together,	
the decision to put Jesus to death. 2They bound him,	a decision. They bound Jesus,		

Matt.	Mark	and Jesus was led before them. 67"If you are the Christ,b" they said, "tell us."

b. 67Or *Messiah*

Matt.	Mark	Luke 22	John

Jesus answered, "If I tell you, you will not believe me, [68]and if I asked you, you would not answer. [69]But from now on, the Son of Man will be seated at the right hand of the mighty God."

[70]They all asked, "Are you then the Son of God?"

He replied, "You are right in saying I am."

[71]Then they said, "Why do we need any more testimony? We have heard it from his own lips."

			John 18:28a
led him away and handed him over to Pilate, the governor.	led him away and handed him over to Pilate.	[1]Then the whole assembly rose and led him off to Pilate.	[28a]Then the Jews led Jesus from Caiaphas to the palace of the Roman governor.

164. Judas's Suicide

Jerusalem; Friday morning, April 7

Matt. 27:3–10

Mark	Luke	John

[3]When Judas, who had betrayed him, saw that Jesus was condemned, he was seized with remorse and returned the thirty silver coins to the chief priests and the elders. [4]"I have sinned," he said, "for I have betrayed innocent blood."

"What is that to us?" they replied. "That's your responsibility."

[5]So Judas threw the money into the temple and left. Then he went away and hanged himself.

[6]The chief priests picked up the coins and said, "It is against the law to put this into the treasury, since it is blood money." [7]So they decided to use the money to buy the potter's field as a burial place for foreigners. [8]That is why it has been called the Field of Blood to this day. [9]Then what was spoken by Jeremiah the prophet was fulfilled: "They took the thirty silver coins, the price set on him by the people of Israel, [10]and they used them to buy the potter's field, as the Lord commanded me."[a]

a. *10* See Jer. 19:1–13; 32:6–9; Zech. 11:12, 13.

165. Jesus' First Appearance before Pilate

Jerusalem; Friday, April 7, about 5 A.M.[b]

Matt. 27:11–14

Mark	Luke	John 18:28b–38

[11]Meanwhile Jesus stood before the governor, and

[28b]By now

b. Probably by sending an urgent message to Pilate that they had seized a dangerous insurrectionist, the Jewish leaders induced the Roman governor to appear at a very early morning hour.

Matt.	Mark	Luke

John 18

it was early morning, and to avoid ceremonial uncleanness the Jews did not enter the palace; they wanted to be able to eat the Passover. 29So Pilate came out to them and asked, "What charges are you bringing against this man?"

30"If he were not a criminal," they replied, "we would not have handed him over to you."

			John

Luke 23:2–7

the governor asked him, "Are you the king of the Jews?"

"Yes, it is as you say," Jesus replied.

12When he was accused by the chief priests and the elders, he gave no answer. 13Then Pilate asked him,

"Don't you hear the testimony they are bringing against you?" 14But Jesus made no reply, not even to a single charge—to the great amazement of the governor.

Mark 15:2–5

2"Are you the king of the Jews?" asked Pilate.

"Yes, it is as you say," Jesus replied.

3The chief priests accused him of many things. 4So again Pilate asked him,

"Aren't you going to answer? See how many things they are accusing you of."

5But Jesus still made no reply, and Pilate was amazed.

2And they began to accuse him, saying, "We have found this man subverting our nation. He opposes payment of taxes to Caesar and claims to be Christ,a a king." 3So Pilate asked Jesus, "Are you the king of the Jews?"

"Yes, it is as you say," Jesus replied.

a. 2 Or *Messiah;* also in verses 35 and 39

Matt.	Mark	Luke

31Pilate said, "Take him yourselves and judge him by your own law."

"But we have no right to execute anyone," the Jews objected. 32This happened so that the words Jesus had spoken indicating the kind of death he was going to die would be fulfilled.

33Pilate then went back inside the palace, summoned Jesus and asked him, "Are you the king of the Jews?"

34"Is that your own idea," Jesus asked, "or did others talk to you about me?"

35"Am I a Jew?" Pilate replied. "It was your people and your chief priests who handed you over to me. What is it you have done?"

36Jesus said, "My kingdom is not of this world. If it were, my servants would fight to prevent my arrest by the Jews. But now my kingdom is from another place."

37"You are a king, then!" said Pilate.

Jesus answered, "You are right in saying I am a king. In fact, for this reason I was born, and for this I came into the world, to testify to the truth. Everyone on the side of truth listens to me."

4Then Pilate

announced to the chief priests and the crowd, "I find no basis for a charge against this man."

38"What is truth?" Pilate asked. With this he went out again to the Jews

and said, "I find no basis for a charge against him.

Matt.	Mark	Luke 23	John

⁵But they insisted, "He stirs up the people all over Judea^a by his teaching. He started in Galilee and has come all the way here."

⁶On hearing this, Pilate asked if the man was a Galilean. ⁷When he learned that Jesus was under Herod's jurisdiction, he sent him to Herod, who was also in Jerusalem at that time.

a. 5 Or *over the land of the Jews*

166. Jesus' Appearance before Herod Antipas

Jerusalem; Friday, April 7, before 6 A.M.

Matt.	Mark	Luke 23:8–12	John

⁸When Herod saw Jesus, he was greatly pleased, because for a long time he had been wanting to see him. From what he had heard about him, he hoped to see him perform some miracle. ⁹He plied him with many questions, but Jesus gave him no answer. ¹⁰The chief priests and the teachers of the law were standing there, vehemently accusing him. ¹¹Then Herod and his soldiers ridiculed and mocked him. Dressing him in an elegant robe, they sent him back to Pilate. ¹²That day Herod and Pilate became friends—before this they had been enemies.

167. Jesus' Second Appearance before Pilate

Jerusalem; Friday, April 7, about 6 A.M.

Matt.	Mark	Luke 23:13–25	John

¹³Pilate called together the chief priests, the rulers and the people, ¹⁴and said to them, "You brought me this man as one who was inciting the people to rebellion. I have examined him in your presence and have found no basis for your charges against him. ¹⁵Neither has Herod, for he sent him back to us; as you can see, he has done nothing to deserve death. ¹⁶Therefore, I will punish him and then release him.^b"

b. 16 Some manuscripts *him." 17 Now he was obliged to release one man to them at the Feast.*

Matt. 27:15–31	Mark	Luke	John

¹⁹While Pilate was sitting on the judge's seat, his wife sent him this message: "Don't have anything to do with that innocent man, for I have suffered a great deal today in a dream because of him."

Mark 15:6–20	Luke	John 18:39–19:16a

¹⁵Now it was the governor's custom at the Feast to release a prisoner chosen by the crowd. ¹⁶At that time they had a notori-

⁶Now it was the custom at the Feast to release a prisoner whom the people requested. ⁷A man called Barabbas was in

³⁹But it is your custom for me to release to you one prisoner at the time of the Passover.

Matt. 27	Mark 15	Luke 23	John 18
ous prisoner, called Barabbas.	prison with the insurrectionists who had committed murder in the uprising.		
¹⁷So when the crowd had gathered, Pilate asked them,	⁸The crowd came up and asked Pilate to do for them what he usually did.	¹⁹(Barabbas had been thrown into prison for an insurrection in the city, and for murder.)	
"Which one do you want me to release to you: Barabbas, or Jesus who is called Christ?"			
¹⁸For he knew it was out of envy that they had handed Jesus over to him.	⁹"Do you want me to release to you the king of the Jews?" asked Pilate, ¹⁰knowing it was out of envy that the chief priests had handed Jesus over to him.		Do you want me to release 'the king of the Jews'?"
²⁰But the chief priests and the elders persuaded the crowd to ask for Barabbas and to have Jesus executed.	¹¹But the chief priests stirred up the crowd to have Pilate release Barabbas instead.		
²¹"Which of the two do you want me to release to you?" asked the governor.			
		¹⁸With one voice they cried out, "Away with this man! Release Barabbas to us!"	⁴⁰They shouted back, "No, not him! Give us Barabbas!" Now Barabbas had taken part in a rebellion.
"Barabbas," they answered.			
²²"What shall I do, then, with Jesus who is called Christ?" Pilate asked.	¹²"What shall I do, then, with the one you call the king of the Jews?" Pilate asked them.		
They all answered, "Crucify him!"	¹³"Crucify him!" they shouted.		
²³"Why? What crime has he committed?" asked Pilate.	¹⁴"Why? What crime has he committed?" asked Pilate.		
But they shouted all the louder, "Crucify him!"	But they shouted all the louder, "Crucify him!"		

Matt.	Mark		John

²⁰Wanting to release Jesus, Pilate appealed to them again. ²¹But they kept shouting, "Crucify him! Crucify him!"

²²For the third time he spoke to them: "Why? What crime has this man committed? I have found in him no grounds for the death penalty. Therefore I will have him punished and then release him."

²³But with loud shouts they insistently demanded that he be crucified, and their shouts prevailed.

Matt. 27	Mark 15	Luke 23	John

²⁴When Pilate saw that he was getting nowhere, but that instead an uproar was starting, he

²⁴So Pilate decided to grant their demand. ²⁵He

took water and washed his hands in front of the crowd. "I am innocent of this man's blood," he said. "It is your responsibility!"

²⁵All the people answered, "Let his blood be on us and on our children!"

²⁶Then

¹⁵Wanting

to satisfy the crowd, Pilate re-leased Barabbas to them.

released

he released Barabbas to them.

the man who had been thrown

But he had Jesus flogged, and handed him over to be crucified.

He had Jesus flogged, and handed him over to be crucified.

into prison for insurrection and murder, the one they asked for, and

¹Then

Pilate took Jesus and had him flogged.

²⁷Then the governor's soldiers took Jesus into the Praetorium and gathered the whole company of soldiers around him. ²⁸They stripped him and put a scarlet robe on him, ²⁹and then twisted together a crown of thorns and set it on his head. They put a staff in his right hand and knelt in front of him and mocked him.

¹⁶The soldiers led Jesus away into the palace (that is, the Praetorium) and called together the whole company of soldiers. ¹⁷They put a purple robe on him, then twisted together a crown of thorns and set it on him. ¹⁹ᵇFalling on their knees, they paid homage to him.

[Luke]

²The soldiers twisted together a crown of thorns and put it on his head. They clothed him in a purple robe

"Hail, king of the Jews!" they said. ³⁰They spit on him, and took the staff and struck him on the head again and again.

¹⁸And they began to call out to him, "Hail, king of the Jews!" ¹⁹Again and again they struck him on the head with a staff and spit on him.

³and went up to him again and again, saying, "Hail, king of the Jews!"

Matt.	Mark	Luke

And they struck him in the face. ⁴Once more Pilate came out and said to the Jews, "Look, I am bringing him out to you to let you know that I find no basis for a charge against him." ⁵When Jesus came out wearing the crown of thorns and the purple robe, Pilate said to them, "Here is the man!"

⁶As soon as the chief priests and their officials saw him, they shouted, "Crucify! Crucify!"

But Pilate answered, "You take him and crucify him. As for me, I find no basis for a charge against him."

Matt.	Mark	Luke

John 19

7The Jews insisted, "We have a law, and according to that law he must die, because he claimed to be the Son of God."

8When Pilate heard this, he was even more afraid, 9and he went back inside the palace. "Where do you come from?" he asked Jesus, but Jesus gave him no answer. 10"Do you refuse to speak to me?" Pilate said. "Don't you realize I have power either to free you or to crucify you?"

11Jesus answered, "You would have no power over me if it were not given to you from above. Therefore the one who handed me over to you is guilty of a greater sin."

12From then on, Pilate tried to set Jesus free, but the Jews kept shouting, "If you let this man go, you are no friend of Caesar. Anyone who claims to be a king opposes Caesar."

13When Pilate heard this, he brought Jesus out and sat down on the judge's seat at a place known as the Stone Pavement (which in Aramaic is Gabbatha). 14It was the day of Preparation of Passover Week, about the sixth hour. a

"Here is your king," Pilate said to the Jews.

15But they shouted, "Take him away! Take him away! Crucify him!"

"Shall I crucify your king?" Pilate asked.

---

a. The "sixth hour" was 6 A.M. John, who wrote in Asia Minor long after the destruction of Jerusalem, apparently used Graeco-Roman time throughout his Gospel; see the footnote on page 34.

				"We have no king but Caesar," the chief priests answered.
			surrendered Jesus to their will.	16Finally Pilate handed him over to them to be crucified.
31After they had mocked him, they took off the robe and put his own clothes on him. Then they led	20And when they had mocked him, they took off the purple robe and put his own clothes on him. Then they led			
him away to crucify him.	him out to crucify him.			

168. Jesus' Journey to Calvary

Jerusalem; Friday, April 7, from 8 A.M.

Matt. 27:32	Mark 15:21	Luke 23:26–32	John 19:16b–17a
			16bSo the soldiers took charge of Jesus.
		26As they led him away,	
32As they were going out, they met a man from Cyrene, named Simon, and they forced him to carry the cross.	21A certain man from Cyrene, Simon, the father of Alexander and Rufus,	they seized Simon from Cyrene,	17aCarrying his own cross,

Matt.	Mark 15	Luke 23	John
	was	who was	
	passing by on his way in from the country, and they	on his way in from the country, and	
	forced him to carry the cross.	put the cross on him and made him carry it be-	

Mark hind Jesus. ²⁷A large number of people followed him, including women who mourned and wailed for him. ²⁸Jesus turned and said to them, "Daughters of Jerusalem, do not weep for me; weep for yourselves and for your children. ²⁹For the time will come when you will say, 'Blessed are the barren women, the wombs that never bore and the breasts that never nursed!' ³⁰Then

"'they will say to the mountains, "Fall on us!"
and to the hills, "Cover us!"'ᵃ

³¹For if men do these things when the tree is green, what will happen when it is dry?"
³²Two other men, both criminals, were also led out with him to be executed.

a. *30* Hos. 10:8

169. Jesus' Crucifixion

Jerusalem; Friday, April 7, from 9 A.M. to 3 P.M.

Matt. 27:33–56	Mark 15:22–41	Luke 23:33–49	John 19:17b–37
³³They came to a place called Golgotha (which means The Place of the Skull).	²²They brought Jesus to the place called Golgotha (which means The Place of the Skull).	³³When they came to the place called the Skull,	¹⁷ᵇhe went out to the place of the Skull (which in Aramaic is called Golgotha).
³⁴There they offered Jesus wine to drink, mixed with gall; but after tasting it, he refused to drink it.	²³Then they offered him wine mixed with myrrh, but he did not take it.		
³⁸Two robbers were crucified with him, one on his right and one on his left.	²⁴And they crucified him. ²⁷They crucified two robbers with him, one on his right and one on his left.ᵃ	there they crucified him, along with the criminals— one on his right, the other on his left.	¹⁸Here they crucified him, and with him two others— one on each side and Jesus in the middle.
	²⁵It was the third hourᵇ when they crucified him.		
	²⁶The written notice	³⁸There was a written notice	¹⁹Pilate had a notice prepared

a. *27* Some manuscripts *left, 28 and the scripture was fulfilled which says, "He was counted with the lawless ones"* (Isa. 53:12)
b. That is, 9 A.M., Jewish time, reckoned from 6 A.M.

Matt. 27	Mark 15	Luke 23	John 19
	of the charge against him		
37Above his head they placed the written charge against him: THIS IS JESUS, THE KING OF THE JEWS.	read: THE KING OF THE JEWS.	above him, which read: THIS IS THE KING OF THE JEWS.	and fastened to the cross. It read: JESUS OF NAZARETH, THE KING OF THE JEWS. 20Many of the

Matt.	Mark	Luke

Jews read this sign, for the place where Jesus was crucified was near the city, and the sign was written in Aramaic, Latin and Greek. 21The chief priests of the Jews protested to Pilate, "Do not write 'The King of the Jews,' but that this man claimed to be king of the Jews." 22Pilate answered, "What I have written, I have written."

Matt. 27	Mark 15	Luke 23	John 19
		34Jesus said, "Father, forgive them, for they do not know what they are doing."a	
35When they had crucified him, they divided up his clothes	24bDividing up his clothes,	And they divided up his clothes	23When the soldiers crucified Jesus, they took his clothes, dividing them into four shares, one for each of them, with the undergarment remaining. This garment was seamless, woven in one piece from top to bottom. 24"Let's not tear it," they said to one another. "Let's decide by lot who will get it."
by casting lots.a	they cast lots to see what each would get.	by casting lots.	

a. *35* A few late manuscripts *lots that the word spoken by the prophet might be fulfilled: "They divided my garments among themselves and cast lots for my clothing"* (Ps. 22:18)

a. *34* Some early manuscripts do not have this sentence.

Matt.	Mark	Luke

This happened that the scripture might be fulfilled which said,

"They divided my garments among them
and cast lots for my clothing."a

a. *24* Ps. 22:18

Matt. 27	Mark 15	Luke 23	John 19
			So this is what the soldiers did.
36And sitting down, they kept watch over him there.			
39Those who passed by hurled insults at him, shaking their heads 40and saying, "You who are going to de-	29Those who passed by hurled insults at him, shaking their	35The people stood watching, and the rulers even sneered at him.	

Matt. 27	Mark 15	Luke 23	John
stroy the temple and build it in three	heads and saying, "So! You who are going to destroy the temple and build it in three		
days, save yourself! Come down from the cross, if you are the Son of God!"	days, ³⁰come down from the cross and save yourself!"		
⁴¹In the same way the chief priests, the teachers of the law and the elders mocked	³¹In the same way the chief priests and the teachers of the law mocked		
him. ⁴²"He saved others," they said, "but he can't save himself!	him among themselves. "He saved others," they said, "but he can't save himself! ³²Let	They said, "He saved others; let	
		him save himself if he is the Christ of God, the Chosen One."	
He's the King of Israel! Let him come down now from the cross, and we will	this Christ,ᵃ this King of Israel, come down now from the cross, that we may see and		
believe in him. ⁴³He trusts in God. Let God rescue him now if he wants him, for he said, 'I am the Son of God.'"	believe."		
		³⁶The soldiers also came up and mocked him. They offered him wine vinegar ³⁷and said, "If you are the king of the Jews, save yourself."	
⁴⁴In the same way the robbers who were crucified with him also heaped insults on him.	Those crucified	³⁹One of the criminals who hung there	
	with him also heaped insults on him.	hurled insults at him: "Aren't you the Christ? Save yourself and us!"	
	a. 32 Or *Messiah*	⁴⁰But the other criminal rebuked him. "Don't you fear God,"	

Matt.	Mark	
		he said, "since you are under the same sentence? ⁴¹We are punished justly, for we are getting what our deeds deserve. But this man has done nothing wrong." ⁴²Then he said, "Jesus, remember me when you come into your kingdom.ᵃ" ⁴³Jesus answered him, "I tell you the truth, today you will be with me in paradise."

a. 42 Some manuscripts *come with your kingly power*

Luke	
	²⁵Near the cross of Jesus stood his mother, his mother's sister, Mary the wife of Clopas, and Mary Magdalene. ²⁶When Jesus saw his mother there, and the disciple whom he loved standing nearby, he said to his mother, "Dear woman, here is your son," ²⁷and to the disciple, "Here is your mother." From that time on, this disciple took her into his home.

Matt. 27	Mark 15	Luke 23	John
⁴⁵From the sixth hour until the ninth hour darkness came over all the land.	³³At the sixth hour darkness came over the whole land until the ninth hour.	⁴⁴It was now about the sixth hour, and darkness came over the whole land until the ninth	John

Matt. 27	Mark 15	Luke 23	John 19

Luke 23: hour,[a] 45for the sun stopped shining.

a. That is, 12 o'clock noon to 3 P.M., Jewish time, reckoned from 6 A.M.

Matt. 27: 46About the ninth hour Jesus cried out in a loud voice, *"Eloi, Eloi,*[a] *lama sabachthani?"*—which means, "My God, my God, why have you forsaken me?"[b] 47When some of those standing there heard this, they said, "He's calling Elijah."

Mark 15: 34And at the ninth hour Jesus cried out in a loud voice, *"Eloi, Eloi, lama sabachthani?"*—which means, "My God, my God, why have you forsaken me?"[a] 35When some of those standing near heard this, they said, "Listen, he's calling Elijah."

John 19: 28Later, knowing that all was now completed, and so that the Scripture would be fulfilled, Jesus said, "I am thirsty." 29A jar of wine vinegar was there, so

Matt. 27: 48Immediately one of them ran and got a sponge. He filled it with wine vinegar, put it on a stick, and offered it to Jesus to drink.

Mark 15: 36One man ran, filled a sponge with wine vinegar, put it on a stick,

John 19: they soaked a sponge in it, put the sponge on a stalk of the hyssop plant, and lifted it to Jesus' lips.

Mark 15: and offered it to Jesus to drink.

Matt. 27: 49The rest said, "Now leave him alone. Let's see if Elijah comes to save him."

Mark 15: "Now leave him alone. Let's see if Elijah comes to take him down," he said.

a. 46 Some manuscripts *Eli, Eli*
b. 46 Ps. 22:1

a. 34 Ps. 22:1

Matt. 27: 50And when Jesus had cried out again in a loud voice,

Mark 15: 37With a loud cry,

Luke 23: 46Jesus called out with a loud voice,

John 19: 30When he had received the drink, Jesus said, "It is finished." With that, he

Luke 23: "Father, into your hands I commit my spirit." When he had said this, he

Matt. 27: he gave up his spirit. 51At that moment the curtain of the temple was torn in two from top to bottom. The earth shook

Mark 15: Jesus breathed his last. 38The curtain of the temple was torn in two from top to bottom.

Luke 23: breathed his last. 45bAnd the curtain of the temple was torn in two.

John 19: bowed his head and gave up his spirit.

and the rocks split. 52The tombs broke open and the bodies of many holy people who had died were raised to life. 53They came out of the tombs, and after Jesus' resurrection they went into the holy city and appeared to many people.

Mark	Luke	John

Matt. 27	Mark 15	Luke 23	John
[54]When the centurion and those with him who were guarding Jesus saw the earthquake and all that had happened, they were terrified, and exclaimed,	[39]And when the centurion, who stood there in front of Jesus, heard his cry and[a] saw how he died, he said,	[47]The centurion, seeing what had happened, praised God and said, "Surely this was a righteous man."	
"Surely he was the Son[a] of God!"	"Surely this man was the Son[b] of God!"		
		[48]When all the people who had gathered to witness this sight saw what took place, they beat their breasts and went away. [49]But all	
[55]Many women were there, watching from a distance. [56]Among them were Mary Magdalene, Mary the mother of James and Joses, and	[40]Some women were watching from a distance.	those who knew him, including the women who had followed him from Galilee, stood at a distance, watching these things.	
	Among them were Mary Magdalene, Mary the mother of James the younger and of Joses, and Salome.		
the mother of Zebedee's sons. [55b]They had followed Jesus from Galilee to care for his needs.	[41]In Galilee these women had followed him and cared for his needs. Many other women who had come up with him to Jerusalem were also there.		

a. *39* Some manuscripts do not have *heard his cry and.*

a. *54* Or *a son*

b. *39* Or *a son*

Matt.	Mark	Luke	
			[31]Now it was the day of Preparation, and the next day was to be a special Sabbath. Because the Jews did not want the bodies left on the crosses during the Sabbath, they asked Pilate to have the legs broken and the bodies taken down. [32]The soldiers therefore came and broke the legs of the first man who had been crucified with Jesus, and then those of the other. [33]But when they came to Jesus and found that he was already dead, they did not break his legs. [34]Instead, one of the soldiers pierced Jesus' side with a spear, bringing a sudden flow of blood and water. [35]The man who saw it has given testimony, and his testimony is true. He knows that he tells the truth, and he testifies so that you also may believe. [36]These things happened so that the scripture would be fulfilled: "Not one of his bones will be broken,"[a] [37]and, as another scripture says, "They will look on the one they have pierced."[b]

a. *36* Exod. 12:46; Num. 9:12; Ps. 34:20

b. *37* Zech. 12:10

170. Jesus' Burial

Jerusalem; Friday, April 7, before 6 P.M.

Matt. 27:57–61	Mark 15:42–47	Luke 23:50–56a	John 19:38–42
	42It was Preparation Day (that is, the day before the Sabbath). So as evening approached,		
57As evening approached, there came a rich man from Arimathea, named Joseph,	43Joseph of Arimathea, a prominent member of the Council,	50Now there was a man named Joseph, a member of the Council,	
		a good and upright man, 51who had not consented to their decision and action. He came from the Judean town of Arimathea	38Later, Joseph of Arimathea asked Pilate for the body of Jesus.
	who was himself waiting for the kingdom of God,	and he was waiting for the kingdom of God.	
who had himself become a disciple of Jesus.			Now Joseph was a disciple of Jesus, but secretly because he feared the Jews.
58Going to Pilate, he asked for Jesus' body,	went boldly to Pilate and asked for Jesus' body. 44Pilate was surprised to hear that he was already dead. Summoning the centurion, he asked him if Jesus had already died. 45When he learned from the centurion that it was so,	52Going to Pilate, he asked for Jesus' body.	
and Pilate ordered that it be given to him.	he gave the body to Joseph. 46So Joseph bought some linen cloth,		With Pilate's permission, he came
59Joseph took the body,	took down the body,	53Then he took it down,	and took the body away. 39He was accompanied by Nicodemus, the man who earlier had visited Jesus at night. Nicodemus brought a mixture of myrrh and aloes, about seventy-five

Matt. 27	Mark 15	Luke 23	John 19
			pounds.[a] [40]Taking Jesus' body, the two of them
wrapped it in a clean linen cloth, [60]and	wrapped it in the linen,	wrapped it in linen cloth	wrapped it, with the spices, in strips of linen. This was in accordance with Jewish burial customs. [41]At the place where Jesus was crucified, there was a garden, and in the garden a new tomb,[b]
placed it in his own new tomb that he had	and placed it in a tomb	and placed it in a tomb	
cut out of the rock.	cut out of rock.	cut in the rock, one in which no one had yet been laid.	in which no one had ever been laid.
		[54]It was Preparation Day,	[42]Because it was the Jewish day of Preparation
		and the Sabbath was about to begin.	
			and since the tomb was nearby, they laid Jesus there.
He rolled a big stone in front of the entrance to the tomb and went away.	Then Joseph[a] rolled a stone against the entrance of the tomb.		
[61]Mary Magdalene and the other Mary were	[47]Mary Magdalene and Mary the mother of Joses	[55]The women who had come with Jesus from Galilee followed Joseph and	
sitting there opposite the tomb.			
	saw where he was laid.	saw the tomb and how his body was laid in it. [56a]Then they went home . . .	

a. The NIV reads "he." By specifying "Joseph," the composite narrative is clarified.

a. *39* Greek *a hundred litrai* (about 34 kilograms)
b. Note the additional information given by Matthew (27:60) that it was Joseph's "own new tomb that he had cut out of the rock."

171. The Sealing of the Tomb

Jerusalem; Saturday, April 8

Matt. 27:62–66

[62]The next day, the one after Preparation Day, the chief priests and the Pharisees went to Pilate. [63]"Sir," they said, "we remember that while he was still alive that deceiver said, 'After three days I will rise again.' [64]So give the order for the tomb to be made secure until the third day. Otherwise, his disciples may come and steal the body and tell the people that he has been raised from the dead. This last deception will be worse than the first."

Matt. 27	Mark	Luke	John
[65]"Take a guard," Pilate answered. "Go, make the tomb as secure as you know how." [66]So they went and made the tomb secure by putting a seal on the stone and posting the guard.			

Matt.	Mark	Luke 23:56c	
		[56c]But the women[a] rested on the Sabbath in obedience to the commandment.	

a. The NIV reads "they." By specifying "the women," the composite narrative is clarified.

172. Preparations to Anoint the Body of Jesus

Jerusalem; Saturday, April 8, after 6 P.M.

Matt.	Mark 16:1	Luke 23:56b	John
	[1]When the Sabbath was over, Mary Magdalene, Mary the mother of James, and Salome bought spices so that they might go to anoint Jesus' body.	[56b]and prepared spices and perfumes.	

PART 13

Jesus' Resurrection, Appearances, and Ascension

Forty Days—Probably April 9 to May 18, A.D. 30

173. The Earthquake

Jerusalem; Sunday, April 9, before dawn

Matt. 28:2–4	Mark	Luke	John

[2]There was a violent earthquake, for an angel of the Lord came down from heaven and, going to the tomb, rolled back the stone and sat on it. [3]His appearance was like lightning, and his clothes were white as snow. [4]The guards were so afraid of him that they shook and became like dead men.

174. Mary Magdalene at the Tomb

Jerusalem; Sunday, April 9, before dawn

Matt. 28:1	Mark	Luke	**John 20:1–2**

Matt. 28:1

[1]After the Sabbath, at dawn on the first day of the week, Mary[a] Magdalene and the other Mary went to look at the tomb.

---

a. Mary Magdalene evidently arrived at the tomb first (see John 20:1), ahead of "the other Mary," who arrived with Salome (Mark 16:1) and other women (Luke 24:10); see sec. 175.

John 20:1–2

[1]Early on the first day of the week, while it was still dark, Mary Magdalene went to the tomb and saw that the stone had been removed from the entrance. [2]So she came running to Simon Peter and the other disciple, the one Jesus loved, and said, "They have taken the Lord out of the tomb, and we don't know where they have put him!"

175. The Other Women at the Tomb

Jerusalem; early Sunday morning, April 9

Matt.	**Mark 16:2–8**	**Luke 24:1–8**	John

Mark 16:2–8

[2]Very early on the first day of the week,

just after sunrise,

Luke 24:1–8

[1]On the first day of the week, very early in the morning,

Matt.	**Mark 16**	**Luke 24**	John

Mark 16 / **Luke 24**

they were

on their way to the tomb ³and they asked each other, "Who will roll the stone away from the entrance of the tomb?"

⁴But when they looked up, they saw that the stone, which was very large, had been rolled away. ⁵As they entered the tomb,

they saw a young man dressed in a white robe sitting on the right side, and they were alarmed.

Luke 24:

the women took the spices they had prepared and went to the tomb.

²They found the stone rolled away from the tomb,

³but when they entered, they did not find the body of the Lord Jesus. ⁴While they were wondering about this, suddenly two men in clothes that gleamed like lightning stood beside them.ᵃ ⁵In their fright the

---

Matt. 28:5–8

⁵The angel said to the women,

"Do not be afraid, for I know that you are looking for Jesus, who was crucified.

⁶"Don't be alarmed," he said. "You are looking for Jesus the Nazarene, who was crucified.

⁶He is not here; he has risen, just as he said.
Come and see

He has risen! He is not here. See

Luke:

women bowed down with their faces to the ground, but the men said to them,

"Why do you look for the living among the dead? ⁶He is not here;

a. Matthew and Mark mention only one angel.

Matt.	Mark	

he has risen! Remember how he told you, while he was still with you in Galilee: ⁷"The Son of Man must be delivered into the hands of sinful men, be crucified and on the third day be raised again.'"

---

the place where he lay.
⁷Then go quickly and tell his disciples:

'He has risen from the dead and is going ahead of you into Galilee. There you will see him.'

Now I have told you."

the place where they laid him.
⁷But go, tell his disciples

and Peter, 'He is going ahead of you into Galilee. There you will see him, just as he told you.'"

⁸Then they remembered his words.

⁸So the women hurried away from the tomb, afraid yet filled with joy, and ran to tell his disciples.

⁸Trembling and bewildered, the women went out and fled from the tomb.

They said nothing to anyone, because they were afraid.

176. Peter and John at the Tomb

Jerusalem; Sunday morning, April 9

Matt.	Mark	Luke 24:12	John 20:3–10
		12Peter, however, got up and ran to the tomb. Bending over, he saw the strips of linen lying by themselves, and he went away, wonderinga what had happened. ――――――――――――――――――――― a. The NIV reading, "wondering to himself," has been abbreviated for the sake of proper grammatical sequence in the composite narrative.	3So Peter and the other disciple started for the tomb. 4Both were running, but the other disciple outran Peter and reached the tomb first. 5He bent over and looked in at the strips of linen lying there but did not go in. 6Then Simon Peter, who was behind him, arrived and went into the tomb. He saw the strips of linen lying there, 7as well as the burial cloth that had been around Jesus' head. The cloth was folded up by itself, separate from the linen. 8Finally the other disciple, who had reached the tomb first, also went inside. He saw and believed. 9(They still did not understand from Scripture that Jesus had to rise from the dead.) 10Then the disciples went back to their homes,

177. Jesus' Appearance to Mary Magdalene

Jerusalem; Sunday morning, April 9

Matt.	Mark 16:9	Luke	John 20:11–17
			11but Mary stood outside the tomb crying. As she wept, she bent over to look into the tomb 12and saw two angels in white, seated where Jesus' body had been, one at the head and the other at the foot. 13They asked her, "Woman, why are you crying?" "They have taken my Lord away," she said, "and I don't know where they have put him." 14At this, she turned around and saw Jesus standing there, but she did not realize that it was Jesus. 15"Woman," he said, "why are you crying? Who is it you are looking for?"

Matt.	Mark 16:9	Luke	John 20
	⁹ᵃ When Jesus rose early on the first day of the week, he appeared first to Mary Magdalene, out of whom he had driven seven demons.		Thinking he was the gardener, she said, "Sir, if you have carried him away, tell me where you have put him, and I will get him." ¹⁶Jesus said to her, "Mary." She turned toward him and cried out in Aramaic, "Rabboni!" (which means Teacher). ¹⁷Jesus said, "Do not hold on to me, for I have not yet returned to the Father. Go instead to my brothers and tell them, 'I am returning to my Father and your Father, to my God and your God.'"
	a. The most reliable early manuscripts and other ancient witnesses do not have Mark 16:9–20.		

178. Jesus' Appearance to the Other Women

Near Jerusalem; Sunday morning, April 9

Matt. 28:9–10	Mark	Luke	John
⁹Suddenly Jesus met them. "Greetings," he said. They came to him, clasped his feet and worshiped him. ¹⁰Then Jesus said to them, "Do not be afraid. Go and tell my brothers to go to Galilee; there they will see me."			

179. The Women's Report to the Disciples

Jerusalem or Bethany; Sunday morning, April 9

Matt.	Mark 16:10–11	Luke 24:9–11	John 20:18
	¹⁰She went and told those who had been with him and who were mourning and weeping. ¹¹When they heard that Jesus was alive and that she had seen him, they did not believe it.	⁹When they came back from the tomb, they told all these things to the Eleven and to all the others. ¹⁰It was Mary Magdalene, Joanna, Mary the mother of James, and the others with them who told this to the apostles. ¹¹But they did not believe the women, because their words seemed to them like nonsense.	¹⁸Mary Magdalene went to the disciples with the news: "I have seen the Lord!" And she told them that he had said these things to her.

180. The Guards' Report to the Sanhedrin

Jerusalem; Sunday morning, April 9

Matt. 28:11–15

| | Mark | Luke | John |

[11]While the women were on their way, some of the guards went into the city and reported to the chief priests everything that had happened. [12]When the chief priests had met with the elders and devised a plan, they gave the soldiers a large sum of money, [13]telling them, "You are to say, 'His disciples came during the night and stole him away while we were asleep.' [14]If this report gets to the governor, we will satisfy him and keep you out of trouble." [15]So the soldiers took the money and did as they were instructed. And this story has been widely circulated among the Jews to this very day.

181. Jesus' Appearance to Cleopas and His Companion

Sunday afternoon, April 9

| Matt. | Mark | Luke 24:13–32 | John |

[13]Now that same day two of them were going to a village called Emmaus, about seven miles[a] from Jerusalem. [14]They were talking with each other about everything that had hap-

a. *13* Greek *sixty stadia* (about 11 kilometers)

Mark 16:12

[12]Afterward Jesus appeared in a different form to two of them while they were walking in the country.

pened. [15]As they talked and discussed these things with each other, Jesus himself came up and walked along with them; [16]but they were kept from recognizing him.

| Mark |

[17]He asked them, "What are you discussing together as you walk along?"

They stood still, their faces downcast. [18]One of them, named Cleopas, asked him, "Are you only a visitor to Jerusalem and do not know the things that have happened there in these days?"

[19]"What things?" he asked.

"About Jesus of Nazareth," they replied. "He was a prophet, powerful in word and deed before God and all the people. [20]The chief priests and our rulers handed him over to be sentenced to death, and they crucified him; [21]but we had hoped that he was the one who was going to redeem Israel. And what is more, it is the third day since all this took place. [22]In addition, some of our women amazed us. They went to the tomb early this morning [23]but didn't find his body. They came and told us that they had seen a vision of angels, who said he was alive. [24]Then some of our companions went to the tomb and found it just as the women had said, but him they did not see."

[25]He said to them, "How foolish you are, and how slow of heart to believe all that the prophets have spoken! [26]Did not the Christ[b] have to suffer these things and then enter his

b. *26* Or *Messiah;* also in verse 46

Matt.	Mark	Luke 24	John
		glory?" 27And beginning with Moses and all the Prophets, he explained to them what was said in all the Scriptures concerning himself. 28As they approached the village to which they were going, Jesus acted as if he were going farther. 29But they urged him strongly, "Stay with us, for it is nearly evening; the day is almost over." So he went in to stay with them. 30When he was at the table with them, he took bread, gave thanks, broke it and began to give it to them. 31Then their eyes were opened and they recognized him, and he disappeared from their sight. 32They asked each other, "Were not our hearts burning within us while he talked with us on the road and opened the Scriptures to us?"	

182. Cleopas and His Companion's Report to the Disciples

Sunday evening, April 9

Matt.	Mark 16:13	Luke 24:33–35	John
	13These returned and reported it to the rest; but they did not believe them either.	33They got up and returned at once to Jerusalem. There they found the Elevena and those with them, assembled together 34and saying, "It is true! The Lord has risen and has appeared to Simon." 35Then the two told what had happened on the way, and how Jesus was recognized by them when he broke the bread. _____ a. To be exact there were only ten of the apostles present, for John states (20:24) that Thomas was absent on this occasion. After the suicidal death of Judas, the expressin "the Eleven" was evidently used with reference to the apostles as a group, even though all the members of the group might not always be present.	

183. Jesus' Appearance to the Disciples—sans Thomas

Jerusalem; Sunday evening, April 9

Matt.	Mark 16:14	Luke 24:36–43	John 20:19–25
			19On the evening of that first day of the week, when the disciples were
		36While they were	together,
		still talking about this,	with the doors locked for fear of the Jews, Jesus
	14Later Jesus appeared to the Eleven as they were eating;	Jesus himself stood among them	came and stood among them and said, "Peace be with you!"
		and said to them, "Peace be with you."	
		37They were startled and	

Matt.	Mark	Luke 24	John

frightened, thinking they saw a ghost. [38]He said to them, "Why are you troubled, and why do doubts rise in your minds? [39]Look at my hands and my feet. It is I myself! Touch me and see; a ghost does not have flesh and bones, as you see I have."

[40]When he had said this,

	Mark	Luke 24	John

he rebuked them for their lack of faith and their stubborn refusal to believe those who had seen him after he had risen.

he

showed them his hands

and feet.

[20]After he said this, he showed them his hands

and side.

	Mark		John

[41]And while they still did not believe it because of joy and amazement, he asked them, "Do you have anything here to eat?" [42]They gave him a piece of broiled fish, [43]and he took it and ate it in their presence.

	Luke	

The disciples were overjoyed when they saw the Lord.

[21]Again Jesus said, "Peace be with you! As the Father has sent me, I am sending you." [22]And with that he breathed on them and said, "Receive the Holy Spirit. [23]If you forgive anyone his sins, they are forgiven; if you do not forgive them, they are not forgiven."

[24]Now Thomas (called Didymus), one of the Twelve, was not with the disciples when Jesus came. [25]So the other disciples told him, "We have seen the Lord!"

But he said to them, "Unless I see the nail marks in his hands and put my finger where the nails were, and put my hand into his side, I will not believe it."

184. Jesus' Appearance to His Disciples—and Thomas

Jerusalem; Sunday, April 16

Matt.	Mark	Luke	John 20:26–29

[26]A week later his disciples were in the house again, and Thomas was with them. Though the doors were locked, Jesus came and stood among them and said, "Peace be with you!" [27]Then he said to Thomas, "Put your finger here; see my hands. Reach out your hand and put it into my side. Stop doubting and believe."

[28]Thomas said to him, "My Lord and my God!"

[29]Then Jesus told him, "Because you have seen me, you have believed; blessed are those who have not seen and yet have believed."

185. A Miraculous Catch of Fish

Probably in early May

Matt.	Mark	Luke	John 21:1–23

[1]Afterward Jesus appeared again to his disciples, by the Sea of Tiberias.[a] It happened this way: [2]Simon Peter, Thomas (called Didymus), Nathanael from Cana in Galilee, the sons of

Matt.	Mark	Luke

John 21

Zebedee, and two other disciples were together. [3]"I'm going out to fish," Simon Peter told them, and they said, "We'll go with you." So they went out and got into the boat, but that night they caught nothing.

[4]Early in the morning, Jesus stood on the shore, but the disciples did not realize that it was Jesus.

[5]He called out to them, "Friends, haven't you any fish?"

"No," they answered.

[6]He said, "Throw your net on the right side of the boat and you will find some." When they did, they were unable to haul the net in because of the large number of fish.

[7]Then the disciple whom Jesus loved said to Peter, "It is the Lord!" As soon as Simon Peter heard him say, "It is the Lord," he wrapped his outer garment around him (for he had taken it off) and jumped into the water. [8]The other disciples followed in the boat, towing the net full of fish, for they were not far from shore, about a hundred yards.[a] [9]When they landed, they saw a fire of burning coals there with fish on it, and some bread.

[10]Jesus said to them, "Bring some of the fish you have just caught."

[11]Simon Peter climbed aboard and dragged the net ashore. It was full of large fish, 153, but even with so many the net was not torn. [12]Jesus said to them, "Come and have breakfast." None of the disciples dared ask him, "Who are you?" They knew it was the Lord. [13]Jesus came, took the bread and gave it to them, and did the same with the fish. [14]This was now the third time Jesus appeared to his disciples after he was raised from the dead.

[15]When they had finished eating, Jesus said to Simon Peter, "Simon son of John, do you truly love me more than these?"

"Yes, Lord," he said, "you know that I love[b] you."

Jesus said, "Feed my lambs."

[16]Again Jesus said, "Simon son of John, do you truly love me?"

He answered, "Yes, Lord, you know that I love you."

Jesus said, "Take care of my sheep."

[17]The third time he said to him, "Simon son of John, do you love me?"

Peter was hurt because Jesus asked him the third time, "Do you love me?" He said, "Lord, you know all things; you know that I love you."

Jesus said, "Feed my sheep. [18]I tell you the truth, when you were younger you dressed yourself and went where you wanted; but when you are old you will stretch out your hands, and someone else will dress you and lead you where you do not want to go." [19]Jesus said this to indicate the kind of death by which Peter would glorify God. Then he said to him, "Follow me!"

[20]Peter turned and saw that the disciple whom Jesus loved was following them. (This was the one who had leaned back against Jesus at the supper and had said, "Lord, who is going to betray you?") [21]When Peter saw him, he asked, "Lord, what about him?"

[22]Jesus answered, "If I want him to remain alive until I return, what is that to you? You must follow me." [23]Because of this, the rumor spread among the brothers that this disciple would not die. But Jesus did not say that he would not die; he only said, "If I want him to remain alive until I return, what is that to you?"[c]

---

a. *1* That is, Sea of Galilee

a. *8* Greek *about two hundred cubits* (about 90 meters)

b. It should be noted that in this dialogue between Jesus and Peter, two different Greek words are translated "love." The previously boastful Peter (Matt. 26:33), deeply ashamed of his denial of Christ (Matt. 26:69–75), now shrinks from using the same strong word for "love" that Jesus used in testing him.

c. Other appearances of Jesus, not recorded in the Gospels, are mentioned in 1 Cor. 15:6–7.

186. The Great Commission

About the middle of May

Matt. 28:16–20	Mark 16:15–18	Luke 24:44–49	John
[16]Then the eleven disciples went to Galilee, to the mountain where Jesus had told them to go. [17]When they saw him, they worshiped him; but some doubted. [18]Then Jesus came to them and said,	[15]He said to them,	[44]He said to them,	

Matt.	Mark	"This is what I told you while I was still with you: Everything must be fulfilled that is written about me in the Law of Moses, the Prophets and the Psalms."

[45]Then he opened their minds so they could understand the Scriptures. [46]He told them, "This is what is written: The Christ will suffer and rise from the dead on the third day, [47]and repentance and forgiveness of sins will be preached in his name to all nations, beginning at Jerusalem.

Matt. 28:16–20	Mark 16:15–18	Luke 24:44–49
"All authority in heaven and on earth has been given to me.	"Go	
		[48]You are witnesses of these things.
[19]Therefore go	into all the world and preach the good news to all creation.	
and make disciples of all nations, baptizing them in[a] the name of the Father and of the Son and of the Holy Spirit, [20]and teaching them to obey everything I have commanded you. And surely I am with you always, to the very end of the age."		

a. *19* Or *into*; see Acts 8:16; 19:5; Rom. 6:3; 1 Cor. 1:13; 10:2 and Gal. 3:27.

Matt.		Luke

[16]Whoever believes and is baptized will be saved, but whoever does not believe will be condemned. [17]And these signs will accompany those who believe: In my name they will drive out demons; they will speak in new tongues; [18]they will pick up snakes with their hands; and when they drink deadly poison, it will not hurt them at all; they will place their hands on sick people, and they will get well."

Mark

[49]I am going to send you what my Father has promised; but stay in the city until you have been clothed with power from on high."

187. Jesus' Ascension

The Mount of Olives, near Jerusalem; about May 18

Matt.	Mark 16:19–20	Luke 24:50–53	John
	19After the Lord Jesus had spoken to them, he was taken up into heaven and he sat at the right hand of God.	50When he had led them out to the vicinity of Bethany, he lifted up his hands and blessed them. 51While he was blessing them, he left them and was taken up into heaven. 52Then they worshiped him and returned to Jerusalem with great joy. 53And they stayed continually at the temple, praising God.a	
	20Then the disciples went out and preached everywhere, and the Lord worked with them and confirmed his word by the signs that accompanied it.	a. A fuller account of Christ's ascension is recorded in Acts 1:6–12.	

PART 14

Conclusion

188. The Purpose of John's Gospel and a Personal Testimony

Matt.	Mark	Luke

John 20:30–31; 1:14b; 16–18; 21:24–25

30Jesus did many other miraculous signs in the presence of his disciples, which are not recorded in this book. 31But these are written that you maya believe that Jesus is the Christ, the Son of God, and that by believing you may have life in his name.

14bWe have seen his glory, the glory of the One and Only,b who came from the Father, full of grace and truth.

16From the fullness of his grace we have all received one blessing after another. 17For the law was given through Moses; grace and truth came through Jesus Christ. 18No one has ever seen God, but God the One and Only,c,d who is at the Father's side, has made him known.

24This is the disciple who testifies to these things and who wrote them down. We know that his testimony is true.

25Jesus did many other things as well. If every one of them were written down, I suppose that even the whole world would not have room for the books that would be written.

---

a. *31* Some manuscripts *may continue to*
b. *14* Or *the Only Begotten*
c. *18* Or *the Only Begotten*
d. *18* Some manuscripts *but the only* (or *only begotten*) *Son*

Scripture Index